Here's Johnny ORR

"If I didn't have a sense of humor, I wouldn't still be here coaching. It's a way to let the steam off. I get uptight some but never have had ulcers or anything like that. When you lose games, it's very difficult to be funny. It comes much easier when you win. The thing about dealing with young kids, well, I wouldn't say it's frustrating, but it's unpredictable. Just when you think you have things going well, something nutty happens. During the season it happens just about every day. Something pops up that's never entered your mind and you can't believe it would happen."

Here's Johnny ORR

GENE McGIVERN

Iowa State University Press / Ames

To my parents, Margaret and Gerald,

who in 1992 celebrate 50 years of marriage.

Their lives, like the writing of a book,

are a remarkable blend of creativity and work ethic.

Gene McGivern is a sports correspondent for United Press International and sports information director at Augsburg College, Minneapolis. As sports editor of the Ames (Iowa) *Daily Tribune* from 1984 through 1988, McGivern closely followed coach Johnny Orr's basketball team and its rise from obscurity into the final 16 squads at the National Collegiate Athletic Association tournament in 1986. He is a 1981 graduate of Iowa State University.

Authorization to photocopy items for internal or personal use, or the internal or personal use of specific clients, is granted by Iowa State University Press, provided that the base fee of $.10 per copy is paid directly to the Copyright Clearance Center, 27 Congress Street, Salem, MA 01970. For those organizations that have been granted a photocopy license by CCC, a separate system of payments has been arranged. The fee codes for users of the Transactional Reporting Service are 0-8138-1289-5 (clothbound edition) and 0-8138-1291-7 (paperbound edition) $.10.

⊗ Printed on acid-free paper in the United States of America

First edition, 1992
Second printing, 1992

Library of Congress Cataloging-in-Publication Data

McGivern, Gene.
    Here's Johnny Orr / Gene McGivern.—1st. ed.
        p.   cm.
    ISBN 0-8138-1289-5 (cloth).—ISBN 0-8138-1291-7 (paper)
    1. Orr, Johnny. 2. Basketball—United States—Coaches—Biography. 3. Iowa State University—Basketball—History. I. Title.
GV884.O77M37   1992
796.323'092—dc20   92-24569
[B]

Contents

Foreword *by Bob Knight*

JOHNNY ORR has been one of the outstanding coaches of my era. I have probably known him longer and been closer to him than anybody in coaching. There is no one I have respected more than John.

Our styles of coaching differ greatly, which made for a lot of interesting games between our teams. His teams have always been a challenge for us to play because of his emphasis on quickness and aggressiveness. While his system is important, the key to his success has been Johnny's ability to get the most out of his players. His style of play has proven very difficult for teams in both the Big Ten and the Big Eight to play against. I have already mentioned that Johnny's approach to basketball is a lot different from mine, which is simply indicative of the fact that there are a lot of ways to play the game well.

The first time I met John, he was head coach at the University of Massachusetts and I was an assistant coach at Army. I took him and his assistant coach out to lunch when they came up to play us in a scrimmage. I liked John right off the bat, and I've increased my admiration for him ever since.

John has done an outstanding job at both Michigan and Iowa State. Iowa State is not a school that is rich in basketball tradition nor is it located in a part of the country where there is a great supply of basketball talent. John accepting the challenge of leaving Michigan to go to Iowa State came as something of a surprise to me. However, the fact that he has taken five Iowa State teams to the NCAA tournament has been no surprise. I believe to this

Head Basketball Coach,
Indiana University
3-Time National Coach of the Year
3-Time NCAA Team Champions

day that John would have remained at Michigan had he been paid anything close to what he should have been for the job he was doing there. Yet the move to Iowa State has been a great one for both John and the Cyclone fans. His personality and his way with people are great assets to the university. I never felt that as a coach and a person he was ever really appreciated at Michigan.

You are about to have a most enjoyable experience reading about Johnny Orr, the athlete, the coach, and the person. For twenty-five years I have looked upon him as an outstanding coach and an ever better friend.

Acknowledgments

Several people offered valuable advice and support throughout this project, including Mark Neuzil, Dave Cline, Tom Kroeschell, Dan Davenport, John Akers, Bob Asmussen and Barbara Lammers. Gretchen Van Houten and the staff at Iowa State University Press were also extremely supportive.

Special thanks to others who helped supply valuable photography and research materials: Romie Orr; Jeff King, Mark Davitt, Denny Waller and Verle Burgason of the *Daily Tribune* in Ames; Dave Starr and Iowa State University Sports Information Office; the sports departments of the *Des Moines Register* and Cedar Rapids *Gazette;* Don Williams of Taylorville High School and the Taylorville *Breeze-Courier.*

History is best told through newspaper and magazine accounts of the day. I thank the following writers and publications for the use of their descriptions of Johnny Orr and his basketball teams:

First the Iowa press. From the Ames *Daily Tribune:* John Akers, Bob Asmussen, Jeff Burkhead. From the *Des Moines Register:* Rick Brown, Bob Dyer, Marc Hansen, Ron Maly, Gene Raffensperger, Buck Turnbull, Tom Witosky. From the Cedar Rapids *Gazette:* Mark Dukes, Jim Ecker, Mike Hlas. From the *Quad City Times:* Craig Cooper, Don Doxsie, Mark Neuzil. Also Bob

Brown, Fort Dodge *Messenger*, and Russ Smith, *Waterloo Courier*.

Next the Michigan corps. From the Ann Arbor *News:* Jeff Mortimer, John Viges. From the *Michigan Daily:* Jim Ecker, Marc Feldman, Mark Mihanovic, John Papenek, Tony Schwartz. From the *Detroit Free Press:* Judd Arnett, Jack Berg, Curt Sylvester. From the *Detroit News:* Joe Falls, Jerry Green. Also Jerry Zimmerman, *Huron Valley Advisor.*

Then there's the Illinois crowd. From the Chicago *Daily News:* Jack Ryan, Clark Shaughnessy. From the *Chicago Tribune:* Roy Damer, Bob Logan, Edward Prell. From the Urbana *Courier:* Eddie Jones, Lynn Ruester. Also Jack Burns, Taylorville *Breeze-Courier*, plus the Chicago *Sun-Times* and Rockford *Register-Star.*

From other publications: Frank Reichstein, Beloit (Wisc.) *Daily News;* Sid Hartman, and Jon Roe, *Minneapolis Star and Tribune;* Dennis Dodd, Kansas City (Mo.) *Times;* John Hannen, Toledo (Ohio) *Blade;* Curry Kirkpatrick, *Sports Illustrated;* Dan Davenport, *Visions* magazine, Iowa State University Alumni Association; Jim Enright, *March Madness;* John Feinstein, *A Season Inside.* Also Richard Shook, United Press International and the New York Times News Service.

And finally, David Israel.

Introduction

Hey, Cyclone basketball fan, relax. The rumor you heard was false. A prominent Johnny did retire in the spring of 1992. But it was Carson, not Orr. Same folksy first name. Same theme song. Same crowd appeal. Just a different last name.

Iowa State's Johnny is heading into his final chapter of a 50-year association with athletics, thus it's an appropriate time to hit the rewind button on his life. What follows is a collection of Orr's reminiscences, his humor, accounts of his successes and failures, his views on college sports, and scores of testimonials. It reveals much about this complex and multifacted man—an animated entertainer at the microphone, yet a reserved, simple man at home.

The Johnny Orr coaching record bulges with accomplishments:

- He's won 432 basketball games (and counting) in 27 years of college head coaching.
- He twice was named National Coach of the Year and twice voted Big Ten Conference Coach of the Year.
- He's one of only two people to hold the distinction of being the winningest basketball coach at two NCAA Division I schools.

He's the all-time victory leader at both Michigan and Iowa State, equaling the feat of Ralph Miller (Wichita State and Oregon State).

- He'll start the 1992–93 season ranked 20th nationally among active Divison I coaches for career victories and 13th nationally in games played among active Division I coaches.

- His 1976 Michigan team reached the Final Four and was national runner-up.

- Two of his Wolverine teams were ranked No. 1 for a spell by the national polls, and several of his Cyclone teams have cracked the national top 25.

- He has coached teams to nine NCAA tournament berths, already has had seven assistant coaches go on to head coaching jobs, and has had nearly a dozen players go on to the NBA.

Orr's scrapbooks read like a walk through the Basketball Hall of Fame. As an 18-year-old freshman at the University of Illinois, Johnny guarded the great George Mikan of DePaul. He later played and coached against legendary UCLA coach John Wooden's teams. Other prominent coaches Orr has faced off against include Adolph Rupp, Ray Meyer, Frank McGuire, Bob Knight, Joe Lapchick, Lou Carnesecca, Al McGuire, Dean Smith, Lute Olson, Jud Heathcote and Larry Brown. As a young coach, Johnny crossed paths at clinics with Rupp, Bear Bryant and Henry Iba. His basketball camp at Michigan was attended by a young Earvin Johnson of Lansing, Mich., a special player who later earned the nickname "Magic." Johnson was among the great players Orr later coached against, joining the likes of Bill Walton, Dan Issel, Alex English, Isiah Thomas, Kent Benson and an acclaimed John Havlicek–led team at Ohio State. Orr has played golf with President Gerald Ford and often shares a stage with prominent figures from the sports and business world. He's been inducted into several halls of fame as a player and coach, and he currently is president of the National Association of Basketball Coaches. He's going strong at age 65 and ranks as the third-oldest active NCAA Division I coach. The 1992 retirement of 67-year-old Lou Carnesecca of St. John's leaves Orr behind the 70-year-old Butch van Breda Kolff of Hofstra and Michigan State's Heathcote, who was born 14 days before Orr.

Away from coaching, Orr has carved a special niche, and this book explores the factors that have made Johnny a hit. Like a skillful politician on the campaign trail, Johnny has a knack for connecting with people—players, fans, the media, the public.

Part of his appeal is his unique personality. On the one hand, his use of profanity at certain speaking functions makes some cringe. He has lost his cool in public on occasion, chasing officials off the basketball court or snapping at a reporter in the interview room. On the other hand, with the same high energy, he's embraced countless charity projects.

Whatever his quirks, Johnny has made many more friends than he has made enemies. If for no other reason, Orr deserves acclaim for his longevity. For 32 years and counting, he's coached in the madhouse environment of college athletics and lived to tell about it. And few can tell a story quite like Johnny. He's at his best when he jokes about his sport, his team and himself. In his self-deprecating style, Orr laments that it's hard to earn the kind of respect afforded Ralph Miller when you're surrounded by characters out of the sitcom "Barney Miller."

To help you realize how far Johnny Orr has come, this book takes you back to the places where Johnny has labored. Orr, a coal-miner's son, grew up in small-town Illinois. After a remarkable high-school athletic experience, the Orr story zips from Champaign, Ill., to Beloit, Wis., and into the National Basketball Association for details of Orr's underpublicized college and pro playing career. The story dribbles through 40-plus years of coaching, from Milton to Hilton. There was his first major-college basketball job in Massachusetts, and his first hiatus from the game when he redshirted his career to recruit insurance agents for a company in Champaign. Then there were good times and good teams in Michigan, followed by a stunning move to Iowa.

Along with the places, the book tries to connect you with the people who have shaped Orr's life. You'll meet his family, notably his colorful wife, Romie. This First Lady of Iowa State basketball definitely agrees with Johnny, even when she never says a word. Among the testimonials is the Foreword, offered by Bob Knight, Johnny's longtime friend, whose hometown, curiously, is Orrville, Ohio.

While documenting Orr's past, the book also peeks into his future. A guy whose head college basketball jobs have come in cities named Amherst, Ann Arbor and Ames just may be working his way through the alphabet. What's the next stop, Johnny? Alaska-Anchorage? Amarillo? Annapolis? Rather than predicting a specific retirement date for Orr, the book examines his impact on college basketball and speculates on how he'll be remembered on the state and national scene.

Why do I write a book on Johnny Orr? Perhaps it's our similar athletic careers. We both had unique basketball experiences during our senior years of high school. Johnny's Taylorville gang went 45-0 to establish an Illinois record. My Davenport Assumption team of 1975–76 went 19-0. (OK, so it was 19 losses and no wins. OK, so I was cut from the team during pre-season tryouts.) My interest in Orr and the seeds for this project were planted with our first professional encounter. It was 1981; I was 22 years old and sports editor of the *Iowa State Daily* when Orr was in his first season as Cyclone head coach. It's debatable which was a worse job to have that winter.

It was a gloomy February afternoon, and Orr had just lost to an excellent Missouri team, 70-56. That wasn't unusual. What was unprecedented was the fact that while the game was in progress, Johnny marched onto the court to protest when an official appeared to ignore a flagrant foul. Johnny was mad as hell, both at the referees and with his helpless feeling of not having the superior athletes. After compiling a decent 7-4 record to start to the season, the Cyclones would win just two of their last 16 games, and this Missouri loss came during the middle of a 10-game losing streak. Johnny's walk on the wild side was greeted with a technical foul, and his tirade with the refs continued for more than one minute. After Missouri pulled away for an easy victory, and Johnny did his regular radio show and met with reporters, the still-seething coach stood alone drinking a pop in the corner of the press room.

A smart reporter would have given Orr a cooling-off period—let's say until about April. Because our next edition of the *Daily* didn't come out until Tuesday, though, I needed a solo interview to get some fresh quotes, and this was the optimal time to get them. I strolled over to the fuming Orr and asked, "Coach, you said you're tired of the way this season is going. What do you plan to do to change things?" This query drew a curt nine-word response. "We're going to go out and get some plaaay-ers," he snapped, then chugged his drink, crushed the cup as if it were an official's torso, and quickly left the room.

That was 12 years ago. Johnny is still the basketball coach, and I'm still a reporter asking questions. Gradually, Orr went out and got the players, and the head basketball coaching job at Iowa State finally became more attractive than the job of *Iowa State Daily* sports editor. You even get your own theme song if you're the coach. So, **Heeeeeeeere's Johnny . . .**

Here's
Johnny
ORR

"This 1991–92 year was one of the most fun seasons I ever had, no doubt. It think it was the most exciting season I ever had, too. We did things no one anticipated. I thought we were one of the better teams, and we proved we belonged. I think we made the NCAA selection committee look good with the way we played out in Worcester."

"Our fans were unreal again. They're going to be juiced up next year. They're really excited about Fred Hoiberg. He'll be the most popular player in school history by the time he finishes. I don't know yet if he's the best player ever from Iowa, as some are predicting. We'll wait and see on that. But he'll shoot better in the coming seasons, he's a great passer, and he's very mature. He's an A-student, too. He's just a hell of a kid. The thing about comparing him to Jeff Hornacek is that Fred was so far ahead when he came here. Jeff improved every year and has continued to improve for 10 years. Now the thing is, will Fred be able to do that?"

"I think (in 1992–93) we'll start out ranked in the top 25 nationally. Iowa will be there, too."

• Who Would'a Thought It?

In August 1991, during a rare lull in Johnny Orr's schedule, I came to the coach's Hilton Coliseum office with a fresh notebook and a mission: to coax a few additional anecdotes and to seek the compelling quote to complete this book. Johnny didn't disappoint.

During 1991 and early 1992 Orr encountered more highs and lows than a weather bureau. Personal conflicts, followed by a near tragedy, added a dramatic backdrop to his 1991–92 basketball season. Then Orr's restocked and Reeboked team laced up its shoes and took fans on its version of the Space Mountain ride. There was a fast start, the expected bumps, some scintillating surges, a sudden nosedive in the late stages, and a zoom back to the top at tourney time. After the cardinal and gold roller coaster ground to a halt in Worcester last March and the dizziness wore off, this much was clear: Cyclone basketball had a bright future, Johnny had renewed spirit, and what's more, this book had a slam-dunk finish. Make that a slam-dunk beginning here in Chapter One.

This was not a jolly Johnny speaking in August 1991. To hear the coach tell of his battles on various fronts, "Orr at War" seemed an appropriate title for the book. Along with the rigors of staying up with the likes of Kansas, Oklahoma State and Missouri on the court, Johnny came into the school year at war over a Big Eight–mandated one-game suspension; at war over sharing practice time at Hilton with the women's basketball team; and at war over the knee-jerk mentality of the NCAA reform movement. Gone were the days when the only thing to ruffle Johnny in the summer was the back nine at Veenker golf course.

Orr faced another potential conflict. The arrival of his 64th birthday that summer, coupled with the possibility of a third straight losing record, fueled an uneasiness among some fans. "It looked like Orr's legendary career was about to end with a whimper," is how *Des Moines Register* columnist Marc Hansen described the mood. "A lot of people in Ames thought Johnny's better years were behind him." The doubters felt Orr's last hurrah would be billed "On Golden Pond." They worried that their revered coach and the Cyclone program would drift along to a quiet but uneventful finale.

So much for the Asleep at the Wheel theory. Forget about the Cyclones' two straight losing records, and never mind Victor Alexander's first-round draft into the National Basketball Association. Once again, Johnny Orr raised a little hell and raised a lot of hopes, this time with a delightful 1991–92 team. Despite those preseason doubts and low expectations, Orr's 12th Cyclone season will be remembered as a winter of magic and milestones.

It was a season

. . . in which a malfunctioning furnace nearly took Orr's breath away, then a youthful basketball team did;

. . . in which Johnny became the second coach in college basketball history to become the all-time winningest coach at two different Division I schools;

. . . that started with a blowout of Maryland-Eastern Shore, a team you've never heard of, and concluded 17 weeks later with a shootout against Kentucky, a household name in college hoops;

. . . when Johnny's roster went international, as culture met agriculture. A team with eight in-state players welcomed a lanky kid from Czechoslovakia known as "Yuli";

. . . out of the 1950s, as newcomers with short haircuts and nostalgic names such as Fred, Howard and Loren provided thrills, not in the Armory, but in Hilton Coliseum;

. . . when Orr went back to play in Massachusetts, the site of his first head coaching job, first for a holiday tournament, and then for the NCAA first-round games;

. . . in which Big Eight basketball and Iowa State earned national acclaim. Cyclone victories over Iowa, Minnesota, Oklahoma, Oklahoma State, Kansas, Missouri and North Carolina-Charlotte put Ames back on the map;

. . . and when Johnny muttered the most notable rebuttal on national television since Joe Friday was holding court on "Dragnet." Bantering live on ESPN with Dick Vitale on NCAA Selection Sunday, Orr countered Vitale's mention of their past Detroit vs. Michigan meeting with "We kicked your ass."

Iowa State's determined upset of Missouri on Friday the 13th at the Big Eight quarterfinals secured the prestigious NCAA tournament bid. Then the Cyclones made a strong showing in the tourney's rugged East Regional to cap a lively 12 months in which virtually all of Orr's emotions were tapped.

• It's Always Darkest before the Dawn

The pride and satisfaction in the 21-13 finish were a far cry from the disillusionment that Orr expressed back in August, however, when he spoke of the downside of coaching college basketball in the 1990s. In a nutshell, Johnny

- Said his opening-game suspension for the 1991–92 season was unwarranted.
- Was irked that after 11 seasons at Iowa State he was being forced to share prime practice time in Hilton Coliseum with the women's basketball program.
- Was frustrated with a budget freeze that prevented his assistant coaches from receiving pay raises.
- Was irritated at what he called misguided talk of reform in college sports, particularly the opinions being offered by people far removed from the scene.
- Disagreed with Iowa State's tighter admissions policies, not only for the potential harm to fielding competitive athletic teams, but also because they deny opportunity to youths who need a chance.
- Bristled at talk that schools, not coaches, should reap the benefit of outside income arrangements.

Standing alone, each of these issues could be classified simply as irritating. Lumped together, they stuck to Orr's skin like humid August air. "I don't feel as relaxed about my job," he said in the interview. "If I was going to start out in coaching today, the way it is now, I don't think I'd go into it. There's no question it's not as much fun. It's too much of a business. As long as I was healthy, I would have wanted to coach until I was 70, no question. But now, I don't know what will happen."

Orr probably felt a little snakebit, too. The sting was fresh from the 1989 Sam Mack fiasco and two disappointing seasons that followed. Mack, Alexander and Mark Baugh were expected to provide the cornerstone of strong Cyclone teams in 1989–90 and 1990–91, and Orr beefed up the schedule accordingly. Mack left the program in 1989 after his acquittal on armed robbery charges, and Baugh washed out academically, so the next two Iowa State teams were overmatched. Iowa State finished 10-18 and 12-19 in those years, the first back-to-back losing seasons for Orr since the building years of the early 1980s. While his 1991 recruiting class was being hailed among the nation's 15 best, Johnny knew his team faced obstacles coming into 1991–92 with only one proven Division I starter (junior guard Justus Thigpen).

On a personal front, Johnny expended great time and energy for several months of 1991 in a venture with friends to try to purchase a golf course at his summer home in Panora. "I was getting all fired up," Johnny said. "I've never spent so much time on something. We did all kinds of research." It would give Orr a chance to stay actively involved in athletics when he retires from coaching. Then a late twist in the negotiations put the purchase on hold.

Something else was in the air—literally. Johnny and Romie Orr discovered the hard way in October the reason they felt so lousy in recent months. Their prolonged fatigue and listlessness had nothing to do with age or attitude, but everything to do with their exposure to a malfunctioning four-year-old furnace. The damper on the flue—the device that channels carbon monoxide from the furnace outside the house—stuck shut, causing deadly gas to back up indoors. As weeks passed, the odorless gas became so concentrated that one morning the Orrs didn't rise and shine. Romie nearly lost consciousness and had to be hospitalized on an oxygen tank for two hours to detoxify her system.

"That morning we really had a hard time getting up," Johnny recalled. "We're usually up by 6:30, but it was like 8:30 or 9:00 and we were just zapped. I thought I was having one of those dizzy spells. Romie thought she was having a stroke, so I called our daughters. They came over and said, 'You've got gas in the house.' "

The Orrs' habit of sleeping with a bedroom window open probably saved their lives. Officials measured the gas in the Orr home at 250 parts of carbon monoxide to 1 million parts other gases, a ratio considered life threatening. A Chicago house where 10 people died in a carbon monoxide tragedy the same autumn measured one half of that toxicity. "We're just lucky we had the window open. They told us that it was as bad as going into your garage and turning your keys on and sitting there. You didn't think anything like that could ever happen to you."

Romie Orr called the incident "spooky," like a bad dream. "John was scared, I was scared, the kids were scared," Romie said. "I think the carbon monoxide had been around a long time. I could hardly get my act together the whole year. I was 63 years old, but I felt like I thought I'd feel when I was 93. I couldn't shake the feeling. We were always so tired. Those are things you never think will happen to you. We try to tell everyone about it whenever we can so maybe people will check their furnace and it won't happen to them."

Romie said there was both a physical and psychological change in their health once the carbon monoxide was discovered and removed. "After this, it was literally like a shade was lifted for John," she explained. "He still gets mad about things, but after this he doesn't take it so personally. Things that bothered him last summer probably don't seem so severe now."

• A Breath of Fresh Air

Johnny clearly came into the 1991–92 season with a revived attitude. There was a new spirit on the Cyclone team, too, with an infusion of talent reminiscent of the 1985 arrival of fresh-faced Jeff Grayer and Gary Thompkins. Johnny welcomed Iowa's best three high school prospects: the state's most versatile player, its best big man, and its best three-point shooter. The Cyclones also brought in two junior-college transfers—a steady center with a reputation for defense, and a guard who was almost automatic at the free-throw line. Johnny capped the recruiting class by signing an intriguing prospect from Czechoslovakia who had attracted serious attention from no less than UCLA.

Like all recruiting classes, this group was a combination of the known and the unknown. The unknown, in terms of Division I readiness, came in the form of two junior-college transfers (Howard Eaton, a 6'6" center, and Ron Bayless, a 6'1" guard), two in-staters (Loren Meyer, a 6'11" center from Ruthven and

Hurl Beechum, a 6'5" forward from Des Moines North), and a rare overseas find (6'11" forward Julius Michalik of Prievidza, Czechoslovakia).

Complementing the unknowns was the known element of the recruiting class. He stood 6-foot-4-inches and weighed 196 pounds, not counting a ton of hometown expectations on his shoulders. Fred Hoiberg's reputation preceded him across town from Ames High. Pick a sport and hear an anecdote: basketball, football, baseball, or track and field. Hoiberg has great basketball genes, too. His grandfather, Jerry Bush, played college ball at St. John's under legendary coach Joe Lapchick and played in the pre-NBA pro basketball era in the 1940s.

"Fred's the type of athlete who would have been outstanding in whichever sport he went," said Bud Legg, a longtime coach and counselor at Ames High. "He showed me a letter he got in which the Minnesota Twins wanted him to try out. (Arizona coach) Lute Olson sat here in my office and made the statement, 'It's hard to believe everything this kid can do. It's frightening to think how good he's going to be when he concentrates on one sport.' "

Hoiberg's 8 × 11 action glossies soon outgrew the *H* folder in the photo files of the Ames *Daily Tribune* and earned Fred his own personal drawer. Hoiberg's exploits peaked as a prep senior during the Little Cyclones' 1990–91 championship basketball season, when Fred's deadly scoring from inside and outside led a deep team. It was Ames High's first gold basketball trophy at state since 1976 when another Iowa State recruit, Chuck Harmison, an eventual Australian pro basketball player, was the star.

Hoiberg averaged 29.2 ppg as a senior, with a school-record 51 points in the sub-state finals against Indianola. He closed his high school career with 108 points (36 ppg) in three state tournament victories at Vets Auditorium. Surpassing Harmison's Ames High career scoring record (1,010 points) in his junior season, Hoiberg closed his remarkable career with 1,760 points and 679 rebounds over three varsity seasons. Although AHS struggled in football in Fred's final year, Hoiberg still passed for 1,574 yards and was a good enough quarterback prospect to be recruited personally by Nebraska's Tom Osborne. In track, he was second in the high jump and ran on three place-winning sprint relays to help Ames High capture its sixth straight boys' state championship. He was the Gatorade Player of the Year in Iowa in both football and basketball.

Ames High has turned out some athletic stars, including the Gibbons brothers in wrestling, the Richard siblings in swimming, and the Burris brothers in track. Its basketball heritage ranks with the Davenports and Marshalltowns. Both Harmison and Steve Burgason played four years on scholarship at Iowa State, and Dick Gibbs, who played his senior year at AHS in the 1960s, went on to play at Texas-El Paso and six years in the NBA with the Washington Bullets. Yet in terms of multisport ability, Fred Hoiberg may be the best athlete Ames High has ever seen. "He's certainly going to be the measuring stick for future Ames High athletes," says Legg, "both with his athletic ability and interpersonal qualities."

Fort Dodge sportswriter Bob Brown, who has watched prep and college sports in the state for 50 years, saw enough of Hoiberg as a prep and a college freshman to predict last February: "Make book on it. Barring any physical calamity, Iowa State University freshman Fred Hoiberg will someday become the greatest native Iowan basketball player of all-time."

Johnny and his staff focused on Hoiberg for more than two years. The pursuit became more intense over the final months when Hoiberg's play in state and national AAU basketball further enhanced his reputation around the country. "The first time I met Coach Orr, I was six years old, and he came over to eat lunch at our house," Hoiberg said. "He came over to visit my grandfather, who used to be the basketball coach at Nebraska. Then (Orr) really recruited me hard when I was at Ames High.

"It's great playing for Coach Orr," Hoiberg now says. "He's fun to talk to off the court. When he came in for my home visit, you could tell he'd be a great guy to play for. I narrowed my choices down to Stanford, Arizona, Nebraska and Iowa State. I eventually canceled my visit to Nebraska. It came down to the night before signing day when I finally decided. I just felt Iowa State was the best opportunity for me.

"I've gotten a lot of great support in the community. People ask me if I feel any extra pressure, but I don't worry about it. I'm just trying to have a good time and play the way I can. I think we have a great four years ahead of us. I think the difference from (the 1990–91 Iowa State team) is that we're playing a lot more together as a team."

Karen Hoiberg, Fred's mother, said the only concern in her mind about Iowa State was whether Johnny would retire before Fred was finished, and what impact Orr's departure would have. "He told me he was coaching for four more years (until 1995)," Karen Hoiberg said. "I got it in writing. Though he went on to say there are never any guarantees—in fact, the Stanford coach already has left. In general Johnny was so honest."

Hoiberg wasn't the only reason Johnny and his coaches were excited when they assembled their 1991–92 team. Besides an abundance of excellent basketball skills, the roster featured exceptional all-around athletic ability. For example, in the preseason timed mile run, the 6-foot-6-inch Eaton clocked 4:53, and the 6-foot-11-inch Michalik ran 4:59, well below the best of previous center Vic Alexander. Alexander came a long way on the court in his career, and his 23.4 ppg average in 1990–91 was mighty. Johnny's best teams revolve around quicker, more mobile post players, though.

With Big Vic now wearing the uniform of the Golden State Warriors, Orr knew he would need more scoring balance, and not just from Thigpen and the newcomers. The coach saw playing opportunities for at least six other returners—guards Brian Pearson and Skip McCoy, front-liners Brad Pippett and Mike Bergman, and forwards Norman Brown and Donnell Bivens. Johnny and his coaching staff were able to blend these veteran players with the newcomers, and the mix immediately produced a positive attitude and winning team chemistry. "This team is fun to be around," Orr said. "They love to play. They love to practice. I like to watch them because they really get after it. They get along so well together."

Even the attention showered on hometowner Hoiberg didn't cause jealousy, and actually was a source of amusement. "At our last practice before Christmas break, I asked the guys if they had their stuff out of the dorms yet," Orr said, "because we had to be out that day. The only guy that wasn't ready was Fred Hoiberg. The guys call Fred 'The Mayor,' and they just said, 'Don't worry, coach. The Mayor won't have any trouble getting his stuff out if he's late. They'll unlock the door for him.' "

The Mayor and his mates had excellent long-range potential, but nobody envisioned consistent success in their first year together. Realistic goals for the Cyclones would be to finish with a record over .500, pull off a few Hilton upsets, and perhaps land an NIT tournament berth. There was no evidence that this would be an NCAA tournament team this soon. Predictions of preseason basketball magazines weren't encouraging.

One publication, *Dick Vitale's Basketball,* picked the Cyclones for seventh in the Big Eight, said it was "very doubtful" they'd make any postseason tournaments, and speculated they'd finish 15-16. Among Big Eight teams, Iowa State's was dubbed the "program under pressure."

Who are these guys? It's the first question that comes to mind when perusing ISU's roster. Victor Alexander is gone. So are Doug Collins, Paul Doerrfeld and Phil Kunz. Led by Alexander (23.4 ppg), the foursome accounted for almost two-thirds of Iowa State's scoring and rebounding last season. The holdovers (just three seniors) are Thigpen and seven players who averaged no more than 3.4 ppg. Orr remains optimistic about his youthful club. For starters, some experts rank his recruiting class in the top 20. But don't ask Orr to name a starting lineup. Right now, he couldn't . . . The win-loss record should improve, even if the team doesn't. And it won't.

The *Big Eight Basketball Yearbook* saw a seventh-place finish, too, noting: "ISU could jell towards season's end, but likely is a team of the future." United Press International's John Hendel also envisioned a seventh-place finish:

Iowa State lost even more (to graduation) than Nebraska. The Cyclones, 12-19 last year, must replace 66.7 percent of their scoring load. Johnny Orr does have Justus Thigpen back, but the pickings quickly slim from there.

Johnny said the seeds for the 1991–92 success were planted during the final half of the previous season when a brutal schedule—ranked the nation's toughest by *USA Today*—contributed to the Cyclones' 1-8 start. But Iowa State played .500 ball after mid-December against some solid foes, with victories over Michigan and NCAA qualifier Temple; a season sweep of NIT finalist Oklahoma; defeats of 20-victory teams Missouri and Oklahoma State; and respectable losses by seven points to NCAA runner-up Kansas and by 11 to Big Ten co-champ Indiana. "We were good (1990–91) at the end of the year," Orr said. "We played really hard, and I think we were a top 30-35 team, but we couldn't get any tournament bid because of that awful start. Just that stigma of starting 1-8 killed us."

Johnny was even more fired up than usual when he spoke at his 1991–92 preseason Media Day. "I'm excited because these are good kids," Johnny told reporters. "They work hard. They don't complain. They really get after it. There hasn't been one single night that I've gone home from practice unhappy . . . Sometimes they're going to set things on fire. And at other times they're going to get their brains beat in. But you can see that they have talent. As old as I am, I can tell that."

Michalik's ability was pretty much a secret outside the Cyclone coaching staff and team. Johnny hinted at Media Day that

Michalik would be a guy to watch. "Just wait until you see (Julius)," Orr said. "He can fire in that three-point shot." Orr wasn't exactly going out on a limb, though, when he said Hoiberg "is going to be a truly great player. When you see him, you won't think of him as a freshman."

The Cyclones' opening two exhibition games at Hilton allowed Johnny to experiment with his personnel puzzle in game situations. They topped an army team from Ft. Sill, Okla., 126-58, then took on a decent Ukrainian national team. Ukraine, an 85-81 loser in Iowa City the night before, was no match for Iowa State in a 91-72 decision.

• Suspension

Johnny came into 1991–92 with a 163-163 record in his first 11 seasons in Ames, and he needed four wins to become Iowa State's winningest basketball coach. He would get the first of those victories from his easy chair at home during the Sunday November 24 season-opener against Maryland-Eastern Shore. Orr had been reprimanded during the 1990–91 season for remarks about officials. When he spoke out about officiating at the 1991 Big Eight tournament, Commissioner Carl James responded with a one-game suspension. Johnny claimed his comments were taken out of context and appealed the penalty, but the appeal was denied and Orr was forced to miss his third game in 12 seasons at Iowa State—the other absences came in 1989 due to the flu and in 1991 with a back ailment. Orr had plenty of company as the year went on, though. Several coaches around the country were slapped with suspensions for their comments or actions regarding officiating, including Cincinnati's Bob Huggins, whose team later reached the Final Four.

Johnny likened his suspension to censorship and said college basketball is changing for the worse. "I think of guys like Adolph Rupp, John Bluedorn and Bones McKinney," Orr told the Ames *Daily Tribune.* "Great coaches. Holy cow, they'd have been thrown out of 50 games. But they were colorful. Now they're taking that away from the coaches. They're all going to have the same personality."

On the game night Cyclone athletic director Max Urick stopped by the Orr house to watch on television with Johnny. After two hours they thought they were viewing "Murder, She Wrote." With assistant coach Jim Hallihan directing the team, Iowa State rolled to a 114-59 victory over Maryland-Eastern

Shore, making ISU 23-4 in season openers since 1965. Thigpen, Bayless, Eaton, Hoiberg and Meyer comprised the starting cast, and all five scored in double figures for what would become one of the most balanced teams in school history.

Johnny returned to the bench two days later as the Cyclones made it 2-0 at Hilton with a 92-75 victory over Creighton. The Cyclone defensive pressure helped create 25 Bluejay turnovers, and once again, the starting five all scored in double figures. In 34 games this season, Iowa State would have 14 games in which four or more starters scored in double figures, and the team finished 13-1 in those games.

• Twilight Zone

Johnny was two wins away from passing Louis Menze as Iowa State's all-time winningest coach. Next up was a tournament in San Juan, Puerto Rico, and out of habit, Orr braced himself for some unusual developments. Sure enough, the travel plans hit a snag. "We found out (two days before the trip) that one of our flights had been canceled," Johnny said. "It seems like every time I go someplace, they cancel our plane. They never cancel the Indiana or Syracuse plane, it's always Iowa State's plane. It took us three days to get back from Hawaii (in 1990–91)."

The team sank further into the Twilight Zone in the tournament opener when it lost a 53-52 decision to Texas Christian. The Horned Frogs, coached by former Nebraska mentor Moe Iba, a master of the deliberate offense, benefited from what Orr said was the season's strangest call by a referee. The Cyclones led 52-50 with 26 seconds left but were whistled for a foul on a potential game-tying jump shot. Johnny was stunned when the official also awarded a goal-tending basket, even though Iowa State's Meyer caught the errant shot six feet from the basket. Instead of simply tying the game, TCU made the subsequent free throw for a three-point play and took a one-point lead. The Cyclones had one final chance, but Hoiberg's game-winning shot rimmed off in the closing seconds. Texas Christian went on to place third in the Southwest Conference and barely missed an NCAA tournament berth despite a 22-10 record.

Iowa State bounced back to win two games in the consolation round in Puerto Rico and give Johnny his record-setting 167th victory. The Cyclones beat American University, 108-74, and Hoiberg broke a school record in the game with seven steals.

They reached Orr's milestone with a tourney-ending 70-63 win over Maine.

The 4-1 Cyclones returned home and hosted Northern Iowa. Under Coach Eldon Miller, a longtime Orr friend, the Panthers had topped Iowa State in 1990–91 in Cedar Falls, 68-62, and broken a 10-game losing streak in the series. UNI hadn't beaten the Cyclones in Ames, however, since 1963, and it went home empty again as the Cyclones forced 30 turnovers in a 84-66 victory. "What I liked about them was their defense," Miller said in postgame remarks.

In their 5-1 start, the Cyclones showed signs their bench would be dangerous. "We had a scrimmage in practice and our reserves outscored our starters, 47-30," Orr said. "We'll be having three-hour practices, and our players don't want them to end." The depth was so promising that senior forward Morgan Wheat, a talented transfer from Vanderbilt who was practicing with the Cyclones, delayed his intention to reclaim his playing eligibility. The former West Des Moines Valley star chose to return in 1992–93 for one full season rather than finish up with just the final semester of 1991–92.

Next at home was a visit from Texas-Arlington, one of those hyphenated schools known to give opposing coaches fits. It was tempting for the Iowa State team to call this a "W" and look ahead to the marquee game four days later with the Iowa Hawkeyes. Arlington may have lacked national visibility, but it led the nation in three-point baskets in 1990–91, and had the kind of athletes who could stay with Iowa State in an up-tempo game. Resisting the urge to coast, the Cyclones scored a 96-82 victory. Michalik made his first start and answered the challenge with 19 points, 11 rebounds, and three blocked shots. Hoiberg scored 17 points, but with less than three minutes left suffered a sprained ankle that jeopardized his status for the upcoming Iowa game.

The Hilton Coliseum fans, beginning to sense an interesting winter ahead, chanted "Beat the Hawks" near the end of the contest. And just in case Iowa coach Tom Davis and his Hawkeye players needed one, Texas-Arlington coach Mark Nixon offered an appropriate warning in his postgame remarks. "Any team that comes in here will have a tough time winning," Nixon said.

Johnny had won four out of five meetings from the Hawkeyes from 1983–88, although the next three decisions went to Iowa and Coach Tom Davis. Eight of the last 14 games in the series were decided by four or less points, including Iowa's 75-73 triumph in 1991 and its 89-87 escape in 1990. The Hawks were a slight favorite to make it four in a row as they came into Hilton ranked 16th nationally with a 6-0 record. "I don't know what concerns me more, their rebounding or their press," Orr said before the game. Davis had similar pregame praise for the Cyclones and stressed that Iowa State's 6-1 record was legitimate. "While they certainly are playing a lot of new players, they're not playing like new players," Davis said. "They're playing pretty heady basketball. I don't think it's a fluke. I think it's a very strong Iowa State basketball team."

• The Hurricane Arrives

On a December night when 14,456 screaming fans showed up, the Cyclone newcomers officially arrived. Hilton magic alone doesn't explain the unranked Cyclones' convincing 98-84 victory, the biggest Iowa State winning margin in the series since 1974. The Cyclones drilled eight three-pointers, and their starters shot 59 percent from the field and combined for 90 points. Hoiberg, whose availability still was in doubt 24 hours before tip-off, played 38 minutes on the sore ankle and finished with 11 points, nine assists and seven rebounds. Thigpen's 28 points led another five-player charge in double figures. For the Hawks, Acie Earl had 32 points and James Moses sank 23, but Iowa was hurt by its 21 turnovers. The Cyclones were in control all night despite a 48-35 rebound deficit and a 35-19 deficit in free-throw attempts.

"We were like a hurricane," Orr said later. "The Michigan win in 1986 will always be my biggest, but this victory over Iowa was probably the biggest victory for Cyclone fans of any victory I've had here. I couldn't get to sleep until about 3:30 in the morning after that game, I was so excited. I've never heard it so loud in that building. It was just deafening. It was just a hell of a game. They played well, we played well. It was the most talked about game, the most watched game. The TV ratings have to be unbelievable."

Thigpen was named *Sports Illustrated*'s National Player of the Week for his 54 points in wins over Texas-Arlington and Iowa. And Iowa State wasn't the only Big Eight team opening eyes across the country. The conference stood 47-5 against non-league foes at mid-December, prompting Orr to joke, "When I first got here (to Iowa State), if you scored 55 points, you stayed up all night and called your friends. Now, if you hold anybody under 100, you're tickled to death."

The Cyclones and their fans had plenty of time to savor the

Iowa conquest. Because Tennessee State pulled out of its December 21 game at Hilton in the fall, the Cyclone schedule had a gaping hole. Nebraska-Omaha was picked up for a December 31 game as a replacement. The December 14 Iowa win was followed by a 13-day layoff for final exams and the Christmas holiday. The next stop was Springfield, Mass., and the Naismith Holiday Classic, featuring Orr's return to the site of his first college head coaching post. Orr and Co. opened the four-team tournament against Fairfield and extended its winning streak to six with a 92-59 decision; a streak that produced a 91.3 ppg scoring pace and an average victory margin of 20 points. The championship game was an expected matchup against Massachusetts but a somewhat unexpected final score. The 10-2 Minutemen showed why they would become one of the surprise teams in America in 1991–92. UMass, which went to the Final 16 of the national tournament and finished 30-5, used a 15-2 run in the first half en route to a 73-53 win. "We're a young team, and this was our first bad game," Orr said in postgame comments.

The Cyclones returned home for a unique New Year's Eve game with Nebraska-Omaha. The sluggish performance at Massachusetts prompted Johnny to work out his team twice the day before and once on game day. The Division II Mavericks felt the brunt of the Cyclones' force, and what followed was a 114-57 victory for Orr's team.

Now 9-2, Iowa State rolled into the 1992 portion of the schedule with a tricky road test at Minnesota in the Gophers' ancient Williams Arena, a building where Cyclone teams were 3-14 all-time. This Gopher team, like Orr's bunch, looked to be a year or two away from emerging nationally, but was tough to beat at home. Minnesota later would beat Final Four teams Indiana and Michigan along with Michigan State at home, but the Cyclones handed the Gophers a rare Minneapolis defeat, 76-73. With the score tied in the final seconds, Bayless' slick lob to Thigpen on an inbounds pass under the Iowa State basket resulted in the winning three-point play. This road win, the first by Iowa State in Minneapolis since 1968, later would prove crucial to the Cyclones' case for an NCAA tournament bid.

"We're 10-2, and I can't believe it," Johnny said after the Williams Arena escape. "We beat a good Iowa team and a fine Minnesota team from the Big Ten. Maybe we should switch leagues."

Orr came back to earth as he prepared for a mid-week game at Hilton against another hyphenated school, Loyola-Chicago. Loyola, 7-2, owned wins over Purdue and Northwestern, and looked dangerous as it trailed the Cyclones just 37-33 at half-time. Iowa State broke open the game with 55 second-half points and claimed a 92-69 win, aided by Michalik's career-high 23 points. The victory let the Cyclones take an unexpected 11-2 record into its Big Eight opener against Oklahoma set for Hilton Coliseum.

• Big Eight Season

Of all the Big Eight foes, Oklahoma was the only school with a winning record (6-5) at Hilton in Orr's 11 years. Coach Billy Tubbs's 1991–92 team came to Ames ranked 21st nationally with a 10-1 record. Its only defeat was an 86-73 decision at Massachusetts, the same team that derailed the Cyclones. Iowa State basketball alumni on hand for a pregame scrimmage shared the Iowa State fans' excitement. "This team reminds me a lot of our team," said Gary Thompkins, a starting guard on the 1985–86 team that made the NCAA Final 16.

All the ingredients were in place: OU was in town, the Big Eight season was here, the "Sit Down, Billy!" signs were out. The building was unusually calm, however, as Iowa State shot just 32 percent from the field in the first half and trailed 39-28 at the break. It looked bleak when the Sooners' lead reached 14 points with 9:23 to go and the Cyclones couldn't sustain any rallies. Orr said later "We were in a funk, boy. I told (assistant Jim) Hallihan, 'We've got to have a complete change here, man.' " The Cyclones replaced funk with spunk and exploded down the stretch to out-score OU 21-5. Michalik's basket and foul shot with 16 seconds left erased a one-point deficit and put Iowa State ahead 73-71. The Sooners couldn't answer in the closing seconds and the Cyclones escaped with a thrilling victory. "How old is that guy?" Tubbs asked in his press conference, referring to the 19-year-old Michalik. Julius played all 40 minutes and contributed 18 points and nine boards in a performance that would earn him Big Eight Player of the Week honors. "That was one of the greatest comebacks I've ever been around," Johnny said.

Cedar Rapids *Gazette* columnist Mike Hlas offered this assessment of the win:

> To no one's shock, Orr was bubbly after the game. His team stole a big game, and he knew it, but Orr also has come to the conclusion he has a ballclub on his hands. "Julius, (Friday) night at our practice, he was absolutely phenomenal," Orr said. "It's the first time that I've felt that maybe this team is pretty good. Be-

cause he was just drilling everything, and making passes, and doing everything in the world."

With this January 11 victory, the 12-2 Cyclones already matched their win total of the previous season. They also earned their first appearance in the national top 25 rankings in four seasons, as they moved in at No. 24 in Monday's ratings. The Cyclones were one of five Big Eight teams ranked, although they would have trouble staying there with the conference schedule kicking in.

The Cyclones extended their record to 13-2 and 11 wins in 12 outings with a 92-55 home win over Division II school Morningside. Next came a trip to Stillwater to play the 15-0 Cowboys, the preseason NIT winner and the talk of the country with a No. 3 ranking. Oklahoma State put its 25-game home-court win streak on the line and promptly dispatched the Cyclones, 85-67, behind Byron Houston's 34 points. "Oklahoma State is good enough to go to the Final Four," Orr said after the game.

Now 13-3, the Cyclones rebounded to bury Drake in Des Moines, 92-61, behind Hoiberg's 24 points and 10 rebounds. Johnny's team broke to a 21-2 lead and gave Drake its worst home loss since 1983. The 31-point win also marked the fattest road victory ever by a Cyclone team. Next came a Big Eight home game with Kansas State, 0-2 in the league and 9-5 overall. Once again, Iowa State started slow and found itself trailing 23-14 early. The Cyclones built a perilous 38-34 halftime lead but shot 76 percent from the field in the second half to post an 85-59 victory. That 26-point win was Iowa State's biggest over Kansas State since 1946. Two nights later, Iowa State made it 16-3 overall and 13 straight at Hilton with a 114-76 win over Chicago State in its final non-conference game. The Cyclones shot 63 percent from the field and they finished the month at 7-1, the best January showing by an Iowa State team since 1978.

The Cyclones' Space Mountain ride took some unexpected dips over the next five weeks. Off the court, two reserve players, Saun Jackson and Bivens, were arrested in incidents involving, respectively, a firearm and shoplifting. Both were suspended from the squad, although Bivens returned to the team one game later. Johnny himself was slowed by a nagging virus—one that would hang on through March—and these police problems did nothing to improve his health. Then came back-to-back road defeats at Nebraska (68-63) and at Missouri (81-71) that reinforced how difficult this Big Eight season would be.

Now facing its first two-game losing streak of the season,

Iowa State stood 16-5 overall and 2-3 in the conference. Orr and Co. faced a string of three games in six days, starting with a Monday night home game against Colorado set for a national telecast on ESPN. The Buffs, 10-8 overall, were mired in the conference cellar, but they played like an NCAA tournament team on this night. The Cyclones saw a 15-point second-half lead evaporate, although their TV viewers missed the exciting moments. The verdict in the Mike Tyson rape trial was announced during the second half, so ESPN abruptly switched away from the Iowa State telecast, leaving basketball fans in limbo. Colorado's furious rally forced a 77-77 tie after regulation ended, but Iowa State outscored the Buffs 19-5 during the five-minute overtime. "Boy if we didn't get this one, I don't know what we'd do with Kansas and Oklahoma State coming up," Orr said.

Two nights later, the fourth-ranked Jayhawks once again made Johnny's trek to Lawrence a downer. Kansas handed Iowa State the worst defeat of the season, 91-60. KU shot 62 percent to Iowa State's 36 percent and dropped the Cyclones to 17-6 overall and 3-4 in the conference. Thigpen picked the wrong night to second-guess Orr's strategy, and Johnny kept his star guard out of the starting lineup the next game, a home encounter with No. 2 Oklahoma State.

The Cowboys had surged to a 20-0 start before stumbling in upset losses at Nebraska and Colorado. Coach Sutton's team wasn't going to be surprised on this day, though. The Cowboys raced to a 38-20 halftime lead, aided by Iowa State's 29-percent shooting and their own 62-percent proficiency. Just when Orr's guys looked like they were headed for their fourth loss in five games, Thigpen charged out of the doghouse to fuel a late rally. Iowa State canned an unreal 24-of-30 shots from the field in the second half, and Thigpen's basket with :06 remaining forged overtime at 67-67. Down six with one minute left in overtime, the Cyclones stormed ahead 84-83 on Hoiberg's basket and foul shot with :09 to go. The Cowboys drew a foul and had a chance to win, but Darwyn Alexander, a 90-percent free thrower the previous season, clanked two off the rim with two seconds left. That let Iowa State escape with its 18th win and even its conference record at 4-4. "I've been coaching 42 years and I've never had a greater comeback, I don't think, in my career," Orr said. Johnny improved his overtime record to 12-6 in 12 seasons at Iowa State with this triumph.

The victory over the nation's second-rated team put Iowa State in good shape for an NCAA tournament bid. Johnny's fun bunch stood 18-6 with six regular-season games left, and apparently needed two more wins to lock up a bid to the NCAA tourney. With Kansas State and Nebraska on the schedule in the next week, the Cyclones even had a chance to climb back into the title chase. Iowa State broke to a 34-26 halftime lead over the Wildcats, but Iowa State's flat 21-point output in the second half and K-State's 17-8 edge in free throws doomed the Cyclones in a 64-55 defeat. All four favored Big Eight teams lost on this night, typifying the conference's unpredictable state in 1991–92.

A return to Hilton the following Saturday for a rematch with 16-6 Nebraska was expected to solve Iowa State's woes. But the Cyclones' postseason hopes were thrown for a loop as the Huskers posted an 80-70 victory and ended Iowa State's 15-game home-court win streak. Johnny's habit of stressing positives with players went out the window after this defeat. "That was as mad as I've ever seen Coach," Hoiberg said. Orr told reporters that he hates to get mad at players, but he went on to say, "You've got to get mad at 'em, damn it, when they're not doing it. And they didn't do it today. Hell, I told them I was mad at 'em. If they don't change, we'll make some changes. The players aren't running the show. I'm running the show. They'll play hard, or they'll be on the bench."

The slumping Cyclones returned to Hilton four days later to play No. 6 Missouri, which boasted an excellent 19-4 record. The Cyclones shot 70 percent from the field in the first half and took a 42-38 halftime lead, but the Tigers prevailed in the final half and went on to post a 75-71 victory. In the postgame press conference, reporters seized on the Cyclones' current 2-6 February record and asked Johnny if the pressure was getting to his young team. "We're playing good teams, not just a bunch of ding-dongs," Orr said in defense.

A February 29 leap day trip to Norman, Oklahoma, was next for the Cyclones, now 18-9 overall and 4-7 in the conference. Fittingly, Johnny endured one of those days he'd only like to experience every four years. The Iowa State slump hit four as Oklahoma broke to a 45-26 halftime lead and went on to score a 96-70 victory. That was the most points Iowa State allowed during the regular season.

Johnny's team ushered in March with a rematch against Kansas at Hilton Coliseum. NCAA tournament speculation was the rage by now, and it looked like the Cyclones needed two more wins to reach the 64-team carnival. A win over Kansas seemed imperative, not only to boost the Iowa State argument at selection time, but to restore some confidence in a team rapidly losing altitude. The Jayhawks, coming off an emotional home victory over Oklahoma State on ESPN just two nights earlier, were ranked No. 3 nationally with a 22-3 record. KU was 7-1 against Iowa State since Coach Roy Williams came on board in 1988–89, including two straight victories in Hilton Coliseum. All of which made Iowa State's 70-66 victory sweet for Johnny and his team. The Jayhawks erased a 60-49 deficit and pulled within 64-64 with 1:50 left, but Michalik scored two baskets and the Cyclones had a big steal in the closing minute.

Three days later, the Cyclones took an 0-6 Big Eight road record to Boulder, where a victory would have pushed Iowa State to the 20-win plateau and gained a sorely-needed road victory. The stubborn Buffaloes wouldn't yield, however, and used a glaring advantage in free throws to post an 87-83 victory. Michalik went scoreless, which is revealing: in games after December 31, the Czech was held under 12 points just seven times, yet the Cyclones were 0-7 in those clashes. Told that Colorado coach Joe Harrington said Iowa State was deserving of an NCAA bid, Johnny said, "Joe isn't on the selection committee."

Iowa State, 19-11 and 5-9, finished in a tie for sixth in the conference with Kansas State, but won the tie-breaker to earn the sixth seed and the right to face third-seed Missouri, 20-7 and rated No. 9 nationally, in the Big Eight quarterfinals at Kansas City. There were arguments for and against a Cyclone bid to the NCAAs, but everyone believed they needed a win over the Tigers. Never before had a 5-9 conference finisher received an NCAA at-large bid, although few conferences ever had a season like the Big Eight did in 1991–92. The conference posted a remarkable 97-13 record against non-conference foes (.882 winning percentage), including a 21-5 mark against teams who played in the 1991 NCAA tourney.

The Cyclones' bubble predicament vaulted them into the national spotlight. Johnny was quoted in a page-one story by Steve Wieberg in *USA Today* on the morning of the Cyclones' Friday the 13th game with Missouri.

> Many teams on the fence are pleading their final on-court cases this weekend. "It puts a lot of pressure on us," says Iowa State coach Johnny Orr, whose 19-11 Cyclones are playing under the committee's noses in the Big Eight tournament in Kansas City, Mo. "They're watching." . . . Also fairly obvious is what's to become of the handful of regular-season conference champions who were upset in their league tournaments (Wisconsin-Green Bay, Louisiana Tech, Richmond and James Madison all are longshots). And how much they'll squawk if the selection committee hands a bid to Iowa State in spite of the Cyclones' 5-9 finish in

the Big Eight. Iowa State counters with the strength of that conference—it was the nation's best this season—and victories over NCAA-bound Iowa, Oklahoma, Oklahoma State and Kansas, plus fence-sitter Minnesota.

Iowa State had lost six of the last seven meetings against Missouri and was 0-4 all-time against the Tigers in the Big Eight tournament. The Cyclones' desire to reach the NCAA was evident with their blistering start. Michalik scored 14 first-half points as the Cyclones swarmed to a 39-21 lead with 2:21 to play in the opening half. But Missouri stormed back with a 27-6 run, including 15 consecutive points early in the second half, to take a 54-49 lead with 12:02 remaining. Iowa State didn't collapse, though. Johnny's guys trailed 73-70 with three minutes left but outscored the Tigers 10-2 thereafter. The 80-75 upset of Missouri was the Cyclones' 20th on the season and was accomplished with 57-percent shooting and five Iowa State starters scoring in double figures. The Cyclones overcame the Tigers' 37-30 edge in rebounds, their 32-16 edge in free throws and the Tigers' modest total of 10 turnovers. "We played our guts onto the floor in the last five minutes," Hoiberg said. "We were playing for our NCAA lives." For the first time since the Oklahoma State win, Johnny and Iowa State fans could sleep easier. "The decision is up to the NCAA Selection Committee," Orr said. "But I'd be nutty if I said I didn't think we belonged in the tournament."

The Cyclones showed the effects of the emotional win and a lack of sleep the next afternoon when they lost in the semifinal round to Oklahoma State, 69-60. After taking a 15-10 lead, they were outscored 16-2 in a stretch before halftime and shot just 28 percent in the first half. "Emotionally, we just weren't sharp after our big win Friday night," Orr said. McCoy scored 11 and was the only Cyclone to score in double figures. The Cowboys sputtered most of the game, too, but capitalized on 46 free throws to Iowa State's 13. A win or a better showing here would have guaranteed an NCAA berth, although Johnny and the Cyclones had plenty of reasons to be optimistic. In the Sagarin computer rankings, Iowa State ranked 29th, one of six Big Eight teams in the top 30. Add in the Cyclone victories over Kansas (a 27-5 finisher), Oklahoma State (28-8 finisher), Missouri and Oklahoma (both 21-9 finishers) and Iowa (19-11 finisher), and the case looked strong.

• NCAA at Last

Johnny and his players returned to Ames Sunday and assembled in the team room of Hilton Coliseum with some pizza to watch the announcement of the NCAA tournament pairings on CBS-TV. Pizza Hut wasn't the only thing that delivered on this afternoon. When the Cyclones saw their school name on the screen matched up against North Carolina-Charlotte, a roar went through the room followed by cheers and high fives. Exactly sixteen weeks after the season started here on a Sunday evening in November, the Cyclones were celebrating and Johnny was off to his ninth NCAA tournament appearance in 19 years.

A few days earlier, ESPN, expecting that Iowa State would be a bubble team, arranged to get a live reaction shot of Johnny and his players at Hilton. The team waited patiently, and nearly 20 minutes after the remaining selections were announced, Johnny was interviewed live on ESPN by John Saunders, Jim Valvano and Dick Vitale. Immediately before the switch to Ames, Vitale said on the air that a team with less than a .500 conference record shouldn't get invited to the NCAA tournament. He quickly added, "Don't get mad at me, Johnny Orr." Also interviewed live was James Madison coach Lefty Driesell, whose team was knocked off in his conference tournament and missed an NCAA berth despite a 21-10 record. The Cyclones' 5-9 Big Eight finish again was brought up, and if the network thought Orr was going to give the diplomatic response, it was wrong. After Driesell, Vitale and Valvano had their say, Johnny countered that if the Cyclones would have played in James Madison's Colonial Athletic Association instead of the Big Eight, "We'd have won 30 games." Johnny argued that if you add two perennial losing programs to the Big Eight, such as Northwestern and Wisconsin, his team might have been 9-9 instead of 5-9. "I used to coach in the Big Ten, and you had Wisconsin and Northwestern, that's four wins every year. We don't have that in the Big Eight."

Johnny went on to say he was sorry for Driesell, and said the remedy is to invite the best 64 teams, period, and throw out all the automatic berths that benefit the smaller schools. Johnny had a parting shot for ESPN's commentators, too. He likely spoke for many Division I coaches in the country when he said, "Hey, Valvano and Dick (Vitale), I want to get me one of those jobs like you've got. You don't go to practices or anything and you just say whatever you want." Valvano countered that he had a lofty NCAA tournament record as a coach (14-6), and Vitale mentioned that he was coaching the University of Detroit team that played Johnny's No. 1–ranked Michigan team in the 1977 NCAA tournament. "Yeah, and we kicked your ass," Orr said. (Johnny said later that he doesn't agree with many statements Vitale makes, but he harbors no bad feelings against Dickie V. personally. "I saw Vitale at the NCAA tournament and we had a good visit," Orr said.)

Johnny told reporters at a Sunday evening press conference, "We think we deserved to go. We beat the nos. 2, 3, 9 and 11 teams in the country. We had four players who had never played Division I before. We've come a long way. We've won 20 games. I don't think any team is more exciting than us in the United States. They've done things that no one, even the coaches, thought they would do."

The flip side of the controversy was that Iowa State gained some excellent national exposure with its invitation to the tournament. The top headline on page one of the *USA Today* sports section the following morning read, "Iowa State stands taller than its record." The story praised Iowa State and Orr's season but questioned whether the super conferences like the Big Eight deserved six berths. Most teams that were left out of the NCAA party, though, did little in the NIT tournament to back up their case. Nine 20-win teams went to the NIT and promptly lost their first game. Driesell's James Madison team lost to 15-14 Rutgers—a team that went 6-10 in its conference—in the first round. Other first-round NIT losers included 24-5 Wisconsin-Green Bay, 22-7 Richmond, 24-8 Ball State, 23-7 Louisiana Tech, 22-7 Southern Illinois, 21-7 Penn State, 20-8 Alabama-Birmingham, and 20-8 Cal-Santa Barbara.

Iowa State erased all doubts whether it belonged in the NCAAs when it shot down North Carolina-Charlotte, 76-74, in the first round game at Worcester, Mass. Charlotte, the school that eliminated Orr's No. 1–ranked Michigan team in the 1977 NCAA regional finals, came in with a 23-8 record after a one-point win over Tulane in the Metro Conference tournament finals. Iowa State trailed 31-29 at halftime but hit six three-pointers on the game and built a 66-57 lead with two minutes to play. Charlotte applied the pressure with some late threes and cut the lead to three in the final minute, but a breakaway pass to Hoiberg produced a clinching slam dunk—reminiscent of the Jeff Hornacek to Elmer Robinson inbound pass and breakaway layup that deflated Michigan late in the 1986 NCAA tournament game. Thigpen had 20 points, Hoiberg had 17 points and eight rebounds, Eaton had 10 points and nine rebounds, Michalik tossed in 13 points and Bayless scored nine.

The Friday afternoon victory earned the Cyclones a Sunday meeting against Southeastern Conference champion Kentucky, 27-6, ranked ninth in the final poll. If you'd have told Orr his team would score 98 points, get a combined 62 points from Thigpen and Bayless, get a 34-of-38 performance at the free-throw line, outrebound the Wildcats 33-27, and commit just 13 turnovers, he'd have taken it in a second. The problem was Kentucky was even better. Coach Rick Pitino's team canned 11-of-22 three-point shots, made 10-of-12 free throws in the final 80 seconds, shot 59 percent from the field, and committed just 10 turnovers. The Cyclones, who trailed all game, pulled within 93-90 late but couldn't get over the hump in a 106-98 loss. Thigpen (32 points) and Bayless (30) turned in one of the best backcourt showings in Iowa State history as they combined to make 24-of-25 free throws en route to scoring their 62 points. Cyclone Brad Pippett closed out his career with 12 points off the bench. Kentucky advanced to the final 16, and after disposing of Massachusetts, the Wildcats had No. 1–ranked Duke in serious trouble in the regional final. Kentucky held a one-point lead with only two seconds left, but an amazing length-of-the-court pass and Christian Laettner's desperation shot hit all net and denied the Wildcats a spot in the Final Four.

Thigpen said that the NCAA berth capped a season that was rewarding in many other ways. "Coach Orr seemed to be a lot more at ease this year," Thigpen said. "This is more his type of team, smaller, quicker, up-tempo style. Last season, we had to slow it down a lot to counter our lack of quickness. Winning has brought a little bit of youth back to him. You can see it when he jokes around with us, and comes out and shoots baskets with us. I've come to see Johnny Orr as a father figure. He's a good person, and you see he can do so much to help you. I'm just happy I got the chance to play for him. He'll get mad at you, but he realizes we're a young team. Sometimes, the losses help you mentally learn more. The way he sees it, losing isn't fun, but if we have to lose in order to win, let's do it."

• The Coaches' Coach

Johnny capped this memorable season with a trip with his entire family to the Final Four in Minneapolis. A highlight of the weekend came on the eve of the Duke-Michigan national championship clash, when Orr was inducted as president of the National Association of Basketball Coaches. An audience of more than

1,300, including a virtual who's who of past and present coaches in the country, listened as Orr closed the program with a brief talk about his vision for the NABC in 1992-93.

At the start of the banquet, master of ceremonies Curt Gowdy told the crowd that Michigan coach Steve Fischer and Duke coach Mike Krzyzewski would speak first so they could leave and return to their teams for further preparations for Monday's title game. Fischer said he wanted to stay, though, explaining, "I don't want to leave right away if I can help it. It's great for me to watch Johnny Orr be inducted as president of the NABC. He's a Michigan man. He's a good guy and he's done great things everywhere he's coached. Both (my wife) Angie and I think the world of Johnny and Romie, so I think we're going to hang around."

Krzyzewski came to the microphone and evoked a roar of laughter when he teased Johnny with the following remarks, "I'm not going to stay tonight. I'm not a Michigan man, and I hate Johnny Orr. I don't think he should be president of our organization. In fact, I think I was the one vote against him getting picked. I think we should have a president who can speak, and when he gets up here, you'll understand what I'm talking about."

When Johnny came to the podium, he said, "I'm an old Michigan man, so Mike Krzyzewski, I've got to be for the Wolves tomorrow night." Johnny offered kind words for both championship coaches. "When you see guys like Mike Krzyzewski and Steve Fischer here," he said, "it just makes me sick when you read all the bad things being written about our coaches' images. These guys are just terrific for the game."

Orr wanted to have a more visible role in the NABC leadership. Knowing that he soon would be retiring from coaching, Orr asked two other vice presidents if he could move ahead of them in the rotation so he could gain the president's chair. "My desk is already covered with letters from coaches wanting help with jobs or other problems," Orr explained. "I'm going to be very active and take part in as many things as I have time for. I have two main goals: (1) to get the legislation changed back so we can have four full-time coaches, and (2) to get the rule back so we can have 14 scholarships. I think it can pass if we do it properly. The Division I coaches are 100 percent unanimous behind these things."

Johnny Orr's 1991-92 season—indeed his five decades in coaching—can be summed up by an anecdote he told at the NABC convention involving NCAA executive director Dick Schultz, the former Iowa Hawkeye basketball coach. "I remember when I worked at Michigan for (athletic director) Don

Canham, brother, he was tight with money. When I went on the road, I'd stay in single rooms to save money. Then I met Ralph Miller, the Iowa coach, and man, he had a big suite. He had a party going on in his room and invited me in, and get this: Dick Schultz (then the Iowa assistant coach) was the bartender. Hell, now Dick is the executive director of the NCAA. It's amazing how far you can go in this business."

"I was never the class-clown type in school. I was an outgoing individual, but always very serious. I wasn't a real funny guy. I think when I got into pro basketball and then got into coaching, I became a lot looser the more I got out into the public. The speaking is something I warmed up to. The more I did it, boom—it just came to me. My public speaking ability is a natural thing. In fact, I'm much better when I don't use notes. About 90 percent of the time I don't. I've talked to every kind of group there is."

"If I didn't have a sense of humor, I wouldn't still be here coaching. It's a way to let the steam off. I get uptight some but never have had ulcers or anything like that. When you lose games, it's very difficult to be funny. It comes much easier when you win. The thing about dealing with young kids, well, I wouldn't say it's frustrating, but it's unpredictable. Just when you think you have things going well, something nutty happens. During the season it happens just about every day. Something pops up that's never entered your mind and you can't believe it would happen."

• Funny Guy

Volkswagen boasts of a European experience called *Fahrvergnügen,* an intangible feeling its cars are said to evoke. Likewise, Iowa State basketball fans have experienced *Orrvergnügen,* thanks to their big wheel of a coach. Orr's style has never been called European, except perhaps for an occasional sideline outburst in French. Yet Johnny clearly comes from a world of his own.

Johnny Orr didn't make wild promises when he moved from Michigan to Ames. Over time, Orr and his teams did make people cheer and feel proud. Best of all, Orr made people laugh. Don't underestimate the latter accomplishment. It's a skill that won't be appreciated fully by Iowa State fans until after Orr calls his last time out at courtside and a successor steps into the job.

A lot of people say funny things. A select few are consistently funny. To know Orr is to know the difference. "When Hayden Fry first moved to Iowa, the state thought he was funny," said former Ames sportswriter John Akers. "And for a summer, he was. But Fry was only delivering material about how bad his first Hawk-eye team was going to be. Orr, on the other hand, has a gift for seeing things in different hues from the greys that most of us see. Orr is as funny when his teams are winning as he is when they're losing."

With Orr, you laugh at his material, you laugh at his delivery, you laugh at his spontaneity, you laugh at his expressions, you laugh at his voice, and you laugh at his vocabulary. You even laugh at his laugh. "Johnny has that look . . . he just looks funny," said former Iowa State wrestling coach Jim Gibbons.

Colleague Rod Wilson emphasized that Orr doesn't need alcoholic spirits to attain his own lively spirit. "Sometimes, he's acting so goofy, people think he's intoxicated," Wilson said. "But he's just being himself. He'll break you up whether he's drinking 7Up or a mixed drink."

Cyclone assistant athletic director Dave Cox said Orr's stand-ups are as entertaining as watching reruns of "Cheers." "I've heard some of those rotten jokes 25 times," Cox said, "and I still laugh at them every time. They're still funny."

Akers noted how difficult it is to capture Johnny's freewheeling comedy monologues in print. "It was the reporter's curse to come back from an Orr luncheon thinking you had great material, only to open your notebook and discover that it wasn't what Orr had said that was funny, but how he delivered it. That delivery—the high-pitched voice, and then the sudden pause, the 'Whoo-ee, coach!' and the cackle. That was a never-fail method to make his audience howl."

"John mixes humor and honesty as well as anyone I know," said Bobby Randall, the Cyclone baseball coach. "Like all those guys with charisma, when they walk in, they're in control. And John is always in control of the situation. John likes the spotlight, but the thing I've always appreciated about John is that he can get the spotlight without stepping on everyone else. (ISU football coach) Jim Walden is an outgrowth of John. Jim has his own distinct personality, but Jim will let John get top billing. They're both top dogs. They're shrewd—very perceptive of what's going on."

Des Moines Register sportswriter Rick Brown said Orr often is funny when he's not trying to be. "At the (1989–90) Baylor game, Johnny was sick and missed the game, and (assistant coach Jim) Hallihan had to coach," Brown explained. "Orr was having headaches, so he had a brain scan taken. He was scared to death that he had a tumor. He got the tests back and found out he was OK, and he was so excited he said, 'They checked my brain, and there's nothing there.' He wasn't trying to be funny, it just came out that way."

Former Cyclone player Malvin Warrick recalls laughing after practices with teammate Lefty Moore over Johnny's high-pitched voice. "Orr would yell at us in certain practice drills, 'Get over there . . . Now get back over here . . . And back over here!' in a shrieking voice. He didn't know it, but it tickled us to death, man."

In Orrspeak, lively words like "nutty," "cuckoo" and "whoo" jump out of his vocabulary like kernels exploding from a hot air popper. Some people say Orr even is funny when he curses. Away from basketball, Orr the speaker is regarded as a savvy entertainer who can take control. Many observers say that Johnny's humor works so well because, like Orr himself, it's genuine. He'll zing himself or his own players as regularly as he gets a dig in on an official or a broadcaster.

Former Cyclone Jeff Hornacek recalled a Cyclone Club outing in State Center when he was given a pie to throw in Orr's face. "I wasn't really going to throw it, but he didn't know for sure whether I would or not, and the crowd had a lot of fun with it. There are not many guys who are that loose that a player can act that way around."

Like comedian and philanthropist Jerry Lewis, Orr roams the spectrum from seriousness to silliness. He puts his time and energy into charity projects like the Variety Club of Iowa or the Muscular Dystrophy Association and earns a reputation as a class act. Then he gets on the golf course or to the podium at the same charity event and becomes the class clown. "Coaches are all like little kids, that's why we coach," said Iowa State assistant track coach Ron McEachran. "John's that way."

Dave Cox added, "John's vain about his age. He thinks he's 18 years old. But during the games and during the season, John's about 95 years old. He's exhausted when the game is over because every eyelash, every corpuscle is invested in that game. But when basketball is over and recruiting is finished, and he can go play golf and go on the outings, that's when you see that 18-year-old come out."

Perhaps the best evidence of Orr's silly side was his role in Iowa State's acclaimed Bartles & Jaymes "Cooler Coaches" promotional campaign. It started as one poster linking Orr and newly hired Iowa State football coach Jim Walden. It played off Orr's and Walden's down-home personalities and their resemblance to the characters in the popular Bartles & Jaymes wine cooler ads. The project mushroomed into additional posters, TV commercials, music cassettes and even a music video. It earned Iowa State positive national publicity—including a photo and write-up in *Sports Illustrated*—at a time when it needed it most. Morale and fan interest had dipped at Iowa State in 1986 after the football program was assessed NCAA penalties and had its head coach fired. "It's hard to say what an overall success this (Orr-

Walden campaign) has been," Cyclone athletic director Max Urick said at the time. "But it sure has lightened the load around here." Orr and Walden returned the next season as singing Old West gamblers, with another poster, a music video and a cassette tape.

Few people with such high public visibility are so brave, especially at age 60. Orr's willingness to join the Bartles & Jaymes gig, willing to play second fiddle to the football coach, no less, again displayed his carefree side. "I don't see a lot of fear in John," said Bobby Randall. "That silly poster and (music) records that Johnny and Walden did, most coaches would never do that. He's not afraid to take risks."

"I thought it was a hell of a promotion," Orr said. "I didn't get kidded about it too much. Everyone who saw it liked it and thought it was a terrific idea. It made the people of Iowa State feel good to see the football and basketball coach getting along so well. It was a fun thing and reached people all over the country. It never really got overdone, although it probably was good we ended it when we did. It would be fun to come back with it again sometime."

Orr's only complaint, offered in jest, is that his back was sore from figuratively carrying Walden through the project. "They called me and asked if I'd get my picture taken with the football coach," Johnny said, tongue-in-cheek. "They told me it would only take a few minutes, but I knew we'd have to be there two to three hours just to get one good picture of Walden. Then we did the TV commercials, and it took like six hours, all because of Walden's ineptness. He couldn't get his lines right, and all he said was 'Thank you for your support.' Then we did the singing and cut the tapes, and we had to do about 100 takes. The guy kept saying, 'John, you're fine, but Jim, we're going to have to do yours over.' "

Johnny has found reams of comedy material in describing his relationships with certain colorful Cyclone players. His occasional "Can't live with them, can't live without them" routine with guys like Ron Falenschek, Sammy Hill, Lafester Rhodes, Elmer Robinson and Victor Alexander played well. Colleagues say it works because Johnny understands the difference between ribbing and ridicule and doesn't cross the line. "Even though in public he makes light of his players and sometimes appears to cut them down, deep down the players know he's there for them," said Iowa State track coach Bill Bergan. "He has their best interests at heart."

"When he used humor, he always used it in a way that

wasn't critical," Hornacek said. "If a guy made a mistake, he wouldn't get down on them." In fact, part of the reason Iowa State's Cyclone Club summer outings and luncheons became so popular are the anecdotes Johnny tells about players, allowing fans to see the athletes' personal side.

Johnny's wit and "whoos" made him a hit with the media, too, especially out-of-state reporters who often encounter more mundane sources. Jon Roe of the *Minneapolis Star and Tribune* once wrote: "Johnny Orr was bubbling, and when the old coach bubbles, the listener feels like he is standing under Niagara Falls." In a coaching world full of cautious types and cliché masters, it's refreshing when Orr is on a roll, like when he hits a press conference with a comment like the one he uncorked at his 1986–87 Cyclone preseason media day: "We're picked in the top 20 in just about everybody's poll. Except Dick Vitale's . . . (pause for effect) . . . and he's an asshole anyway."

"Johnny gets away with saying things nobody else gets away with," said Iowa State play-by-play broadcaster Pete Taylor, who admits he's been close to tears more than once when Orr's at the microphone and rolling. Gibbons added, "The truth is funny, and that's why Johnny's so funny."

Like the time Orr said that former player David Moss "had the longest arms he's ever seen on a white guy." Only Johnny would make such an off-the-wall observation. Or the time he said his Fort Dodge recruit Tom Peterson "can really jump for a white guy." The remark was perceived by some as being racist or derogatory to his player, but Peterson said he always considered the remark "a compliment." Peterson, who played on Johnny's second through fifth Cyclone teams, explained that behind the occasional banter, the coach treated all of his players with respect, both blacks and whites, in-staters or out-of-staters. "If people don't understand Coach Orr, it's a shame they don't see him in certain situations, like before practice when he's asking you about your family and your classes," Peterson said. "He's really a caring person."

Orr's best one-liner? There could be several nominations, but several reporters recall another preseason media day comment, prior to the start of his third Iowa State season. Fort Dodge sports editor Bob Brown was inquiring about the weight of 6-foot-11-inch center Ron Falenschek. A classic wide-bodied post player recruited by previous Cyclone coach Lynn Nance, Falenschek wasn't the mobile, 6-foot-8-inch racehorse-type center that Orr prefers. Yet Johnny is quick to say that his first Cyclone team suffered greatly when Falenschek was sidelined for 10 games with a foot injury. Brown asked at the press conference, "John, where's Falenschek's weight at?" referring to the total on the scale. "Where's his weight at? Where's his weight at?" Orr repeated. "It's all in his ass, that's where it is." The fact that Orr was needling a player wasn't necessarily funny. The humor came through not only in the spontaneous and blunt nature of the response, but in the coach's ability to joke through the early rebuilding years at Iowa State.

Bergan said Orr has a skill of using humor, not only for its therapeutic value, but as an outlet for his own frustration. "Johnny uses humor as a way to air his concerns," Bergan said. "If he's upset about something, he'll say it in such a way that it's funny, but at the same time get his point across. That way people don't say, 'I get tired of hearing Johnny Orr gripe all the time.'"

Like a professional comedian, Orr seems to warm up better to audience feedback. Johnny never seems as funny—or tries to be as funny—on his TV or radio shows as he does in front of an audience or reporters. In fact, neither Pete Taylor nor former TV show host Mark Mathew recalls consistent humorous gems by Orr on their shows compared to what you get in person or at a speech. "The best part of the Orr shows is during the commercials," Mathew said. "That's where he takes off on subjects and says some things he won't say on the air. He has the cameramen and people in the studio roaring."

As assistant coach Hallihan said, "People like to be around Johnny, to put it simply. Whatever it is, a magnetism, people like to be around him. When he goes into the room, he's the center of attention." Just as the most popular comedians are appealing to all age groups, Hallihan noted that Orr is equally appreciated by recruits, players, the media and fans of all ages.

Orr is not averse to joining in a practical joke, either. Tom Evans, now an Ames business executive and an active Cyclone Club officer for many years, replaced Orr as Dubuque high school football coach. Evans remembered a game when he heard a loud voice from the stands criticizing his play calling. Thinking it was a disgruntled parent, Evans eventually turned around to discover the heckling actually was coming from . . . Johnny Orr.

Johnny also got Indiana basketball coach Bob Knight to pull a joke on Mathew. Knight and his Indiana team came to Hilton Coliseum in Ames to play, and Orr asked the Indiana coach to play along with a setup.

"I adore Bobby Knight," Mathew explained. "In my heart I think he's the best basketball coach I've seen in my life. Well, Orr knew this, so the first time Knight was here, I told him, 'God,

John, I'd like to get an interview with him.' Later, Orr calls me and says I can interview him after the Indiana shoot-around workout. I go over there, and Orr says, 'Yeah, come on in to his practice.' I knew his practices weren't open to outsiders, so I'm walking about 20 steps behind Johnny, feeling uncomfortable. All of a sudden, Knight sees me and his eyes are glued to me. Orr walks up and says something to Knight—after awhile I realized that's when he set me up. Well, pretty soon Knight stops his practice and yells, 'Who the **** are you? What are you doing here? Get the **** out of here!' Well, Orr is laughing his butt off. I'm feeling like a little kid with my tail between my legs, and I beat it out of there.

"My cameraman and I stood out in the tunnel for about 20 minutes, then finally a manager came back and said, 'OK, you can come back for your interview.' Well, we start the interview and every other word out of Knight's mouth is a profanity. We can't use any of it. So after about the third question, I say, 'Coach, please, can you give me something I can use?' Knight looks at Orr and says, 'Who the **** is this guy, Orr?' Johnny tells him that I used to play basketball. Knight said, 'He wouldn't make a pimple on a basketball's butt.' He's just insulting the hell out of me. He finally takes the microphone, puts his arm around Johnny and gives me about five minutes of uninterrupted comments. He sings the praises of Iowa State basketball. Then he says to me, 'Is that good enough, because that's all you're going to get.' Knight and Orr walk away and get one step from the door, and Knight turns around and comes back to me. He throws out his hand and says, 'Mark, it was a pleasure. I'm glad you can take a little kidding.' "

Orr knows about Knight's practical jokes. He fell for one back in 1976, after Orr's Wolverines had qualified for the Final Four with Indiana, Rutgers and UCLA. A telephone call came to Orr's home supposedly from a representative of the President of the United States, asking him to stay on the line for the president. Since Michigan graduate Gerald Ford then was in the White House, it made sense to Orr when he took the call and waited to talk to Ford. After about 30 seconds of congratulations, Johnny realized it wasn't Ford but Knight playing a prank. "I know who this is," Orr finally said. Johnny got his payback, though, when he arranged to have the Indiana team bus driver pay $5 to park when he came to Michigan's Crisler Arena.

Orr also got a little more of his own back at Knight at the Johnny Orr roast held on April 23, 1992, to raise money to promote teaching excellence at Iowa State. The guest roasters were

George Raveling, Jud Heathcote and Bob Knight. Responding, Orr announced, "My biggest worry about this whole affair was whether Knight was going to call this banquet off or not. I'm glad he decided to let us have it. . . . I've played against Knight several times. He gets all the credit for throwing that chair. When I played him one time *I* threw a chair. The referee turned around and I pointed up to the stands and said, 'See what those SOBs think of you?' "

Mathew recalls another situation, all true and unarranged, that produced a good anecdote for Orr on the banquet circuit. It occurred during the 1987–88 season when Iowa State played during the holiday break at the Toledo Blade City Classic. Mathew at the time hosted Johnny's weekly TV show and did play-by-play announcing on WOI-TV's telecasts of Cyclone basketball. Mathew took his family to Toledo for what turned out to be a nightmare of a vacation.

"The hotel restaurant closed at 10 p.m. We were the last ones to go in there," Mathew explained. "We came in there to get a bite to eat, but what we got was food poisoning. Every hour about one of us got sick as a dog, and it lasted all night. By 5 or 6 in the morning, none of us could move, so we called downstairs and asked for a doctor. They called the emergency services and got some paramedics to come up. They ended up calling ambulances for all of us to go to the hospital. At the time, it was snowing, so they had us on stretchers, and they pulled the sheets up over our heads to keep us warm. When the team heard all the sirens and commotion, one of the Iowa State basketball managers came down to see what was going on. The manager went back and told Coach Orr, 'Mark Mathew and his family got sick from the food.' About that time, Orr looks out the window and sees them taking four bodies out of there on stretchers, with the heads covered up. Orr says, 'Oh, my God, they killed Mark Mathew.' Well, he told that story at the Cyclone Club outings for months."

One of Orr's pranks involved former Des Moines sportswriter Bob Dyer and a vocal Iowa Hawkeye fan from Des Moines. "John agreed to help me play a practical joke on this big Iowa fan that I know," Dyer said. "This guy is on the I-Club board of directors, and he's always telling me that Orr can't coach. I knew this guy was going to be at this bar in Des Moines watching an Iowa basketball game, and Orr and I had to get together to talk about his upcoming basketball banquet that he wanted me to emcee. Johnny gets there, and I ask him if he'll help me play a joke on this guy. So he walks right up to this table of Iowa fans and points right at the guy and says, 'Are you the SOB who's going around saying I can't coach?' The guy was speechless. Orr gets that twinkle in his eye and starts laughing, and the guy sees me come over and knew he was set up. It broke everyone up. Orr stayed there with these guys for a couple of hours and watches the game, and even the big Iowa fan admits he likes the guy."

Here's a sampling of Johnny Orr humor, offered with the usual disclaimer: It won't read as funny in print as it sounded in person.

• High School

ORR ON HIS HIGH SCHOOL SPORTS CAREER AT TAYLORVILLE:
"We only had 13 guys on the football team, and if you got hurt you had to play anyway because there wasn't anyone else. Our running track was covered with ground-up cinders from the boilers. I was a high hurdler, fell once and cut myself pretty bad, and said, 'The hell with this.'"

• The Michigan Years

ORR ON HIS INITIAL JOB INTERVIEW AT MICHIGAN, AND HIS CONVERSATION WITH LEGENDARY ATHLETIC DIRECTOR FRITZ CRISLER: *"Fritz said, 'Where did you come from, Orr?' 'Beloit,' I answered. 'Where's that?' he said. Later Michigan had named Robben Fleming, a former Beloit College basketball and track star, as its new president. Next time Crisler sees me, he says, 'Where did you say you came from?' 'Beloit,' I answered. 'That's a great school,' he says this time."*

ON HIS SURPRISE HIRING AS MICHIGAN'S HEAD COACH: *"Everyone wanted to know who I was. That was a strange feeling hiring a guy like me. I would have wanted to know who I was, too."*

ON PLAYING JOHNNY WOODEN'S GREAT UCLA TEAM IN 1973–74 WHEN THE BRUINS WERE SHOOTING FOR THEIR 83RD STRAIGHT WIN: *"I knew we were in trouble when the referee went up to Bill Walton and asked for his autograph at halftime. I never say a bad word about John Wooden. He put his subs in with 32 seconds left in the game, and we were only 35 points down."*

ON EX-MICHIGAN BOSS DON CANHAM'S SALARY PHILOSOPHY (THE QUOTE LATER APPEARED IN SPORTS ILLUSTRATED'S "THEY SAID IT"): *"I got my contract renewed by Canham: from 30 days to a year. Hell, with Canham, that's tenure."*

ON MICHIGAN'S HARD-TO-PLEASE FANS: *"They even boo the football team. I remember my wife used to stand up during basketball games and she got criticized for it. Unless a guy does a 360-degree turn and dunks it with his toes, they don't cheer much."*

AFTER UNRULY UNIVERSITY OF DAYTON FANS THREW TOILET PAPER ONTO THE COURT DURING THE MICHIGAN-DAYTON GAME, AND SOME HIT ORR: *"It seems to me if I was a little younger, I would have gone up into the stands and kicked some kid in the ass."*

ON HIS MICHIGAN PHENOM CAMPY RUSSELL: *"Campanella can do anything a basketball player should. People ask me if he can adjust to my style. Hell, I'm adjusting to his style. He'll be great, even with my coaching."*

"Campy called me into his office and told me, 'Coach, you just sit back and relax. We're going to make a great coach out of you.' "

ON MICHIGAN PLAYERS C. J. KUPEC AND TOM KUZMA: *"If I had 11 guys like C. J. Kupec, this job would be a pleasure. I don't even have to go out and find him for practice."*

"We've got one player, Tom Kuzma, who's had open heart surgery. I've never had a player with open heart surgery before. He's the only player I've ever had that doesn't want to play the whole game. I told him he'll play 2–4 minutes a game."

DEAD PANNING: When asked if Michigan star Phil Hubbard's presence in the Wolverine lineup helps star teammate Mike McGee: *"Yeah. And it helps me a lot, too."*

ON COACHING DEFENSE AT MICHIGAN: *"We're not too good in the man-to-man. So far we haven't been too good in the zone, either. I don't know what else we could try. Maybe*

we'll have to invent something. (Assistant coach Bill
Frieder whispers, "Combination.") *Combination? Hell, that
would just confuse me.*"

**ON A SUMMER TRIP TO EGYPT HE TOOK WITH HIS MICHIGAN
TEAM:** "*About five minutes after I had landed I knew I
didn't want to be there. But we were there for 18 days.
Our rooms were on the 18th floor and it was always 90
degrees. The bugs coming in the windows woke us up in
the morning. We couldn't drink the water, so we had to
brush our teeth with either beer or Coke. Tough decision.
And—get this—there is only one gymnasium in the entire
country. The Egyptians would have their end of the floor
cleaned at halftime, but not ours. I asked them to clean
ours, but I was nice. I had a lot of players who came from
the ghettos, but they told me compared to this trip, the
south side of Chicago was heaven.*"

**ON HIS INCREASED PUBLIC VISIBILITY AFTER HIS 1976 MICH-
IGAN TEAM REACHED THE NATIONAL FINALS:** "*At first
when I was invited to play in a celebrity golf tournament,
they'd have me teeing off at 6:30 in the morning. They
didn't even turn off the sprinklers. The guy who was supposed to introduce me wasn't there, and the two or three
guys I played with asked who the hell I was. Now tee-off
time is at 1:30. Now they introduce me by saying all this
stuff, even if it isn't true . . . It's like President Ford. When
he played at Michigan, he played on the worst damn
teams, but once he became president, he was an All-
American.*"

**ON FORMER PRESIDENT GERALD FORD, A MICHIGAN GRADUATE,
WHO CAMPAIGNED ON THE ANN ARBOR CAMPUS IN 1976:** "*I
played golf a couple of times with Gerald Ford. When he
was running for president he was back in Ann Arbor and
had a press conference, and Bo Schembechler and I were
there. That's the first press conference I've ever been to
where I didn't get to say a word. At one point, Bo turned
to me and said, 'What the hell are we doing here?'*"

ON HIS OVERACHIEVING 1978 WOLVERINE TEAM: "*When you
see us, you'll wonder how we have won eight games.
We're so small that our basketball shorts look like hockey
pants.*"

• Iowa State Times and People

ORR ON HIS VISION FOR THE PROGRAM AFTER HIS 1980 HIRING AT IOWA STATE: *"Someday, Iowa State is going to win the Big Eight, and they're going to the postseason tournament, and I hope that I'm the guy to take them there. Then, man oh man, we'll have to renegotiate* (my contract).*"*

ON RECRUITING STRATEGY: *"We will go to Hawaii and Alaska if that's where the players are. However, if we get any players from Alaska, the assistants will recruit them. We're looking for players who can run, shoot, dribble, pass, play defense and have an intense desire to win. Of course, so are 800 other colleges."*

ON BEING REJUVENATED: *"I was the dean of the Big Ten coaches, and now I'm the rookie of the Big Eight. I feel 20 years younger. My wife said, 'Prove it.' "*

AT HIS INITIAL IOWA STATE PRESS CONFERENCE: *"You have great people here, unless you're lying to me."*

ON HIS FIRST FRONT-LINE RECRUIT SIGNED AT ISU FOR 1980–81 TEAM: *"It's important we signed* (6-foot-7-inch Derrick) *Thomas. Now when our team walks into airport lobbies, we'll look like a basketball team, not a bunch of wrestlers."*

ON SALARY: In 1980, responding to the initial publicity of his salary being higher than Iowa's Lute Olson and Hayden Fry: *"You writers make a big deal about that. One wrote that I made more than Lute Olson. Hell, I should. I've beaten him 10 of the last 12 times we've played. When I was at Michigan, it was like going on vacation to go to Iowa. We beat the Hawks 16 of 21 times when I was at Michigan. They write that I make more than Hayden Fry. Hell, I should. He was only 5-6 last year, and he has to sell hats."* (Reference to Fry's brief association with selling Hawkeye memorabilia in 1979.)

ON THE 1980 CYCLONES: Relating one of his first conversations with newly hired assistant coach Charlie Harrison, who had been studying films of the previous season: *" 'How's it* *look, coach?' I asked. And Charlie says, 'Don't look at the films, coach.' "*

AT HIS FIRST PRESEASON MEDIA DAY AT IOWA STATE: In November 1980, Orr made light of the predicament of football coach Donnie Duncan, whose team started 5-1 that fall but was in the midst of a four-game November losing streak: *"Our goal this season is to win one game. Of course, that's Donnie Duncan's goal, too, and that's not very funny right now."*

PREDICTION OF HIS FIRST IOWA STATE TEAM: *"We may not throw it to the right people or run in the right direction, but we'll be exciting. I like that. I'll be excited . . . until I look up at the scoreboard, that is."*

ON POLLS WHICH PICKED HIS FIRST CYCLONE TEAM TO FINISH NEAR THE BOTTOM IN THE BIG EIGHT: *"We've been picked to finish seventh in the Big Eight. The only reason we weren't eighth is that we had a vote. There's one thing about getting picked to finish last, though. If you get fourth, they pick you Coach of the Year."*

AT THE START OF HIS THIRD SEASON AT IOWA STATE: *"Romie and I have lived in Ames now two years, and I think we like it more now than when we got here. If you guys can keep on taking losing teams, I think we'll get along great."*

ON BARRY STEVENS, WHO IN 1985 LED IOWA STATE TO ITS FIRST NCAA TOURNAMENT BID IN 41 YEARS: *"That Barry, he can stroke it. But he does some strange things sometimes. He drives you nutty."*

STARTING HIS FOURTH ISU SEASON: *"I'm excited, but I'm always excited in July. I could tell you anything and you'll forget it by the time the season has started . . . everyone forgets it, that is, except the writers."*

ON HIS 1984 RECRUITING CLASS AT IOWA STATE: *"We've got Elijah Parker, and Lafester Rhodes. If we would have gotten (Pitt signee) Demetrious Gore, we would have everyone in the Bible."*

ON DIFFERENCES BETWEEN PLAYERS: *"That Elmer Robinson is such an honest kid. He said, 'Coach, there are two things I don't like to do: run, and go to class.' And I said, 'We're going to have a couple of conflicts, man.' "*

"Now Sammy Hill, he's just the opposite. He doesn't always tell you the truth. You ask him if he's going to class and says, 'Yeah, coach, I'm going.' "

NEEDLING IOWA STATE FOOTBALL COACH JIM WALDEN ON HIS TEAM'S PLAY: *"I tried to leave at halftime to put me out of my misery, but there was so much traffic from people trying to leave, I had to go back in and watch the rest of the game."*

PRAISING COLLEAGUE BILL BERGAN'S SUCCESS AS HEAD COACH OF THE CYCLONES' TRACK AND FIELD PROGRAM AND BERGAN'S ABILITY TO RECRUIT INTERNATIONAL ATHLETES: *"Bill Bergan has done a phenomenal job. I don't think anyone realizes what they've done. They got second in the NCAA indoors, and we don't even have an indoor track. He could get Coach of the Year in five different countries."*

ON THE PROSPECT IN 1990: *"I want to be the winningest basketball coach in Iowa State history. We'll get it, too, even if we have to schedule dogs."*

AT THE APRIL 1992 JOHNNY ORR ROAST: *"I tell you the greatest thing I ever did was come to Iowa State. If I'd have stayed at Michigan I would have retired at about $33,000 a year. Now I'll retire at $135,000. But I really don't like money* (pause). *That's a damn lie."*

• Random Thoughts

ORR ON THE COACHING PERSONALITIES IN THE BIG TEN DURING THE 1970s: *"When I was in the Big Ten, the only coaches who talked to each other were Bobby Knight and me. Some people wanted to get rid of Freddy Taylor as an announcer* (on conference TV games), *and they knew he was Knight's old coach and a good friend of mine. Knight called me and said, 'Do you like the job Freddy's doing on*

TV?' I said yes. He said, 'You get up and say you want him dropped, and I'll second it. It's the only chance we have of saving him.' So believe it or not, I got up (at the coaches' meeting) *and said, 'I don't think Freddy Taylor has been doing a very good job. I think we should drop him.' Knight seconds it. And you know what the vote was? It was 8-2 to keep him."*

IN 1974 ON SPORTSWRITERS AND BROADCASTERS: *"When I get fired, and someday I will, I know a field that's wide open: sportswriting and sportscasting. Those guys need help. You don't have to know anything. You just start writing. Man, that's for me."*

AT THE 1978 UNIVERSITY OF WISCONSIN POSTSEASON BASKET-BALL BANQUET: Referring to ex-Badger coach John Erickson, Orr's former Beloit teammate, then an official with the Fellowship of Christian Athletes: *"I talked to John Erickson and he told me to tell you he's been praying for you all year* (Wisconsin finished 8-19). *So you know how much pull he has with the Lord."*

ON MAGIC JOHNSON IN 1979: *"The greatest player I've ever seen. He's not only great, he has great charisma. I know we beat them this year, but it was great coaching that did it. During the warmups, Johnson told me they were going to kick our butts. I turned to our* (chaplain) *and said, 'Get ready, we're going to need you.' "*

IN 1980 AFTER COLLEGE BASKETBALL REINSTATED THE DUNK: *"I'd much rather see the dunk just in warmups and not in the game. I've seen too many critical shots missed when guys are trying to dunk . . . If people are so fascinated with the dunk, do it in warmups, have a slam-dunk contest and give the winner a subscription to the* Iowa State Daily."

CRITICIZING TV EXPOSURE: In 1985, Orr felt that ESPN was giving too much to some obscure eastern schools: *"I watched a game last night on ESPN. There were so few people at the game you could have shot a machine gun through the stands and not hit anybody."*

ON HECKLING HE RECEIVED AT NEBRASKA: *"At Nebraska, all the students sit near the floor, and the worst ones sit be-*

hind our bench. You have to have certain qualifications to sit there. You have to say really bad things, like when they asked me when I was going to get a haircut. And that was one of the nicer things."

ON BASKETBALL OFFICIALS: "The conference doesn't want me to talk about the officials, so I'll say they were super good. (Orr pauses, grins). I'm going after the sportsmanship trophy."

ON OTHER OFFICIATING PROBLEMS: "It's not always how well you play, it's who you play, where you play, and who's refereeing the damn games."

"I should be like my friend Bobby Knight at Indiana. He gets tossed out of a game when he's 30 points ahead. My problem is I never get 30 ahead."

ON THE FRUSTRATIONS OF RECRUITING: "Doggone it, coach, isn't it just terrible? You go out and recruit good players. Real plaaay-ers! And then the rest of the league goes out and gets better ones, too."

"People talk about what a good guy John is and everything, and his family and all that bull, but let me tell you this: Orr would have traded his wife so fast for nine points at the end of that Kentucky game."

—BOB KNIGHT

"My biggest worry about this whole affair was whether Knight was going to call this banquet off or not. I'm glad he decided to let us have it."

—JOHNNY ORR

"Taylorville was a unique place. It reminds me of a lot of places in Iowa. When I was growing up, I wanted to be mayor of Taylorville. The mayor lived in the nicest house in Taylorville, and I thought it would be a great job. Then I found out it only paid $500 a year, and I said the hell with that. It's grown a lot today, but there only were about 6,700 residents when I was in school. It was strictly a coal-mining town. You'd definitely call it a blue-collar town, as the majority of the people were employed in the mines. There were a lot of good athletes, a lot of coal miners' kids and some white-collar people mixed in, and that was good. It was a beautiful high school—the WPA built it during the Depression. The people there were so involved in the sports programs. If they saw you out on the town at 8:45 at night, they'd send you home, because they knew you had to be home by 9."

"Once you played for (Coach) Dolph Stanley—I don't know, you can't explain it—you just had a great faith in him and you wanted to play for him. It was something natural. It didn't matter if you scouted us and knew what we were going to do. That didn't bother Dolph. If we ran the play right, we knew we were going to get the basket. We had so much pride. We threw the ball around and never took a bad shot. I'd been in some games where we wouldn't have even one turnover. That's unbelievable today, but it's not surprising when you've been raised that way from sixth grade on. I'd say about 80 percent of the practice drills I use today are things I learned from Dolph, with some modifications."

"The thing about Dolph, though, is that you always wanted to shower and get out of the locker room in a hurry, because he had this old car that would never start in cold weather. You always had to help him push that thing. Sometimes you'd push for two or three blocks before it would start. But then he'd give you a ride if you helped. That was a good deal, because you always had to walk to practice—you walked everywhere."

• Whoo-siers!

Who could overlook the charm of the Hickory Huskers team in "Hoosiers," the 1981 film inspired by the real-life 1952 state championship basketball team from a tiny Indiana high school? Hollywood, had it looked further, could have found an equally fascinating story in nearby Illinois.

A state with a remarkable basketball heritage, Illinois has an even greater penchant for arguments. The state that brought us Siskel and Ebert and the Lincoln-Douglas debates won't concede that Indiana has a better roundball tradition. There are several great native Illinois players and teams to boast about. Old-timers recall athletes like George Mikan, Ray Meyer, Lou Boudreau, Robin Roberts, and the famed University of Illinois Whiz Kids. Also, a gentleman named Adolph Rupp had his first coaching job at Freeport, Ill., and did well enough there in four basketball seasons (58-17) to land a coaching job at the University of Kentucky, where he became an institution in the college game.

Baby boomers recognize homestate players like Dan Issel,

Jim Brewer, Don Nelson, Cazzie Russell, Jerry Sloan, Doug Collins, Dave Robisch, Preston Pearson, Clyde Turner, Quinn Buckner, Jack Sikma, Isiah Thomas, Rickey Green, Hersey Hawkins, Mark Aguirre, Terry Cummings, Kevin Gamble, Ronnie Lester and Jeff Hornacek. And finally, the NBA World Championship came to Illinois in 1991 with the Chicago Bulls.

With due respect to Air Jordan, a much simpler Illinois basketball championship was acomplished decades earlier, back in the days when Keds were king. Hollywood would have discovered that mid-century charm of "Hoosiers" in the downstate Illinois town of Taylorville during the magic season of 1943–44. A young Johnny Orr, his closeknit teammates, their inspirational coach, and a united community worked together that winter to post an unprecedented and since unmatched 45-0 record. The Taylorville gang did it without a player taller than 6-foot-3-inches. They did it with an up-and-coming coach, Dolph Stanley, who implemented the acclaimed slip-and-roll offense, which is better known today as the pick-and-roll. They did it with an explosive fast break. They did it with a relentless pressing defense. They beat a tough Champaign team four times during the season and also beat state champions from 1943 (Paris) and 1942 (Centralia) on the way to their unbeaten championship season. They did it with 31 of the 45 games away from home.

Nearly 50 years later, Taylorville continues its evolution from coal mines to combines to fast-food signs. Located 30 miles southeast of Springfield, the town today is a regional hub of commerce in an area dominated by farming. The downtown square displays a quaint county courthouse, built in 1900, with its striking clock tower that still is wound by hand once a week. The original county courthouse, built in 1840, was located in a rural farm lot, and a young Abe Lincoln tried cases there. Coal mining once thrived in the Taylorville area, although most of the mines have since been closed. The region had some of the first fields in the country to succeed in growing soybeans, an alternative crop of the early 1900s. Edward Purcell, born in Taylorville, was the co-winner of the Nobel Prize for Physics in 1952. Another notable native is former major-league baseball pitcher Pat Perry.

None of this hometown trivia is mentioned on highway signs that greet visiting traffic, though. The green road signs at the city limits brag about the Purple Tornado squad of yesteryear, the first Illinois high school team to finish an unbeaten basketball season (45-0) since the first state tournament was sponsored in 1908. Taylorville's winning streak peaked at a state-record 48 games with three more wins the next season, and it was 26 years before that record was surpassed. Quinn Buckner and his great Dolton Thornridge teams won consecutive state championships in building a 58-game streak from 1970 to 1972.

• Boyhood Days

Taylorville was a special place for Johnny Orr. The unique sports environment there helped open doors for him that took him where he is today. Johnny was born June 10, 1927, in Yale, Kansas, a coal-mining region. His parents, Bert and Anna Orr, moved to the southern Illinois mines shortly thereafter, settling in Taylorville. During the Great Depression, it was an economic struggle to have a bigger family, which is the primary reason Johnny didn't have brothers and sisters. "My dad had eight brothers, but I grew up in the Depression, so you just didn't have many kids," Johnny said.

Johnny's wife, Romie, said her husband received much of his personality and sense of fairness from his dad, Bert, who was the seventh of 11 children. "Dad was a pistol," Romie said. "I absolutely adored him. I never knew John's mother (Anna Jane Orr died of cancer in 1947 at age 43 during Johnny's first year at Beloit College), so Bert was my contact to John's early life. Bert was so funny. He used to say that when he walked down the street, people would say, 'There goes Bert.' Now they say, 'There goes Johnny Orr's dad.' He always had a cigar in his mouth, but after he had his heart attack he had to quit. He hated that. When he was younger he was a real fireball. He never let things get him down."

Following his career as a coal miner and a police officer, Bert Orr worked as precinct captain for the Democratic party and was the local boxing commissioner (he was a boxer himself as a youth). Bert suffered a heart attack at age 46 that prevented him from working in the coal mines. Johnny's parents moved 50 miles west to work at the Illinois state mental hospital in Jacksonville, where Bert was head of security and Anna was the hospital's head nurse. "Bert was perceived as a very, very, very fair man," Romie said. "After he got out of the hospital job, he was a magistrate judge. He would hear cases and often would excuse the fines. John would ask him, 'How can you fine these people, then forgive the fine?' And Bert would say, 'They can't afford to pay it.' "

Romie said Johnny adopted his mother's passion for cleanliness. "Mother was fanatic about cleaning, and she was such a hard worker," Romie said. "So John was extremely neat. Once in college he kicked a roommate out of the room for being sloppy."

Johnny matured earlier than most kids because of circumstances encountered during his teen years, when the family was living in Jacksonville. Rules prohibited children from living on the hospital grounds in the staff housing, though, and after living for a spell as a boarder in Jacksonville, Johnny eventually returned to Taylorville to live with his grandmother. That arrangement went on for more than six years. Legend has it that Grandma Anna, who later came to live with Johnny and Romie in their Dubuque years, would cook a pregame meal for Johnny on game nights, then accompany him on the two-mile walk through town to the high school gym.

Walking was one of the realities of a boyhood set in the years following the Great Depression. Orr said kids didn't have televisions or cars in his youth, and it was one reason why athletics were such a popular outlet. "Sports was all I ever thought of, to be honest," he said.

Johnny and his pals played football and baseball, but the town had a special love for basketball. Orr's first coach in organized basketball was a woman—Jane Wright, who was his grade-school coach during his brief stay in Jacksonville. His love of sports was nurtured in Taylorville, thanks to some tireless citizens in the community who organized youth sports teams. Boyd Dappert, a civil engineer in town, supervised open gym sessions on weeknights and was as influential as anyone in Johnny's early athletic development.

"Boyd Dappert picked us up every Tuesday and Thursday night from the sixth grade on, and we went to the high school to play basketball," Johnny said.

"Boyd always had a key to the gym," added Harold "Slick" Parrish, a close friend and basketball teammate of Johnny's. "He let us play basketball but didn't allow messing around. If anyone started fooling around, he'd send us to the showers."

Parrish said that even as a teenager, Johnny Orr was destined to become a coach. "He was like a brother to me," said Parrish, who still resides in Taylorville. "I lived just a block from him on East Adams Street. I was either down at his house or he was down at mine. We'd go down to his house in the morning and he'd have everything lined up. We took his grandma's broken broomstick for a bat and filled a tobacco sack with rags for a ball. If you hit it so far, it was a double, a single or a home run. In the afternoon we'd go to the park and play baseball or shoot baskets. He was the only child in his family, so he had his own ball glove

Even as a toddler growing up in small-town Illinois, Johnny was destined to become a big wheel. [*below*] Johnny (5) and his junior-high friends benefited from a strong sports program in Taylorville.

Just 16 years old for most of his senior year, Johnny Orr helped Taylorville High's class of 1944 gain a statewide reputation as an athletic power. [*below*] Johnny (43) led Taylorville High to a 45-0 record in 1944 and also led the state of Illinois in scoring with 675 points.

Congratulations from cheerleaders following Taylorville's
state championship victory over Elgin. The Taylorville aces
Ron Bontemps and Orr (*seated left*) were first-team all-
staters and went on to star at Beloit College, where
Bontemps was dubbed "Mr. Inside" to Johnny's nickname
of "Mr. Outside." [*below*] Speaking at the welcome home
pep rally following the state championship in 1944, "We
sure made monkeys out of those sportswriters who said it
couldn't be done," Johnny told the gathering.

Johnny, who also wore jersey no. 43 in football, was a starting end who made several clutch plays in the Purple Tornadoes' 8-0 regular season. In his senior year Taylorville outscored foes 264-32.

Coach Dolph Stanley (*back right*) had five different schools qualify for the Illinois state tournament in his remarkable 52-year coaching career, but he said this 1944 Taylorville championship team was his best (*Orr second from left, front row*).

tried football at the
versity of Illinois
to hang out with
Taylorville pals. His
etic ability and
petitive fire helped
beat out eight
r players and grab
of two starting
s at end.

Orr started in
basketball as a
freshman at Illinois on
a 13-7 team that upset
a George Mikan–led
DePaul squad. Orr
received All–Big Ten
mention in both
football and basketball.

Orr would have been
the youngest Illini
athlete to letter in
football, basketball
and baseball, but he
dropped out of baseball
early in the 1945
season to enroll in the
Navy.

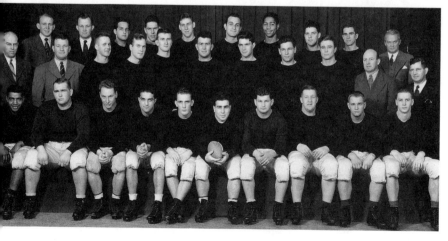

University of Illinois 1944 football squad. Orr (*far right, first row*) recalls that former Illinois football stars like Red Grange would visit the locker room to inspire Illini players on game days.

Orr (*right*) was instrumental in this 43-42 upset of then 10-0 Iowa, as he scored eight points and played his usual strong floor game. An Urbana sportswriter wrote that Johnny "took a beating and dished it right back to any ambitious Hawkeyes who wanted to mix it up."

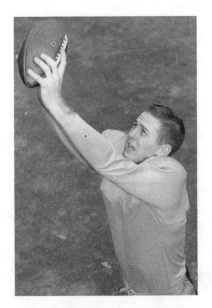

Johnny was selected second-team All–Big Ten in football as an end. "We had some great players, so I didn't get a lot of chances to score," he recalls. "I scored my only touchdown against Iowa—man, we beat the Hawks 40-6." [*right*] Orr was president of Sigma Chi fraternity when he wasn't starring on the basketball court at Beloit College.

and ball bats, but he wasn't someone who wouldn't share—he shared with everyone. I probably wouldn't have played basketball if not for John. I thought I was too small to play, but he taught me better. As a senior I was only 5-foot-9-inches, but I played center."

When Orr wasn't playing sports or in school, he was working part-time jobs. "When the war started, there was no shortage of jobs," Orr explained. "I worked as an usher at the theatre and I cleaned the barbershop, Bob's Barbershop. I used to shine shoes in the barbershop—I made them pay me first, or I wouldn't shine them. I also worked at the coal mines in the summers."

As prominent as Johnny Orr has become as an athlete and coach, he has to share top billing in local lore with Taylorville teammate Ron Bontemps and the remarkable Dolph Stanley, who later coached him to All-American distinction at Beloit College. Bontemps starred with Johnny at Beloit and earned a spot on the 1952 U.S. Olympic basketball team. Bontemps later was named the nation's amateur basketball player of the year by the AAU in 1954 and played professionally.

• Coach Dolph Stanley

Stanley, who died in 1990 at age 85, was a pioneer in the coaching profession. His longevity and successes as a high school and small-college coach rival those of legends like Paul "Bear" Bryant at Alabama, Adolph Rupp at Kentucky, and John Wooden at UCLA. Regarded as a genius of roundball and a fiery competitor, Stanley was a man ahead of the times. He became famous with his perfection of the tipping zone defense, the pick-and-roll offense, and the four-corners delay. The latter style was the rage in college basketball during the late 1970s before the shot clock was added, and those who credited Dean Smith with inventing the tactic would be surprised to know that Stanley was using it back in 1930 at Equality High School.

Dolph Stanley won 957 games in his remarkable high school and coaching career that spanned parts of six decades (52 years) and seven schools. Stanley set an Illinois coaching record when he qualified teams to the state tournament at five different schools, and he alone was the recipient of the title of all-time "Illinois High School Coach" by the *Chicago Tribune* in 1990. A book on the country's greatest high school basketball coaches included Stanley in an elite group of six. Stanley twice was nominated for National Coach of the Year, and a *USA Today* story ranked him second nationally for career wins among active coaches. Stanley didn't have a losing record in his first 27 years in coaching. When he left coaching in 1987 at age 82, three years before his death, Stanley had compiled a 957-420 overall record. Stanley's career record actually is 982-395 if you include 25 wins his Rockford Auburn team later forfeited due to an inadvertent use of an ineligible player.

Stanley's first memory of Johnny Orr on the court? "When Johnny was playing in a third-grade basketball game in Jacksonville," Stanley recalled, "his father sat high in the stands and watched. There came a time when Johnny took a shot at the basket, and the ball went in. Quick as a shot, Johnny left the floor and dashed up into the bleachers, threw his arms around his father, and said, 'Daddy, Daddy, I made a basket.' " In a 1990 interview, Stanley told writer Dan Davenport that Johnny "was always full of vinegar" as a youth. Stanley also declared Johnny to be a born coach. "People always recognized his bearing, his calmness. It wasn't egotism, it was confidence," Stanley said.

"Dolph wanted me to be a coach ever since I started playing for him," Johnny said. In fact, through their association at Taylorville and later at Beloit College and beyond, no one had a greater influence on Johnny Orr's career development than Dolph Stanley. "Everything I ever did in basketball goes back to him," Johnny said.

Orr emulated Stanley, even with his off-court habits like his love of golf and his preference for short haircuts. And Johnny's on-court coaching style strongly reflects the philosophies of Stanley, notably his teams' running and pressing styles, and the use of shorter, more mobile pivot men. "I've never coached an overly tall team," Stanley said in an interview with Jim Enright for the 1977 book, *March Madness.* "To me basketball is speed, skill, finesse, polish, poise and pattern play. I don't discount the big man's place in the game, I just like speed and finesse more than height when we play our three-guard game. I've always felt there was a place for the good little man in basketball." In fact, Stanley's 1944–45 Taylorville team, which returned no starters from the 45-0 team of 1943–44, finished with a 29-5 record despite a starting five with the following heights: 5'9", 5'8", 5'8", 5'4" and 5'4". Stanley also recalled that the few big men he did have rarely worked out. Stanley quipped to writer Steve Tarter, "I had a 6-foot-11-inch center in college one time—he broke his toe and fell in love at the same time and never came back."

Orr said Stanley was a success because he kept things simple and the players understood what was expected of them. "I don't think I ever heard him give a pep talk," Johnny explained. "You always knew you were supposed to win. He never said much if you didn't play well, he'd just say, 'I don't think you were up to par tonight, men.' "

Don Williams, the current Taylorville athletic director who played for Stanley and later coached with him at Rockford Auburn, said Dolph was like a father figure. "He was very stern. You weren't afraid of him, but you never doubted what he said. He could tear you down, but he always would build you up. On game nights, he had a great understanding of the game. As a player you'd say, 'Why are we doing it?' But it worked. He just had a great understanding of youngsters."

Johnny stayed in regular contact with Stanley throughout his career, especially when he needed advice on taking a new job. "I remember thinking about going back to school and getting a master's degree, but in that time, the only guys that did that were guys that couldn't get jobs," Johnny said. "So Dolph said, 'You're going to be a bum. Get out and get a job.' So I never wanted to get a master's."

After Johnny's greatest win in coaching, his 1986 NCAA tournament victory with Iowa State over Michigan, he dialed up Rockford, Ill., and shared his success with Dolph, who was then age 81. "I rarely pray for games, but I did that one," Stanley told Orr, as reported by the Rockford *Register Star*. "Your teams make me homesick."

Stanley ran a tight ship at Taylorville. "The players were more strictly disciplined in those days," he said in an interview with the Chicago *Sun-Times*. "They took care of their bodies. I made them drink orange juice at every meal, eat a lot of fruit and lean meat and told them to get nine hours of sleep every night. I made sure they were doing all this because I checked with their mothers. They were always glad when the season was over because they didn't have to squeeze any more oranges."

Johnny learned one lesson about diet the hard way. "One time I left school on the day of a game and stopped and got a big bag of candy on the way home," Orr recalled. "Well, Dolph saw me, so I just said 'Hi.' I knew I was in trouble, because we weren't supposed to have candy, so I ran home. Dolph never said anything to me. Well, I ate all that candy, and I got so sick that at halftime I thought I was going to die. But Dolph made me start the second half. He never took me out the whole half, even though we had a big lead. Never again did I eat candy on the day of a game."

Except for those occasional teenager splurges, the players

did whatever Stanley suggested, from eating prunes and liver at meals, to taking vitamins, to wearing crew-cut hairstyles and donning suits and ties off the court. "Dolph even taught you how to tie your shoes," said Parrish. "I still tie them the same way. You tie them backwards with the knot square, and the knot won't come untied."

In an interview with Tarter, Stanley said he was born with the traits that made an effective coach. "I'm a Christian man, and I believe I was selected for this work. I just love it. I've been offered every big college job in the country, but I stuck with the high school ranks because you get to do very little teaching in college. In high school, you get a chance to take a kid headed for the penitentiary and save them. Basketball makes them into fine men."

Stanley admits he didn't always have everyone's undivided attention in his first few years at Taylorville. He told writer Jim Enright that his search for "the good Christian boy" and the discipline he preached caused some conflicts. "They didn't know that I was from the same type of mine operations in Marion that they had in Taylorville," Stanley told Enright. "Whereas I worked mainly with reserved farm boys in Equality and Mt. Pulaski, I had an entirely different group in Taylorville. They were rougher-speaking youths, and when I made some changes, I knew there was talk that I would be fired. In the process of elimination, we came up with some outstanding boys. They were leaders in the classroom as well as on the basketball court."

Orr added, "Dolph had a terrible time at first. He dumped a lot of guys at first who didn't want to play by his style, and everyone wasn't so fired up about him. He'd work your butt off." Stanley's first three Taylorville teams finished 22-7, 19-13 and 21-11, but Stanley's fourth through eighth seasons at Taylorville produced a 155-18 record for a phenomenal .896 winning percentage.

Orr said Stanley knew how to balance discipline with motivation. "I remember Dolph telling me, 'Never make a rule that's going to cost you a game. Don't ever get yourself in that position,' " Orr recalled. "I remember that on our trips to games, the bus used to leave from the town square, and you had to be there by 5. When I was a freshman, two of our starters, Benny Wilhelm and Johnny Jones, weren't there, and boom, right at 5, Dolph turned to our bus driver, Ned, and said, 'Let's go.' Ned tried to close the door as slow as he could and give them a little time. We saw those guys coming and yelled to coach, 'Here they come,' but Dolph just told the bus driver to keep on going. I never saw a guy late again. We knew that if he'd leave (star player) Benny Wilhelm, he'd leave anybody. He knew he could beat (rival opponent) Pana without those guys, and I think he knew he had a good team coming up in our group, and we were a little wild. He had a lot of players, so if he disciplined you, it didn't affect the team."

• Senior Year

Orr was all of 16 years and 3 months when he strutted into his senior year at Taylorville High. A member of the Chem Club and a contributor to the school newspaper and yearbook, Orr was profiled in the school paper as a skilled athlete who liked to eat steak and had an obsession with getting to school on time. Johnny was about to embark on the kind of senior year people dream of. Besides the great basketball season, Johnny would contribute to unbeaten regular-season teams in football and baseball and earn all-state consideration in all three sports.

These Purple Tornadoes' 1943–44 successes provided townsfolk with a nice diversion from World War II, which was raging in Europe and in the South Pacific and later would call Johnny and many of his teammates to service before its conclusion. The first local victory of the school year figuratively came in August when school officials announced that Taylorville High would escape the drastic effects of a wartime teacher shortage that was felt elsewhere in the country. More than 75,000 teachers nationwide left the classrooms to fight the war, including Taylorville's football coach.

Stanley was picked to coach the football team for that 1943 season. He took his 28 players on to great heights that autumn, giving the locals their money's worth for the 40-cent price of admission.

The Taylorville High football season started with a 48-0 scorching of Kincaid, one of five shutouts in an 8-0 regular season. Johnny, a starting end who wore No. 47, hauled in two touchdown passes to aid the opening victory. Following a subsequent 6-0 win over Springfield Feitshans and a 26-0 defeat of Gillespie, the 3-0 Tornadoes played rival Decatur. Taylorville trailed the Reds 13-7 after three quarters before Orr's two fourth-quarter touchdowns sparked a 26-13 comeback win. Here's an account from the Taylorville *Breeze-Courier* newspaper of Orr's heroics:

Decatur's next desperate march was halted at the 5-yard-line by some excellent line play by the Stanley men. Orr chose the moment to make the longest run of the year on the local gridiron when he took a lateral from Jack Richards, who had fought his way to the seven-yard-line. Tucking the pigskin lovingly under his arm, Orr dodged and twisted his way down the field for 93 yards while mass hysteria gripped the Taylorville bleachers.

The following week, Orr had a 51-yard touchdown run on a triple reverse in a 65-0 win over the Hillsboro Hilltoppers. By then, the 5-0 Tornadoes were getting attention around Illinois. In a column in the Chicago *Daily News*, Jack Ryan wrote of Stanley's success:

> "The finest compliment that has been bestowed on this year's squad has come from our opponents," Stanley said. "Team members we have played definitely have told me that ours was the cleanest team they had met. Each boy takes his game jersey home and washes it himself. Each player paints his helmet each week and each player shines his shoes once a week . . . No player is allowed to sit during time outs, unless they are injured. No water is permitted during a game. No team bashing or player bashing comes from our players. Neither do we permit friendly conversation with opponents during games."

Taylorville climbed to 6-0 with a 53-0 whitewash of Pana, then escaped Mt. Olive, 13-6, thanks to Johnny's last-minute heroics. Orr completed three halfback passes then scored the winning touchdown in dramatic fashion. He caught a 50-yard TD pass with 11 seconds to play, prompting this account from Jack Burns in the *Breeze-Courier:*

> John Connolly drew back his trusty wing and heaved the pigskin to Orr 50 yards away. Orr was instantly surrounded by three husky Mountaineers, but they were only wasting their time for Orr leaped high in the air and brought the ball down out of the blue with one hand, unlimbered his 6-feet plus and rolled across the goal line. Jones drop-kicked the extra point, and one play later the final whistle brought the game to a howling end.

Taylorville then stopped Benld, 26-14, to close the regular season 8-0 and claim the school's first football championship of the South Central Conference. The Tornadoes' combined scoring margin of 264-32 put them among the state leaders, and they were one of 18 unbeaten football teams in Illinois. In an unusual move, Stanley arranged a challenge game pitting Taylorville against the excellent team from Champaign High, to be played in Champaign. This is believed to be the first time high school teams played at Memorial Stadium on the University of Illinois campus. Champaign won 7-0 on a muddy field, although the *Breeze-Courier* wrote: "John Orr played his usual good game . . . Orr pulled down a Connolly pass with three Champaign men literally hanging on his neck."

The football success was a good launching pad for basketball. Stanley's 1942–43 cagers had finished 28-3 and beat eventual state champion Paris, but four of those starters had graduated and a new group would try to continue the Stanley success in 1943–44. The rangy Bontemps was the only returning starter, but Orr, Schultte Bishop and Dean Duncan showed promise. Stanley recruited Don Jansen from gym class, and he would turn out to be a pleasant surprise on a team that would be unforgettable.

"It was always crazy," Bontemps told the *Sun-Times*, referring to the 1943–44 season. "Every game, either at home or on the road, was a sellout." Teammate Dean "Diz" Duncan added, "The people would start lining up for tickets three hours before the game started. They lived to see those games. My father, who was a coal miner, used to bet socks on the games."

Williams said the community even pitched in valuable gas ration coupons to help transport the team to games. "Being the World War II years, there was a great deal of cooperation getting teams to the games," Williams said. "There were a lot of miners and farmers, and they were on the priority list for gas rationing stamps. People would chip in their rationing stamps for the teams to travel to away games, and people likewise would get together and car pool to games." Parrish added, "I probably shouldn't say this, but we even used one of the sheriff's cars to travel to games. Everyone wanted to ride in the sheriff's car so they could blow the siren as we drove down the road."

Led by Orr's 19 points, Taylorville opened the magic season with a 60-22 win over Feitshans and immediately claimed the state's No. 2 ranking. Next, Orr's 21 points broke open a close tussle with Vandalia in a 39-29 win, and the team vaulted to No. 1 in the Associated Press poll. Victories over Shelbyville (60-20), Effingham (46-26) and Mt. Pulaski (49-19) pushed Taylorville to 5-0, and a 39-28 triumph over Paris, paced by Orr's 21 points, showed that this team was for real. An account of the win in the *Breeze-Courier* said: "The (Paris) Tigers were obsessed with the idea of holding down the tall center (Ron Bontemps), forgetting Orr, who sank shot after shot. Bottling Orr last night would have been as simple as bottling Niagara Falls."

Taylorville zipped to a 12-0 record with victories in the remaining games before Christmas and solidified its position as the state's No. 1–rated team. Orr averaged 13 points a game in that stretch, which included wins over Carlinville (67-20), Staunton (43-28), Mt. Vernon (50-35), West Frankfort (65-25), Mattoon (44-15) and Champaign (49-34). Next up was the Centralia tournament, perhaps the state's toughest holiday tournament at the time. Taylorville rolled to a 4-0 record to claim the title as Orr totaled 78 points to establish a tournament record. Charleston (59-40), Pontiac (79-42), DuQuoin (46-33) and Champaign (41-33) were the victims as the Tornadoes finished the 1943 portion of their schedule with a 16-0 record.

Taylorville was becoming the talk of the state. One newspaper sports editor from a rival town even called Dolph Stanley and asked why the athletic Bontemps and Orr weren't serving in the Army. Dolph had to explain that his star seniors were in fact 17- and 16-year-old players, not 18- or 19-year-old players as the rumors claimed. Stanley did loosen up enough to drop his rule against photo sessions with players on game days, but some superstitions lived on. In fact, Orr had one ritual of his own—he had washed dishes at home for his mother on the day of the opening win, Nov. 25, and he continued dunking dishes as a pregame practice thereafter, so as not to jinx his team.

The blowouts continued as Clinton (60-34), Pana (53-21), Salem (58-33), Nokomis (66-31), Hillsboro (67-39), Centralia (63-26) and Staunton (67-28) were the next teams to fall to the now 23-0 Tornadoes. The third meeting with Champaign produced a close call, with Taylorville escaping 36-32. After Collinsville (44-16) became victim No. 25, Taylorville had a rare situation in its game with Mt. Vernon—Stanley's gang fell behind 9-5 and had to call its first time out of the season. They went on to win 45-26, though, and later hit 30-0 with victories over Nokomis (72-19), Pana (54-34) and Quincy (37-21).

Next up was another spotlight game against Canton, the 1943 state runner-up. Canton brought a 16-2 record into the contest and jumped to a 32-24 halftime lead, but the Tornadoes roared back behind Orr's season-best 22 points to win 53-43. The *Breeze-Courier* wrote:

> The Canton fans rubbed their hands in glee and gloated that here, at last, was the team that would stop the Tornadoes. Whatever lightning it is that Coach Stanley exposes his team to between halves worked overtime, however, and the Purple came

onto the floor and left little doubt in the minds of the fans as to the final outcome. Led by Orr, the Taylorville five sailed the sphere through the hoop with disturbing regularity to overtake and pass the Little Giants.

Taylorville's first-half slump was caused in part by what could be described as Johnny Orr's least successful shoe contract. Johnny had foot problems and had mailed away for a special shoe to ease the discomfort. The *Breeze-Courier* told of Orr's adventure of trying the new shoes against Canton:

> Tis reported that the big boy (Orr) recently purchased very fancy made-to-order basketball shoes to encase his talented tootsies and duly wore them at the Canton game. They didn't live up to his expectations, however, and Taylorville fans watched him limp around the floor in agony all through the first half of the game while Canton sailed into the lead. With Canton's lightning break working beautifully, Bontemps smothered by close guarding, and Orr tortured by new shoes, the immediate future for Taylorville was extremely hazy. Coach Stanley, with his usual foresight, had brought along Orr's old shoes, and during the (halftime break) the big forward changed into them and capered onto the floor at the start of the third quarter a new man. From then on they couldn't stop him. Please John, leave your new shoes under your locker (Wednesday night) against Pinckneyville.

The 31-0 and top-rated Tornadoes, one of five teams in Illinois still unbeaten, next played No. 7 Pinckneyville. According to an account in the Taylorville High yearbook, *The Drift,* this Taylorville-Pinckneyville game was the highlight of the regular season: "On the night of the game, people commenced arriving before school was dismissed, and tickets went like wildfire. People from all over the state came to this game. 'Standing room only' characterized the gym, which practically bulged with the largest number of people ever crowded into it."

For the second—and last—time of the year, the Tornadoes trailed at halftime, this time by a 16-12 score. But the second-half surge pulled out a 40-29 defeat of Pinckneyville, behind Orr's 16 points. The *Breeze-Courier* said Orr "played one of his best defensive games of the season holding Rothenberger of Pinckneyville to a single basket."

Taylorville completed a 36-0 regular season record with subsequent victories over Clinton (54-31), Salem (39-32), Hillsboro (53-25) and Centralia (57-21). Johnny scored his 500th point of the season in game 33, the Clinton victory.

There was one fear in Taylorville as the No. 1–rated locals braced for the state tournament bid: the fact no Illinois high school basketball team ever had completed an unbeaten season and won the state crown. Three teams previously had reached the finals unbeaten, but all lost the title game. A popular belief was that Stanley's gang should have lost one game along the way to erase the pressure that mounted as the winning streak climbed. "Back then, people thought it was good for you to lose one to take the pressure off," Don Williams recalled. "Well, they didn't know Coach Stanley. He didn't believe in losing any games."

Taylorville stormed through the regionals and sectionals to victories over Nokomis (93-24), Morrisonville (72-31), Kincaid (62-39), Springfield Cathedral (57-26) and Jacksonville (72-27), and advanced to the state tournament Sweet Sixteen in Champaign with a 41-0 record. They would play at Champaign's Huff Gym, and the only thing more scarce than tickets there that weekend were vacant motel rooms.

The Tornadoes won the first-round opener over East St. Louis, 52-34, tying the 1940–41 Centralia team's Illinois state one-season record win streak of 42 in the process. Orr had 17 points, "some of them breathtaking and sensational," according to the *Breeze-Courier*. The newspaper also reported that because radio reception was poor for that first-round game, Taylorville residents swamped the local telephone company for score updates.

Taylorville set the winning streak record in the state quarterfinals with victory 43, a 51-30 disposal of Kewanee, powered by Orr's 20 points. Next up was a tricky semifinal game with Champaign, which already had lost three games to Taylorville but hung close each time. The fourth meeting was tight throughout, and Champaign pulled within 38-36 in the final minute before Orr iced the 40-36 Taylorville win with a breakaway layup.

The field of 875 teams that started the sectional round of the Illinois State High School Basketball tournament two weeks earlier was now reduced to two—Taylorville (44-0) and Elgin (21-3). Elgin had escaped Chicago South Shore by a single point in the semifinals, denying South Shore's bid to become the first Chicago school to play in a state championship game. Elgin had tradition on its side—it captured back-to-back titles in 1924 and '25 and was fourth in the 1943 state tourney. This Elgin club was no match for Dolph Stanley's team of destiny, however. In the Saturday, March 18, 1944, championship game, Taylorville outscored Elgin 19-4 in the final quarter—fueled by Orr's eight fourth-quarter points—and the Tornadoes sailed home with a 56-33 triumph and a trophy.

The 45-0 finish and 45-game winning streak shattered the all-time Illinois record of 44 straight wins (over two seasons) set by Dundee, and Taylorville's 23-point margin of victory in the title game was the second biggest in state finals history. Orr scored 19 points against Elgin and finished the four-game state tournament with 66 points, two shy of tournament leader Paul Schnackenberg of South Shore. Taylorville's 45-0 season also included an Illinois state record for points, with 2,475 in 45 games. That topped Centralia's 2,388 in 46 games. Orr finished as the state's leading scorer with 675 points (15 ppg), while Bontemps had 613, good for fourth in the state, although Bontemps played two fewer games (14.2 ppg). Orr and Bontemps were named to the first all-state team—the first time since 1934, when Thornton's Lou Boudreau and Dar Hutchins were honored, that two teammates landed first-team all-state berths. Taylorville's Schultte Bishop was picked on the second all-state team.

According to the Taylorville High school newspaper, the *Pel-Mell*, the Tornadoes celebrated their accomplishment first with a dip into the swimming pool on the Illinois campus. The lone snag in the fun, came when one of the players lost a tooth in the water. Fortunately, a thorough search recovered the tooth. The *Pel-Mell* went on to note that "after the championship game Saturday night, each of the teams scattered to various parts of Champaign-Urbana with their girlfriends. Some time later, one by one, they all returned and met in Orr's room, where they had a big bull session."

The *Chicago Tribune* was scooped on both the lost tooth and bull session stories, but its reporter Edward Prell did write:

> The thousands who watched the Taylorville boys during the three days of the tournament had best described them as robots. These Tornadoes swept through to the title in a most nonchalant, almost bored manner. They were perfectionists, their faces masked like poker veterans . . . (At the pep rally) today they were just another group of boys—dressed in baggy trousers and duck coats, the hallmark of the time's high school boy . . . Their scholarly coach, Dolph Stanley, (was) unbent in the midst of their enthusiasm, but those who know him were saying that before the night's over he will be plotting the Tornadoes' 1944–45 campaign . . . Playing for Coach Stanley is work. He won't let the boys sit during time-outs. He won't let them take a drink of water during the game. "Why?" someone asked him. "Why not?" he retaliated. "They play only 32 minutes."

The *Breeze-Courier* headline the following Monday called the Tornadoes "The team that had everything." Stanley later told a reporter that he had two vivid memories of this gifted team: exceptional playing skills, including the execution of behind-the-back passes, plus the joy they shared when they came home to Taylorville Sunday with the state championship. After a victory dinner of T-bone steaks and pie a la mode, the 150-car Taylorville caravan started the 70-mile trek home. They were greeted by thousands of fans at the edge of town, despite a blizzard described as the worst of the season. "It was snowing like mad," Parrish recalled. "Yet we were riding through the town on the fire engine." At a ceremony at the high school, Co-captain Orr told the crowd, "We sure made monkeys out of the sports writers who said it wasn't possible."

In all the euphoria following the championship game, the team neglected one thing—it forgot to bring the shiny first-place trophy back from Champaign. The Taylorville bus driver, Ned, zipped back to retrieve the stranded hardware, but he had car trouble en route and didn't make it back in time for the ceremony.

Even though they forgot the trophy, there was no forgetting the 1943–44 Purple Tornadoes of Coach Dolph Stanley. "Back in the one-class system, it was everything. The oldtimers around here never forget," Don Williams said.

"When I first went into the (military) service, people would ask where I was from," Parrish recalled. "You'd say 'Taylorville' and they'd say, 'That's the basketball capital of Illinois, isn't it?' That championship really put Taylorville on the map. Those are good memories. Something they can't take away from you. It's something you always cherish."

Heard at Johnny's Roast

"I've probably known John longer and been closer to him than anybody in coaching. There's nobody I've enjoyed more, there's nobody I've respected more."

—BOE KNIGHT

"I've played against Knight several times. He gets all the credit for throwing that chair. When I played him one time I threw a chair. The referee turned around and I pointed up to the stands and said, 'See what those SOBs think of you?'"

—*JOHNNY ORR*

"I had worked in coal mines in the summer, and I just wanted to get a good job so I could escape that. I never thought much about going to college. No one in my family ever went to college. It wasn't until my last year when I started thinking about going to college to play basketball."

• Man for All Seasons

Johnny Orr's stirring athletic seasons as a Taylorville High senior had a great impact on his life. Johnny was considered by many to be Illinois' best all-around prep athlete of 1943–44, with his exploits in football, basketball and baseball.

That's right, baseball. With his batting, baserunning and fielding savvy, the lanky Orr deserves mention alongside George Bush in the category of famous former first basemen. Although Orr didn't compete in college baseball, he played well enough in high school to be wooed by pro scouts. Johnny's 1944 Taylorville team went unbeaten in baseball until the postseason tournaments. When you add the Taylorville football, basketball and baseball records together, Johnny's senior year produced a 65-2 record, with both losses coming in postseason.

Orr received invitations to play in elite Illinois high school all-star games in basketball and baseball. Johnny was enough of a big shot that he had his picture taken with Illinois Governor Dwight Green at the prep all-star basketball luncheon. The baseball affair, held at Comiskey Park, held tryouts for most lineup spots, but Orr was given an automatic berth and was the first designated starter for the downstate team. In announcing Johnny's selection, writer Clark Shaughnessy of the Chicago *Daily News* called Orr "one of the greatest all-around athletes ever to be produced downstate." Johnny proved his athletic versatility again in the summer following his graduation when he emerged from the University of Illinois' summer football practices as No. 2

on the depth chart at end. A Champaign newspaper account of Orr's progress with the Illini noted that "his pass catching was brilliant and he scored often in intra-squad scrimmages."

Sometimes it took more than a human effort to stop him. In one 3-2 Taylorville baseball victory over Athens during his senior season, Orr was robbed of a home run by a large tree that towered over left field. Here's the local *Breeze-Courier* account:

> With the score tied 2-2 in the top half of the seventh, with the Tornadoes howling for a hit, Orr came through with a line triple to left field and if a tree in the wrong place had not stopped the ball's flight, big John would have had a home run.

Orr scored the winning run on a subsequent single.

Taylorville was 12-0 on the diamond before losing in the sectional tournament to Springfield Lanphier, 5-3. It took a big effort to knock Taylorville from the tournament—Lanphier's winning pitcher, who also hit the deciding two-run homer, was Robin Roberts, who went on to major league baseball stardom. Similarly, in the football postseason challenge game of unbeatens, Champaign had topped Taylorville, 7-0, behind young quarterback Bob Richards, who went on to international fame as an Olympic champion pole vaulter.

Collegiate recruiting of the 1940s was much simpler than it is today. The mail was the primary vehicle of communication, and it wasn't unusual for students to choose a school without traveling to campus for a visit. Johnny was pursued by Illinois and Southern Illinois and even was contacted by prestigious Yale University. Orr laughs today when he recalls his chance at being an Ivy Leaguer.

"I had never heard of Yale—I thought it was Yale, Kansas," Orr said, referring to the place of his birth. After the exposure Johnny and Bontemps received as basketball all-staters, prominent Yale alumni brought them to Chicago to try to sell them on the school. "To get accepted at Yale we had to take the ACT test. I had never even heard of that test. There were certain places to go to take it, so Bontemps and I drove to Mattoon. We took the first part of the test in the morning, and they told us the rest of the test was optional. Well, we didn't want to hang around if we didn't have to, so we went home without taking the rest of the test. Well, it wasn't optional, and our scores were half of what they should be. Yale people called us up and thought we were really dummies. Bontemps wasn't fired up about going to Yale, anyway, and we didn't see the campus except in pictures, so it was just as well."

Orr said athletic scholarships of the 1940s were much different than today, where more restrictions are put on the specific benefits. "Southern Illinois tried to get me to play," Johnny recalled, "and they said they'd get me the job running the concession stand, and I could keep all of the money that was profit. That kind of thing was legal in those days. In fact, that's the job I ended up getting at Beloit. All of the scholarship aid was tied in with jobs, and you had to show up and work."

In fact, the University of Illinois scholarship Johnny eventually accepted paid the $80-a-semester tuition, but athletes had to work for their books and room and board. "Everybody worked two days in the bookstore to pay for your books," Johnny explained. "Then to cover the rest of your scholarship, you washed dishes, waited tables, swept the streets on campus, or were a door checker."

• University of Illinois

Orr could have signed a minor league pro baseball contract out of high school with the Chicago Cubs and also was pursued by the St. Louis Browns. In a story in the Chicago *Daily News,* Cubs scout Ray Schalk called Orr "a brilliant prospect." Yet Johnny chose to accept a scholarship to play football, basketball and baseball at the University of Illinois, joining a trio of Taylorville classmates.

"(Illinois football coach) Ray Eliot came to my school to recruit four of us for football—Frank Hurtte, Schultte Bishop, Red Janssen and myself," Johnny said. "He bought us a hamburger, fries and a milkshake and told us, 'You're Illinois boys, you should come to Illinois.' So we did. Well, three of us started—and that was unheard of for a small town like Taylorville; that will never be duplicated again—Frank at left guard, Red at left tackle, and me at end, and Schultte was second-team quarterback." Taylorville's Chuck Riester also went to Illinois and played football, and Bontemps enrolled at Illinois to play basketball.

Orr said his Illinois experience, particularly his exposure to Illini football coach Eliot and basketball coach Mills, had a great impact on his decision to pursue a career as a teacher and coach. "Doug Mills and Ray Eliot were great coaches," Johnny recalled. "Ray was very inspirational, just a tremendous speaker. Being with him definitely affected my personality, and after the way he motivated me, I was never afraid to speak in public."

Ironically, Orr said he never envisioned himself as a college football player. He explained that he tried out for the Illini team primarily to be around his Taylorville pals. "I liked to play football, but I didn't like to practice it. I went out because all my friends were going out," Orr explained. There was plenty of practice, too, because in that era colleges had six weeks of summer workouts for football.

"There were some great players at Illinois then—Buddy Young, Lou Agase, Don Greenwood—guys that later went on to play in the NFL," Johnny explained. Young tied the world indoor record for the 60-yard dash as a freshman at Illinois and would make second-team All-American as a running back in 1944 after scoring 13 touchdowns. "Buddy Young had all the (Illini) offensive records and held them up until about 15 years ago," Orr said. "There were a lot of guys out for football, though. There were 27 guys who started out at the end position and that dropped to about 10 by the beginning of the season."

Johnny told Tom Witosky of the *Des Moines Register* that Coach Eliot was such a great motivator he'd inspire you to "do anything. You'd even go out and bite somebody." Orr recalled the time Eliot sat him down during his freshman season training camp and challenged him. "He called me in before practice and said, 'Orr, if I told your dad the way you were playing, he'd be embarrassed. You've got to play harder,' " Orr said. "I was mad after that, so we had a big scrimmage, and I went out and had a pretty good day and did everything right." Orr caught six passes for 143 yards and two touchdowns in two summer scrimmages that concluded drills, and quickly gained respect for his athletic ability. Urbana *Courier* sportswriter Eddie Jones wrote:

> There is no pass catcher on this squad superior to Orr. There may never have been, here at Illinois, a receiver with such sticky fingers . . . The Taylorville boy thrilled the audience with a catch of a pass thrown by Chuck Starks . . . Orr timed the throw perfectly, outjumped and outguessed the Blue defenders and gathered it in for a touchdown.

Johnny said he still didn't expect to play as a freshman. "When it was time for the first game," Orr said, "Eliot would get all the great former players like Red Grange to stand out in the hall near the locker room. Then he'd put 11 chairs in the front of the room and he'd announce the starting lineup. He's get real dramatic and say 'Starting at end, from Taylorville, Illinois, John

Orr.' Then you'd run up there, and everyone stood up and cheered like hell. Then he'd do that for all 11 starters.

"When he called my name to start, I was fired up. Then the starters would lead the team out, and you'd walk pass Red Grange and all these great players, and they'd shake your hand and wish you good luck. Ray was just a great inspiration, and I got so I really liked football. I started all year, but we had some great players so I didn't get a lot of chances to score. I scored my only touchdown against Iowa—man, we beat the Hawks 40-6."

Orr recalled that he started both ways and even played 59 of the 60 minutes against Ohio State for a respectable Illini team that finished 5-4-1. Johnny was chosen second team All–Big Ten in football and was one of four Illini players tabbed honorable mention All-American.

Without taking even one day off, Johnny jumped into basketball and at season's end earned honorable mention All–Big Ten in that sport. "I played my final football game on Saturday, took the train home from Chicago and got back Sunday, started basketball practice on Monday, and we had our first game on Tuesday, and I started," Orr said. "I started every basketball game the entire year."

Orr played well and contributed to some impressive Illini upsets in a 13-7 basketball finish. The Illini upset the Great Lakes Bluejackets twice; handed an unbeaten, George Mikan–led De-Paul team its first loss; and stopped a 10-0 Iowa Hawkeye team, the latter victory coming by a thrilling 43-42 score. Orr tallied eight points against the Hawks, and a newspaper account in the Urbana *Courier* credited Johnny's aggressive play:

> It was rough-and-tumble Orr who carried on the fight in the first half as Iowa built up a large lead before the Illini scored a basket. And it was Orr in the second half who continued his mad gait. Johnny was in his element, playing in the rough and hard-fought game. The swashbuckling forward from Taylorville High took a beating and dished it right back to any ambitious Hawkeyes who wanted to mix it up.

Orr's competitive fire impressed *Courier* sportswriter Lynn Ruester, who wrote:

> The friendly Orr, who bubbles over with confidence, claims his football letter was "accidental." He came to Illinois direct from Taylorville's championship basketball team to play more basketball. He went out for the football team "just to horse around and try and get into shape. One day Coach Eliot called me into his

office. He told me I had possibilities of making the team, but that first I would have to get down to business, and really work hard. That night I went out to practice and really went to work. I put everything I had into every tackle and set a couple of guys down pretty hard. The next thing I knew some guy took a swing at me and I was in a fight."

Ruester's story concluded,

John's success at sports is due partly to his natural ability, and largely to his fierce competitive spirit. He'll fight at the drop of a hat and he'll fight long after there doesn't remain a fighting chance. When he's on the other side, spectators and players don't like him. When he's on your side, you think he's great. But that's the way Orr is. If he can do anything to help along a winning cause, he'll do his best to do it. It may sound a little rough, but that's the way competitors get to the top. Besides, he's going to enlist in the Marines in May.

Johnny's Illini accomplishments are more remarkable considering he was only 17 years old his entire freshman year. (He was advanced one grade in elementary school and turned 17 two weeks after his high school graduation.) Orr was on the verge of becoming the youngest Illini freshman ever to letter in three sports in the same year when he decided that spring to give up baseball. "I played two weeks of baseball at Illinois," Orr said, "but I ended up quitting because of all the time demands of classes. I also was having too good of a time socially, and I knew I was going into the (military) service in a couple of months, anyway."

• In the Navy

Orr couldn't be drafted into the armed service for World War II until he turned 18, and that time loomed near the end of his freshman year. "My 18th birthday was June 10, and they had a deal that if you enlisted 30 days before your birthday, you could go into the Navy. Otherwise, you'd get drafted, and in 1945 the only place draftees went was the (Army) infantry. Well, nobody wanted to take the risk of being in the infantry. So on May 9, I joined the Navy and got out of school early to leave for boot camp."

World War II was building to its climax when he joined, and Johnny's military career actually turned into an extended athletics experience. He was assigned to boot camp at the Great Lakes Training Center in Waukegan, Ill., and immediately was recruited to play football there. "They played a regular football schedule then, against a lot of college teams, like Navy or Army would now," Orr explained.

"That was a great deal, but there was some investigation of why all these big athletes were playing football instead of out fighting the war," Orr stated. "Just one day after we got our football uniform, pow!—they shipped us all out to the desert (to a base in California). We were out there in amphibian training, picking up Marines on the beach, when they dropped the atomic bomb in Japan."

The war ended shortly thereafter, and Orr was sent to Mare Island, Calif., Navy base to fill out his tour. "I got called in and was asked, 'How'd you like to be the athletic director on the base?'" Orr recalled. "I said, 'What are my choices?' They said I could either go to Guam for 18 months or stay there at Mare Island and be athletic director. So I said, 'I think I'll be your athletic director.'"

Thus Johnny Orr, at the ripe age of 18, had his first management job in athletics. He cleaned the gym, took care of the athletic equipment, managed the golf course, and served as a player-coach of the basketball and baseball teams. The basketball team finished 19-5 against some top-flight college competition in the San Francisco Bay area. Among the friends Orr made on the Mare Island base were twins Mel and El Tappe from Quincy, Ill., who later played for the Chicago Cubs as pitcher and catcher. El Tappe went on to manage the Cubs.

"They asked me to join the Navy reserves, but I said I just wanted to finish my time and be out for good," Orr explained. "About three months later, I got out, and that was a good deal, because a lot of those guys signed up for reserves and were discharged, but they got called back into the Navy during the Korean War. A lot of my buddies had to go back, and some of them were killed in battles."

• Beloit College

With the war over, the University of Illinois athletic teams were overstocked with talent when Orr was discharged from the Navy in late summer 1946. A glut of experienced players had returned to campus simultaneously to finish their degrees, including the famed basketball Whiz Kids, regarded as the best

Illini cage team in history. The thought of taking a redshirt year didn't excite Johnny. "I went back to Illinois, but I hurt my wrist in football practice," Orr said. "I wasn't good enough to start in football because all the players had come back from the war at the same time. There were like 14–18 All-Americans back. They wanted me to sit out one year, and then I would be able to play football the next three years. In basketball, the Whiz Kids were back for their final year, and they wanted me to sit out one year, too. Dolph (Stanley) was coaching at Beloit College now, and he called me to see if I'd play for him. I thought about it and told him, 'Come get me.' I stayed with him for three years, and I loved it."

Johnny said he couldn't have afforded Beloit's private-school tuition without the GI Bill, which not only paid for fees at Beloit, but also provided some extra expense money. "I even got a check each month—I can't remember if it was $85 or $125, but I'd send it home to my dad and grandmother," Johnny said.

While the level of athletic competition at Beloit was less competitive than at Illinois, the academics would present a stiffer challenge. "The difference at Beloit was that you had to take hard courses," Orr said. "At Illinois, I started out in prelaw (studies), but with all the time I spent in sports, and considering how tough the classes were, I got put on academic probation. So I switched to a physical education major, and I made the Dean's List there. But at Beloit, you had to take all the toughest classes— zoology, geology, government, economics, philosophy and one foreign language. Because I was a little older then, and I knew what my goals were, I was able to handle the academics better than when I was at Illinois. I wanted to play professional basketball, and if that didn't work out, I wanted to be a coach, so I had to do what was necessary to have that happen. I never missed classes much, and most of them started at 8 a.m."

Johnny Orr and Beloit proved to be a great match. The guy known as "Whitey" by his fraternity brothers met his wife and many of his best friends at the Wisconsin private college. Beloit also was where Johnny planted the seeds for his career in teaching and coaching. "It's so much different here than at Illinois," Johnny said after becoming a Beloiter. "At an Illinois University banquet, you are pushed into a corner, you eat and then you are introduced. Here, I know most of the people in the room. Almost everyone in town knows me, and I know a lot of them." Johnny said he had the best of both worlds at Beloit. He had a friendly, small-school atmosphere, just like he knew in Taylorville, and had a chance to play for Dolph Stanley, regarded as one of the nation's best coaches. Johnny's familiarity with Stanley made his basketball transition easier, and his skills were polished under the scrutiny of the wise coach.

Although Stanley stressed a disciplined, team-oriented style, he rarely stifled players' personalities. "I taught my boys that when they were on the court, they were actors on the stage. John was always one of the best," Stanley said in an interview with Witosky of the *Des Moines Register*. Orr said Dolph never allowed showboating by his high school teams, but he loosened up when he coached at Beloit. "At Taylorville, he never let you do anything fancy," Johnny said. "Later in college, he changed that, and he got into more showmanship. Our warm-up drills were really fancy—we'd spin the ball off our fingers like the (Harlem) Globetrotters and kick-pass the ball. We worked on that stuff at the end of practice. I think he saw that it gave us a lot of confidence and a lot of pep."

While he stressed discipline, Stanley also tried to find positive means of motivating his players. During Johnny's sophomore season at Taylorville, when the team finished 28-5, Stanley promised to get his hair cut as short as that of the shortest hairstyle of anyone on the team if the guys won their first 10 games. They did. He did. It's a good thing Stanley didn't promise buzz cuts every time one of his teams had a winning streak; he would have looked like Kojak by the time he took his clipboard to Beloit. Stanley's first Beloit team (1945–46) finished 15-6, and 10 of his next 11 teams did even better. Known for playing tough schedules in his 12 seasons at Beloit, Stanley coached 300 games and won 242 of them for an .807 winning percentage. His home-floor record was even better—146-11 for a .930 winning clip. Included were victories over national powers like DePaul, Louisville, Seton Hall, Marquette, Loyola, and a John Wooden–coached Indiana State club. Stanley guided Beloit to a berth in the National Invitation Tournament (NIT) in 1951, which was remarkable given that Beloit was the smallest school ever invited to the tournament. Another of Stanley's Beloit teams ended Evansville's 21-game home-court winning streak. After his team won 40 consecutive Midwest Conference games, Beloit was voted out of the league by a 6-3 margin for, in effect, being unbeatable. Another testament to the Stanley legend occurred when a scheduling mistake left Beloit with two games in one night. They played both games anyway, beating Hillsdale at 7 p.m. and Ottawa at 9 p.m. with the usual fast-break and pressing intensity. Stanley's roster eventually consisted entirely of Illinois players, with five Taylorville graduates on the team in Orr's senior season.

The Beloiters earned the nickname the "Bucket Brigade" as they became the terrors of the Midwest Conference and developed a national reputation for excellence. Orr made an immediate impact in his debut as a sophomore in 1946–47. He was tabbed Midwest Conference MVP and averaged 17.1 points per game (ppg) to rank fourth nationally in scoring in a 22-5 Beloit finish. The Goldmen reached the 32-team National Association of Intercollegiate Basketball (NAIB) tournament in Kansas City— the forerunner of today's National Association of Intercollegiate Athletes (NAIA) national tournament.

Orr wanted to have a big junior season in basketball, and to that end he gave up football that fall because of a knee injury incurred as a sophomore. Beloit came into the 1947–48 basketball season with a new 3,500-seat field house, the result of an imaginative $300,000 construction project. The steel sections of an army airplane hangar were purchased, shipped to Beloit by rail and assembled to form the primary frame of the new facility. The project tripled the seating capacity of the previous gym, yet tickets still were scarce due to the rabid interest throughout the Beloit community. The Goldmen packed the stands with their up-tempo offensive style that produced the nation's second-best scoring average (69.5 ppg). With Orr averaging 15.1 ppg, Beloit zipped to a 27-3 record and returned to Kansas City for another berth in the NAIA national tournament. Orr's play was rewarded as he received the distinction of becoming the school's first All-American. Johnny's reputation grew with his school-record 31-point performance in an 85-76 semifinal-round loss to Louisville, the eventual NAIA champion.

Johnny would repeat as an All-American as a senior in 1948–49, although the arrival of Bontemps that year as a transfer changed Orr's primary role from scorer to playmaker. Bontemps earned the nickname "Mr. Inside" to Johnny's moniker "Mr. Outside." Orr's unselfish play helped Bontemps break two of Orr's school records, as big Ron posted a 42-point individual game and a 617-point season. The Goldmen ranked third nationally in scoring at 73.5 ppg, including a record 82.6 ppg clip in Midwest Conference games. A 71-51 loss to a potent Duquesne team snapped Beloit's 28-game home-court win streak, yet Stanley's gang still was ranked as high as No. 20 nationally. Because of a technicality, Beloit star John Erickson saw his eligibility end at the end of the first semester, yet Stanley's team still went on to post a 29-4 record. A nine-point loss to eventual champion Hamline in the semifinals at nationals dashed the Beloiters' title hopes, and they eventually placed third.

Frank Reichstein of the Beloit *Daily News* covered the national tournament and wrote of Johnny's poise, on the court and off. After Orr's 20 points helped Beloit edge Eastern Illinois in the national quarterfinals, 65-64, Reichstein wrote:

> Without (Orr), we would have been licked. Orr was nothing short of tremendous. He directed teammates around the floor like chessmen. When Eastern Illinois took a lead, it was Orr's long, long, booming shot which came through to put Beloit back in the game.

Reichstein later wrote that Orr impressed the Kansas City crowd when he stepped to the microphone to accept his All-American award after the tourney:

> Most of (the players) sputtered acknowledgement to the plaudits, with at least one exception—Johnny Orr. Dolph Stanley was questioned after the ceremony whether or not Orr had taken speech and/or dramatics. Orr speaks freely and completely at ease before an audience, and without a trace of braggadocio.

Beloit came home from nationals and played a season-ending charity game against Loras College. It gave the school a chance to honor Orr and the squad's other senior, Don Sudkamp. Johnny finished with 16 points in Beloit's 10-point win, but the cool public speaker understandably was overcome with the emotions of saying goodbye. Here's Frank Reichstein's account:

> The ceremony at the end of the contest overshadowed the game for drama. Orr, who never had been ruffled in any game, no matter how much depended on the outcome, broke down at the microphone and wept. Orr had been accustomed to jeers when he stepped to the free-throw line . . . but facing a Beloit audience for the last time was too much. He thanked his teammates and everyone who helped him attain success.

In his three seasons at Beloit, Johnny scored 1,347 points in 88 games (15.3 ppg). Orr was the second Beloit player in history to hit the 1,000-point scoring plateau, reaching the milestone one week after teammate John Erickson did. Beloit's final thank-you to Johnny came through a gift from the local Kiwanis Club—a set of golf clubs.

• St. Louis Bombers

After his senior season, Johnny became engaged to Romie Robinson, a former Beloit student who now was attending the University of Missouri. Eight weeks before his wedding, the 21-year-old Orr learned that the St. Louis Bombers of the Basketball Association of America had won his professional draft rights, outbidding the National Basketball League and the Peoria Caterpillars.

Johnny and Romie were married that summer following graduation, in 1949. Johnny landed a summer job selling insurance before embarking on his pro basketball opportunity with the Bombers. Orr's rookie year in pro hoops was his toughest season to date in athletics. For the first time, his newspaper clippings were less than glowing, primarily because he rode the bench for the first time since early in high school. St. Louis writers didn't help his morale when they wrote that Orr was "a disappointment." Orr responded, "I haven't played enough for anyone to tell."

Orr's sparse playing time and the Bombers' deliberate, slow-tempo offense—a totally different style than the Dolph Stanley up-tempo system Orr excelled in—made him ponder a career switch. His long-term goal of teaching and coaching looked better every day. "The pro ball is fun, but nothing like I thought it would be," Orr told a reporter. "We practice every day, and everything is all business."

Orr was one of two players cut late in the season by the Bombers, a team that subsequently folded after that year. Orr was picked up by the Waterloo Hawks for the final month of the 1949–50 campaign, although it merely delayed the inevitable. "When I graduated, I knew I wasn't going to be a very good pro," Orr said. "And the pay range wasn't like $150,000 then, it was like $2,000 or $3,000." Orr looked to the new decade as an ideal time to start a new chapter in his life.

Basketball had been very, very good to Johnny Orr, the player. Now it was time for the game to benefit Orr, the coach.

"I don't believe that you people know how lucky you are to have Johnny as your coach. I call him coach. He calls everybody 'Coach.' But I'm thrilled he calls me coach, and I'm also thrilled we both call each other friends."

—JUD HEATHCOTE

"Jud and I had some great battles at Michigan State."

—JOHNNY ORR

"When I turned down a coaching opportunity right out of Beloit to play pro basketball, Dolph (Stanley) was so mad at me he could hardly speak to me for a while. After I was offered the coaching job at Milton, Wis., I went back to see Dolph. He said if I was going to be a coach, I should go to Milton and coach everything. He said, 'If you have some success, then we'll tell if you'll be a good coach.' The way he put it was like a challenge, so I thought, 'Well, I'll show you.' "

"I went up there fired up. I was assistant coach in football and baseball, head coach in basketball, taught five classes and study hall, all for a salary of $3,000. When I started that fall in my first experience in coaching, I worked for the head football coach, Andy Anderson. When I first met Andy he told me he wanted me to come to these coaching meetings, and I just laughed. He gave me these note cards that showed me different techniques and footwork we'd teach, and I never even thought of that. He was so organized. Well, the football team won the conference championship, and I was so excited. When it came time for basketball, Andy was my assistant coach, so I thought I'd better find out about those practice plans he had, because I'd have to show him I knew what I was doing. So I drove down to Beloit and sat with Dolph to get some practice plans. Andy was so impressed with that, and he worked his butt off for me."

• Climbing the Ladder

Leave it to Dolph Stanley to influence another phase of Johnny Orr's life. Ever the strategist, Dolph wouldn't let Johnny coast on his reputation. He offered support and advice but ultimately challenged Johnny to sink or swim on his own. The site of Orr's first job offer, Milton, Wis., was a perfect place for Johnny to begin learning the coaching and teaching craft.

Milton made Taylorville look like a metropolis. The high school had 200 kids in four grades, and its gym was so small that Johnny's team had to practice and play across town at Milton College. Orr recalls that the Milton community was dominated by Seventh Day Adventists and Seventh Day Baptists, who regard Friday as their holy day. Thus, Milton High had to play its basketball games on Tuesdays and Thursdays, which turned out to be a blessing for Johnny.

"That was good, because I could play semipro basketball on Friday and make $50–$75 a night," Johnny explained. In trying to supplement the modest teaching salaries that Romie and he earned, Orr took on an ambitious semipro basketball schedule, playing for the Racine Knights of Columbus and the Fond du Lac Rockets. He earned $3,000 that winter of 1950–51 for his semipro games and pocketed an additional $5,000 when he helped organize the Beloit-Illini all-star team for a tour of Illinois and Wisconsin. They played various all-star teams, including the Big

Ten all-stars and Bradley University, the national runners-up the previous year. "That's the only way we survived," Johnny said of the semipro income. "When we moved to Milton, the apartment we got reminded you of a dollhouse. It was like a guest house, two rooms, very small bedrooms. If you came to visit us, you had to sit on the floor—it was like going into a Japanese tea house or something. We bought some furniture from Wally Heil in Taylorville. That way we were able to buy it on credit and pay a little every month, and somehow I got him to drive all the way up to Milton to deliver it."

After Orr helped coach the Milton football squad to the conference title, he took his competitive fire to the coaching box in basketball. Despite a mediocre basketball tradition, Milton finished 15-7 that season, the school's most wins in 15 years. The highlight was earning the school's first trip to the state tournament. "The superintendent gave me the spring off from coaching baseball because we had such a good basketball season," Orr recalled.

• Dubuque Senior

Already anxious to tackle a bigger coaching challenge, Johnny pursued a coaching vacancy back in his home state at Rock Island High. Orr recalled that he was one of two finalists, but the Quad Cities school tabbed a college head coach for the job. Johnny made a good enough impression, however, to prompt the Rock Island officials to recommend him when the superintendent at Dubuque (Iowa) Senior High called for advice on his coaching opening. Dubuque liked what it heard and called on Johnny in Milton.

"I remember I was taking a nap and there was knock on the door, and it was the superintendent from Dubuque Senior," Orr recalled. "I talked to them awhile and later went down for a formal interview." Orr recalled that he didn't know much about Dubuque. He was pleasantly surprised when he discovered that it was a town of 56,000 people, and Senior High had 1,400 students in the top three grades. There were more than 50 applicants for the Dubuque coaching vacancy, but Orr made another good impression in his formal interview. He was offered the job—pending formal approval by the board of education—and he accepted. The gentlemen's agreement caused some anxious moments, though. "They said they'd call me next week," Orr said. "So I resigned at Milton, but then a week, 10 days passed and I didn't hear from them at Dubuque. Whoo, I was getting worried, so I called them to see if it was still on, and they offered me the job."

Orr received an attractive pay raise with the 1951 move—from a $3,000 annual salary at Milton to $4,200 at Dubuque Senior High—although his work schedule was every bit as demanding. Besides duties as head basketball coach, Orr was assigned to work as assistant football coach (and later sophomore football coach) as well as golf coach for boys and girls. He also took on a busy teaching load. Romie landed a teaching job at Dubuque's Jefferson Junior High School, although women's salaries were noticeably smaller during that era. "In those days, a married woman was considered a permanent substitute," Johnny explained, "and you only got paid $2,200, whether it was your first year or your 25th."

"When we moved to Dubuque, we paid $72.50 a month rent," Johnny recalled. "To buy a house then, you had to have $1,000 for a down payment, but that was a lot of money, and you couldn't raise it overnight. We finally got an uncle of Romie's to lend us the money." Orr fondly recalls that his first house was what was called a "John Deere house"—basic housing units built to accommodate the rapidly growing work force at the Deere farm implement plant in Dubuque. "They were built on a slab with no basement, but they had a nice garage," Orr said. "We paid $13,800 for that house."

Johnny remembers learning that he was the fourth basketball coach in four years at Senior High, a school not known for great basketball. On the plus side, Orr had 70 players try out for his first team. No one expected much, Orr said, given the school's sleepy basketball tradition and his team's modest height and relative inexperience. Only five lettermen were back from a 1950–51 team that started 4-0 but finished 7-14.

1951–52, first season

Johnny brought a new look to Senior basketball. True to his lessons from Stanley, Johnny preached to his team the importance of a strict diet and a nine-hour sleep night. According to a story in the Senior High student newspaper, more of Stanley's influence came through in Johnny's penchant for detail and neatness in the off-court aspects of basketball. The story said Orr had proposed a thorough remodeling of the locker room:

> (The coach) will be able to supply the boys with clean practice uniforms every other night. Along with this, there will be a few pictures and amusing quotations in the locker room. The boys'

names will be painted on their lockers by Orr's faithful managers . . . In the locker room, there will be a box at the bottom of the benches with foot powder and tough skin in them. Tough skin to an athlete is like hand cream to girls—they use it to prevent sores. If Senior doesn't have one of the best teams in the state, it should have one of the neatest.

Johnny won a lot of friends—and more importantly, gained a lot of confidence—when his first Dubuque team qualified for the 1952 Iowa state tournament, the school's first trip to state. That feat is significant considering that Senior is the oldest high school west of the Mississippi River, and 1952 marked the 41st year a state tournament was held. "The people were ecstatic," Orr recalled. "We were 13-10—it was the first winning season in several years. I was riding on cloud nine."

The Dubuque Senior Rams flirted with a losing record until they caught fire in the postseason. They upset Marshalltown and Mason City in the substate games, winning each by one-point margins, and became one of 16 teams advancing to the one-class tournament in Iowa City. Senior's Bill Beyer, a 6-foot-4-inch rebounding and defensive ace, was profiled in the *Des Moines Register*'s Prep Parade for his clutch play during the substate drive. The *Register* story noted that Orr benched Beyer earlier in the season "for not hustling," and Beyer responded to Orr's challenge to lead the team to its state tournament berth. The 1952 Iowa state tournament field also included two-time defending champion Davenport High, which had topped Dubuque twice during the season, as well as Story County teams Roland and Ames High. Roland, the 1951 runner-up team, was paced by all-stater Gary Thompson, who later was an All-American player at Iowa State and today is a prominent basketball broadcaster.

Senior's Cinderella season ended in the first round at state, however. Tiny Dinsdale, a Tama County town of 75 with a school enrollment of 22 boys and 24 girls, posted a 58-50 victory before a capacity crowd of 8,500 in Iowa City. Senior's chances were hurt when Beyer and guard Dave Stevens fouled out early in the fourth quarter, paving the way for Dinsdale to win its 33rd straight game.

Later seasons

Orr's 1952–53 Dubuque team started the season on a strong note at Freeport, Ill., and upset the tradition-rich Freeport Pretzels, 58-43. That win snapped Freeport's home-court winning streak at 41 games and was only Dubuque's third victory against

Freeport in 31 all-time meetings. The Rams went on to a 16-6 record in Orr's second season and accumulated an 18-4 record in 1953-54. En route to that 18-4 finish, the Rams earned a share of the Missisippi Valley Conference championship—Senior's first since 1932—with a 63-55 victory over Davenport. That victory snapped Senior's 18-game losing streak to the Iowa prep power-house dating back to 1944; the Rams had trailed the all-time series with Davenport 64-7 prior to the game. Dubuque and Davenport shared the Mississippi Valley title with 9-1 records, and Senior posted the school's first 17-win season in 22 years.

The Rams topped those achievements during Orr's fourth season, 1954-55, as they unveiled a new $1 million athletic facility with the school's best basketball season to date. Senior's 20-7 record in 1954-55 included a return to the state tournament, with a postseason run highlighted by a thrilling 57-55 district tourney win over crosstown rival Loras Academy, the forerunner to Dubuque Wahlert High. In the inaugural state tournament held in Des Moines, Dubuque Senior reached the semifinals before losing to Ames High.

Johnny spoke out to criticize the state tournament pairings, which in those days had a built-in process to guarantee small-school representation. There were three classes, and teams competed for a set number of qualifying berths within their class. Five Class A teams, five Class B teams and six Class C teams advanced from local pools, then the 16 survivors played a one-class state tourney. Although there were some outstanding small-school teams during the 1950s, Orr said he thought it was fairer and more logical to pool all the teams together from the start for a true one-class tournament. "The way the tournament in Iowa is run stinks," Orr told a gathering in Dubuque. The comments later were picked up around the state, and a quote-maker was born.

Former *Des Moines Register* sportswriter Bob Dyer, who grew up in Dubuque, remembers that Orr's competitive fire was evident during his high school coaching career. "I was a student at Wahlert, and we used to sneak into the gym at Senior High, and Orr and (his assistant coach) Rhys Hutchinson used to throw us out all the time," Dyer said. "We used to call John 'Mt. Vesuvius,' because he'd get those veins pumping in his neck and get real red when he was mad. I still think he was the reason for the (coaches') seat-belt rule in Iowa high school basketball." The seat-belt rule, which requires coaches to remain seated except in a few specified situations, was added to improve the courtside behavior of coaches.

One run-in with the referees sticks in Johnny's mind because it came the day his daughter Jenny was born, February 6, 1954. "I think we played at Iowa City that night and had a one-point win," Orr said. "I came back home late and the lights were on and Romie said, 'Let's go to the hospital.' She had the baby about 3:30 in the morning. I didn't get much sleep, and we had another game the next night down at Rock Island—I think that was against one of the Rock Island teams that (NBA coach) Don Nelson played on. I got into a big argument with the official, and he almost ejected me, but Johnny Hurlburt, one of my players, told the ref, 'Don't throw the coach out—he just had a baby last night.' That saved me."

In all, Orr's first six Dubuque basketball teams had winning records, and his eight-year basketball record there was 103-71.

Football coaching

Johnny's success at Dubuque wasn't limited to basketball. He helped turn the football program into a winner, too. Orr said he has fond memories of being a varsity assistant in football and recalls his concern when Dubuque head coach Dale Harris, his boss the first five years, left in 1956 to take a coaching job at Ottumwa.

"I was working for the school district that summer," Orr recalls. "We were knocking steam radiators out and converting them to oil heat. I happened to be in the superintendent's office working, so I told him, 'Be sure you get me a good coach to work for.' A couple of weeks later, the superintendent called me in and asked me if I wanted the job. I said I'd take the job if they'd pay me all my football coaching salary on December 1—that way I'd always have a nice Christmas and be able to buy gifts for my family."

By Orr's third season as football coach, in 1958, Senior emerged as a contender for the mythical state championship (it would be 14 years until a high school football playoff system was implemented). The 1957 Rams finished 3-4-1, but hopes for 1958 were high because of the caliber of underclassmen returning. The optimism started to unravel, though, during the off-season when two key assistant coaches plus a couple of top players moved from Dubuque. Coach Dick Hobbs, a longtime junior high coach, left for a head coaching post at Bloomfield, and longtime Orr colleague Roger Isaacson moved to a job at Oak Park, Ill., taking along touted sophomore quarterback Terry Isaacson. "I figured Terry might be my first all-state football player," Orr told Jack Ogden of the Cedar Rapids *Gazette* in a 1958 preseason interview.

Even with those setbacks, Johnny molded a Senior team that far exceeded its sixth-place poll prediction in the Mississippi Valley Conference. Keyed by a tough defense and the elusive running of all-state halfback Ken Montgomery, Orr's Rams celebrated the school's centennial year by zooming to a 6-1 start before settling for a 6-2 final record. Dubuque recorded several shutouts, none sweeter than a 44-0 blasting of perennial power Davenport High. In handing the Blue Devils their worst loss in school history, Ram quarterbacks Bob Buelow and Jim Phillips finished 13-for-13 in passing for 286 yards. The victory propelled Senior into a final-game showdown with Cedar Rapids Washington for the Mississippi Valley title. Senior, whose only previous loss was a 10-7 setback to Illinois foe East Moline, was rated No. 2 in the state and needed to tie or beat Washington to claim the school's first MVC football championship in nearly two decades. But the Warriors prevailed, 7-0, and earned Cedar Rapids' first MVC football title after 20 years in the conference.

Dubuque finished the season ranked third in the state in both the Associated Press (AP) and United Press International (UPI) polls, and five Rams were named to the nine-school all-conference team, an unprecedented feat. In addition, Orr was chosen Coach of the Year in the Mississippi Valley. Montgomery, who set a school record in rushing with a 208-yard game, rushed for 956 yards and scored 14 touchdowns to earn all-state honors. Ironically, he was second in eastern Iowa scoring behind a Bettendorf High junior who later would become a close friend of Orr's: Dave Cox. Now the Iowa State assistant athletic director, Cox had a prolific junior season at Bettendorf with 22 touchdowns, highlighted by a five-touchdown performance in the final game.

"I had some hellish football teams with some good players," Johnny said of his three years as Ram head coach. "Craig Starkey was captain at Arizona, Mike Reilly was a star at Iowa, Dion Kempthorne and Ken Montgomery were on a Rose Bowl team at Wisconsin, Terry Isaacson was a star at Air Force Academy."

• On to Madison

Orr figured Dubuque would be the place he'd retire, so he moved into a roomy, split-level home following his eighth year there. "I was 32 years old, and I thought I'd probably stay in Dubuque all my life," Johnny recalls. "I had a good job, I was doing what I liked to do. So we built this split-level home, but we didn't live there but four months and we got the chance to go to Madison. My old Beloit teammate John Erickson was hired as Wisconsin head basketball coach, and we always said if one of us got a good college coaching job we'd take the other one to be the assistant coach. I asked the Dubuque superintendent if there was a chance I could make any more money, and he said I was about as high as I was ever going to go. I always wanted to be a college coach, and here was my chance to go into the Big Ten. I always said that someday I was going to have one of those good jobs, and by going to Wisconsin I felt the opportunity would be easier to come by."

Romie and Johnny both say the decision to leave Dubuque for a college job in Madison was harder than their later decision to leave Michigan for Iowa State. "I got the chance to go to Wisconsin to coach, but I hated to leave Dubuque, and I hated to give up football," Orr said. "The thing was, it was so easy to coach football because it was a shorter season, I was organized, and I had good athletes. I'd have to take a pay cut, too, because by now I was making $10,500 at Dubuque in 1959, but I only got $7,200 to come to Wisconsin. But I had a chance to be an assistant coach in both football and basketball at Wisconsin, and I think I'm the last guy ever to do that in the Big Ten."

The Badger basketball program had endured five consecutive losing seasons, including a 1958–59 record of 3-19, prior to Erickson and Orr's arrival in 1959–60. From that last-place spot in the Big Ten, the Badgers rose all the way to second in the conference in just three seasons, with a 17-7 record in 1961–62, the school's first winning record since 1955 and its best conference placing since 1950. The highlight of that Wisconsin season was an upset of the great Ohio State team that featured All-Americans Jerry Lucas and John Havlicek. The Badgers' stunning triumph ended Ohio State's 17-game overall winning streak and a 27-game Big Ten winning streak. Wisconsin came back with another winning season in 1962–63, as Orr's recruiting efforts continued to reap benefits.

Although the term wasn't coined then, Johnny practiced the art of networking while at Wisconsin. That complemented the time-honored job-hunting techniques of patience and persistence. "I met some great people at Wisconsin," Johnny explained, "like athletic director Ivy Williamson. Besides basketball, I was freshman line coach in football. Fred Jacoby, who now is a famous (administrator) in college athletics, was the head freshman coach. The people were closer at Wisconsin than anyplace I've ever been. I loved it."

Eager to fulfill his dream of becoming a head coach in college, Johnny enlisted the help of his colleagues for job references, and that led to an interview for the head basketball job at New Mexico. "I thought I was going to get it, and I even went back and put my house up for sale," Orr said. "Then they called me and told me I wasn't going to be their coach. I had a great interview, but they hired Bob King. I was really depressed. I felt then I had to be a head coach somewhere to get hired as a head coach."

Orr said he began to believe that football might be the better route to achieve his goal of becoming a college head coach. An opportunity almost arose with Badger assistant coach Clark Van Galder, whose son Tim Van Galder later came to Iowa State and set school records as a quarterback. "I lived down the street in Madison from Fuzzy Thurston, the star lineman of the Green Bay Packers," Orr said. "Van Galder almost got the Stanford and Yale head coaching jobs, and if he got either of those jobs, he was going to take me as his defensive line coach and Fuzzy Thurston as his offensive line coach. They turned him down at Stanford, though. He was only 46 years old, and they said he was too old. Can you imagine that?"

• Massachusetts

Orr was gaining respect as Erickson's top recruiter, and basketball coaching opportunities continued to surface. Orr interviewed for the basketball vacancy at Massachusetts, with the help of Wisconsin colleague Milt Bruhn, who was a close friend of the UMass athletic director. That was among three jobs on the East Coast he interviewed for in 1963. Prominent St. John's coach Joe Lapchick, who had hired Orr to do some scouting for him in the Midwest, wrote a recommendation on Johnny's behalf, which buoyed his chances. "I interviewed for head coaching jobs at Rutgers, Massachusetts and Connecticut," Johnny said. "Rutgers hired Bill Foster. I liked both Massachusetts and Connecticut. I felt whoever offered me the job first I would take it, it didn't make a difference. When Massachusetts hired me, I was excited—my first head coaching job. I enjoyed it."

Orr accepted the UMass offer, and on April Fools' Day 1963, at age 35, he was introduced as the new coach of Redmen basketball. Except for a spell in the military in California, this lifelong midwestern guy made a bold move as he crossed the country with his family and took residence in Amherst, a town of 10,000 about 85 miles west of Boston. He would come to love the people, although it was clear that UMass would never replace the Boston Celtics as the state's marquee basketball team. In fact, one of his first challenges was recruiting against a former Celtics star. Bob Cousy retired from pro basketball and became the new coach at Boston College the same time Johnny started at UMass.

Johnny's first Yankee Conference game came at home against conference power Connecticut, and although it produced a narrow victory, it was marred by a bench-clearing brawl during the final minute. Orr's up-tempo offensive style produced results, and his first UMass team went on to set a school record in scoring more than 83 ppg. Johnny said his three seasons at the Amherst school had good moments, thanks to the people he met and some moderate success with records of 15-9, 13-11 and 11-13. A bright spot was the presence of assistant coach Jack Leaman, his successor who's known today as the coach who discovered and coached the great Julius Erving at Massachusetts. "Jack Leaman was one of the better minds I'd ever been around," Johnny said. "He knew basketball." Johnny also landed a radio job as color commentator for the UMass football games.

"Amherst was a beautiful town, and we made some terrific friends," Orr said. "But when I came, it was our first year in Division I. There wasn't much interest in basketball. As an example, friends would invite us to dinner—on the night of a game. That's not good. And we always bused to games; I think we had one airplane trip. We'd make those bus rides to Maine, Virginia, all over the coast. We had a terrible gym that seated about 4,000, and we never had any money in our budget. You didn't have all the stuff you have today, so you did it all. We made those recruiting trips into New Jersey and New York. You didn't have any budget, you'd take your car everywhere. They wouldn't pay for a player's campus visit unless he was coming there for sure. So you had to sell them in their schools and in their homes. I didn't think I could go anywhere from there, so I started looking at some other options."

• Insurance for the Future

With a wife and four daughters at home, and his 40th birthday coming up, Johnny started wondering if the college coaching life was worth it. Then an opportunity in the business world came Orr's way. The Fidelity Union Insurance Company saw Johnny's expertise in recruiting, his contacts with coaches, and his ability as a public speaker and decided he was just the guy to go out and hire them some new insurance sales representatives. "I was making $12,500 at Massachusetts, and Fidelity came in and offered $19,000 a year plus all the best benefits, including a nice expense account," Orr said. "So I took the job, went to Dallas for training, and they said I could go anywhere in the country I wanted to work. I picked Illinois, and I worked out of Urbana as the four-state director of recruiting agents in the Midwest." Among the agents Johnny signed on with Fidelity was Ev Cochrane, now a prominent businessman in Ames who at the time was head coach at Northern Illinois.

The salary and benefits were great, but it didn't take Johnny long to discover he missed coaching. A strange turn of events involving TV broadcaster Bill Fleming brought Orr back to recruiting prep players instead of adult sales reps. "It didn't excite me, I liked the basketball too much," Johnny recalled. "I used to go to all the University of Illinois games. Bill Fleming, the TV announcer, was in town to do the Michigan-Illinois game. I was the first guy he interviewed in broadcasting, at halftime of a Wisconsin game when he was first starting, and he remembered me and called me. I later found out he was a Michigan graduate, and he was friends with Michigan head basketball coach Dave Strack, so we all went to breakfast before the game. Strack started saying things weren't going well for his team—they had a long losing streak going, two of his assistants were leaving, and the only guys staying with him were young guys. He was looking for an older, mature guy to be his assistant. I told him I go all around the state watching coaches for my job with Fidelity, and if I see someone he'd be interested in, I'll call him.

"I thought it was one of those things you say out of courtesy, and I thought that was the end of it. So I was shocked later when he called me. I thought he had forgotten. He asked me if I'd found any good guys, and I told him I knew a good guy—me. He said, 'You're kidding! You'd come?' I told him if they'd pay me enough to live on, I'd come, and I'd be loyal. I wouldn't apply for another job. He said he'd pay me $10,000, so I said I come up if they'd pay my moving expenses. I think they finally found $700 for that, so I decided to come." Johnny moved Romie and their four daughters from Urbana to Ann Arbor, and he served as Strack's assistant coach in 1967–68. Then another twist of fate produced the break Orr had sought throughout his 18-year career.

• The Michigan Miracle

"Fritz Crisler had resigned as Michigan's athletic director, and it looked like football coach Bump Elliott was going to get the job, but there had been a problem with some football players getting free passes to movies. Well, Michigan doesn't like bad publicity, and that hurt Bump's chances. It looked like a set-up deal just to keep Bump from getting the athletic director job, because it was something he had no knowledge of. Don Canham was the track coach at the time, and he called me and told me he was the new AD. And he said Dave Strack was his new business manager.

"Well, I was quite surprised, because I didn't know Dave wanted out of coaching. Canham asked Dave who they should get as basketball coach—he was thinking big-time guys like Frank McGuire, John Wooden, etc.—but Strack said, 'You'll never get those guys. The guy you ought to hire is right here—Orr.' Canham turned to me and said, 'You want the job?' I said, 'Yes!' and boom!—I was the coach. I didn't know what to say. I can't tell you how excited I was. They offered me $15,500."

Orr said Canham earned his respect, despite being tight with salaries and a tough administrator. There were nearly two dozen personnel changes early in Canham's term as athletic director, including Bump Elliott's move from head football coach to assistant athletic director and the hiring of Bo Schembechler as Elliott's successor.

Orr's journey up the coaching ladder illustrates how skill, hard work, persistence, timing and luck must come together to land a major-college coaching job. "It wasn't all easy," Johnny said of the pursuit of his coaching goals. "But if you hang in there long enough, it seemed like something would break. And when we did move, we never went backwards."

•

"Johnny Orr has one of the most interesting shoe deals I've ever heard of. Reebok is paying Orr $50,000 a year to endorse Nike."

—GEORGE RAVELING

"I tell you the greatest thing I ever did was come to Iowa State. If I'd have stayed at Michigan I would have retired at about $33,000 a year. Now I'll retire at $135,000. But I really don't like money [pause]. *That's a damn lie."*

—JOHNNY ORR

"My first year at Michigan as an assistant coach, we got a new field house, and Kentucky came in with Coach Adolph Rupp to play us and dedicate that building. They came up and bounced us good."

"I was shocked when I got the Michigan head coaching job. I thought I'd go up there a couple of years as an assistant and then I'd try to get another head coaching job. When they hired me, the papers wrote 'Johnny Who?' just like when they hired Bo Schembechler from Miami of Ohio, and they wrote 'Bo Who?' The alums wanted to hire guys like Joe Paterno and George Allen when they hired Bo, and a big-name guy like Frank McGuire when they hired me. After Canham offered me the job, he took me around in two days to meet people in Detroit, Grand Rapids, Benton Harbor and Chicago. I met a lot of guys; they were big guys, rich guys. I realized later that if there had been any objections, Don might not have given me the job."

"I can't tell you how excited I was. I couldn't even believe I could be the basketball coach at Michigan. The tradition and nostalgia surrounding Michigan athletics was overwhelming, and it was a tremendous honor to be working there. I was determined to have a good basketball team."

• The Pivotal Season

Under Coach Orr, Michigan won two Big Ten titles, finished second three times, earned four National Collegiate Athletic Association tournament bids, and reached the NCAA championship game in 1976. But perhaps Orr's greatest claim was his ability to survive in the pressure cooker that was Ann Arbor for 12 years—a tenure no other Michigan basketball coach has surpassed—and the fact that when he did leave, he left on his own terms.

Certainly, coaching at Michigan has its advantages. Its athletic tradition, the school's national visibility, and the tremendous in-state recruiting talent combine to make it one of America's most attractive coaching jobs, in football or basketball. The advantages in the 1970s didn't necessarily carry over into salary, which was quite modest by Big Ten standards, but there was a stability with the presence of Don Canham, the Michigan athletic director. Without Canham as an insurance policy, Johnny might have been back finding insurance salesmen. Canham had a reputation of loyalty to coaches. For a newer head coach like Johnny, who was trying to establish that he could meet the high expectations, it was critical to have the patient and prudent Canham as an ally.

Close scrutiny comes with the territory in major-college sports. But in Johnny's day at Michigan, it didn't take much for scrutiny to turn into mutiny. Where else would a kid run for a student government office on a fire-the-basketball-coach platform, as a guy did in the fall of 1973? That vocal minority in the stands and along press row would find fault with John Orr or John Wooden or John Thompson or Pope John Paul. In modern days, it's known as the call-in-show or letter-to-the-editor mentality. Because Michigan is respected nationally in academics and athletics, the standard is high to begin with. Throw in the fact that its football program was then, and remains today, a perennial national force, and you see how the pressure builds for basketball to achieve the same acclaim.

There was one puzzling thing about Michigan basketball fans of the 1970s: Their support and enthusiasm at home games never matched their desire for excellence. Sellouts were rare, and Crisler Arena lacked the sixth-man atmosphere necessary to intimidate opposing teams. Tony Schwartz of the *Michigan Daily* student newspaper wrote during the 1972–73 season that Michigan basketball fans

> Are a surprisingly uptight and unresponsive group. And the basketball team is acutely aware of it. Most of (the players) emphasize the tremendous crowd reaction the home team gets at other schools. (Sophomore guard) Joe Johnson, for one, is more blunt: "Playing at home is like playing on a neutral court . . ." The fans came into the (1972–73) season with sky-high expectations, and even before the first game was over, boos were heard and the perennial plea to "Dump John Orr" had begun anew.

The lukewarm atmosphere wasn't a one-season occurrence. Five years and a couple of Big Ten championships later, apathy still lingered. Jeff Mortimer of the Ann Arbor *News* wrote that the majority of fans at a 1978 game in Crisler Arena "was acting as if Tom Watson were putting for an eagle on the 18th hole at Augusta National. That's about par for Crisler. You'll hear more noise at the movies than you will at a Michigan home game. It's almost as if the customers think it would be too rude to be too loud."

Contributing to a Michigan coach's challenge are the media dynamics of being at a major university in a major conference and located in a large metropolitan area. Sportswriters and sportscasters generally hold the coaches and athletes to the same bottom-line standards of the local professional teams. For example, *Sports Illustrated*'s Curry Kirkpatrick made this assessment of Johnny in his basketball preview story for the 1972–73 season: "An excellent fellow to talk to, Orr has never been accused by his peers of being an excellent coach."

• 1972–73 Season

Orr's fifth season with the Wolverines, 1972–73, would be a pivotal one. He had posted three winning seasons at Michigan, including a 19-7 finish in 1970–71, and a 14-10 record and a third-place tie in the conference in 1971–72. By now, Orr was establishing a reputation as a pleasant, witty and entertaining chap, and a good recruiter of coaches and players. More importantly, he had held the respect of his boss, Canham. What wasn't firm in the minds of many fans and some in the media was Johnny's ability to win championships. A specific question was whether he had the ability to get the most out of exceptional talent. With All-American Rudy Tomjanovich scoring 30 points per game (ppg) as a senior in Johnny's second season (1969–70), Michigan finished just 10-14.

A good beginning

Johnny's 1972–73 season started well enough. The maize and blue optimism sailed in with a newcomer who had a revered last name, a rarely used first name, a lovely middle name and a catchy nickname: Michael Campanella "Campy" Russell. Although he was no genetic relation to Michigan basketball legend and All-American Cazzie Russell, who led Michigan to three straight Big Ten championships from 1964 through 1966, Campy nonetheless was adopted as a Cazzie clone. Regarded by many as the nation's best high school senior in 1971, Campy backed up that reputation in 1971–72 on the Wolverines' freshman team in the final season that freshman weren't eligible for varsity play under NCAA rules. The 6-foot-8-inch forward, an autoworker's son and the fifth of 10 children, honed his skills on an asphalt playground court in nearby Pontiac, Mich. After being dubbed all-everything at Pontiac Central High, Campy enrolled at Michigan and promptly averaged 30.2 ppg and 12 rebounds per game (rpg) in leading the Wolverine frosh to a 12-0 record.

The question with Campy wasn't whether he'd be a star, but how long would he wait before leaving college for professional basketball? Orr's biggest concern was that Campy would jump to the lucrative American Basketball Association after his first varsity season. "I bet he gets more mail than Bo, Canham and me combined," Johnny told Jerry Green of the *Detroit News*, referring to the agents, advisers and others trying to gain a relationship with Campy in 1972. "I can't believe some of the mail Campy gets. I don't let the mail get out. Here he's never played a college game and he's getting mail from all these untrustworthy characters. Boy, he gets some bad advice. And when he starts playing, watch his mail go up."

On arrival with the Wolverine varsity in 1972–73, Campy would mix with four returning starters: All-American guard Henry Wilmore, a 23.4 ppg scorer as a junior; 6-foot-10-inch inside threat Ken Brady; and senior forwards John Lockhard and Ernie Johnson. Also up from the unbeaten freshman team were 5-foot-10-inch foot point guard Joe Johnson and 6-foot-8-inch Charles Jerome (C.J.) Kupec, a tough Chicago kid who played tight end in football that fall for a Michigan team that shared the Big Ten championship. Johnny wasn't afraid to label the 1972–73 squad as "potentially our best team," and the fans and media understandably got caught up in the Campy craze.

Writer John Papanek of the *Michigan Daily* went so far as to write:

> Believe me, there is no place like (the present) if you're a Michigan basketball freak . . . Michigan is loaded with playing talent. Wilmore is a two-year All-American, and according to Orr, he has adjusted his tremendous ability to playing guard, a position he had difficulty handling on a few occasions last year. With slippery little Joe Johnson doing the bulk of the ball-handling and play making, Wilmore will be free to use his never-ending collection of shots and moves on clear-outs and one-on-one drives. Campy Russell may be the best player in the country. At 6-8 he has the speed, hands and shot to play guard, but in the corner he's as dangerous as they come. Nobody can beat him one-on-one, and the beautiful thing is that if the opponent tries to trap him in a zone, Michigan still has Wilmore on the outside . . . So this is it. This is the year Michigan must do it. The Wolverines make two trips to New York, where good teams become great teams, and not-so-good ones get buried; the media sees to that. It also could be John Orr's last chance.

Sports Illustrated, which pegged the Wolverines 13th nationally in its preseason rankings, came out early in December with Campy splashed on its cover to accompany its preview story of the Big Ten race. Perhaps this was another in the string of *Sports Illustrated* notorious cover jinxes waiting to happen. *SI*'s Curry Kirkpatrick wrote:

> In Ann Arbor, basketball is treated in the same loose manner as student government, where last week the council narrowly defeated a proposal to establish a student dope co-op. The Wolverines' Johnny Orr, a frank and fun fellow who some rivals claim has trouble leading his team out of the dressing room, reflected on his coaching strategy the other day. "Last year we had one offense—Henry Wilmore," he said during a press conference. "Now we have two—Campy and Wilmore . . ." Defensive techniques are guaranteed to be absent. As Notre Dame's Digger Phelps said before the game (with Michigan) Saturday, "Orr's idea of defense is to beat you 91-89." Which turned out to be nearly on the button (Michigan won 96-87).

In retrospect, the fans and media were getting the bandwagon ahead of the horse, even if the horse averaged 30 ppg on the freshman team. Campy and the fellow sophs had yet to play a varsity game. There was a question about the team's chemistry, particularly how offensive standouts Campy and Wilmore would blend together. Wilmore was moving to guard from forward, in part to accommodate Campy and in part to expose him to a position he hoped to play in pro basketball. Injuries hurt the team the previous season, and fingers were crossed that big man Brady was over his knee injury that slowed him in 1971–72. The team lacked a proven take-charge guard, like Danny Fife, who led Michigan's 19-7 finish in 1971 and went on to a pro baseball career. There were three new coaches on Johnny's staff. Ace recruiter Fred Snowden had left as Michigan assistant to take the head coaching job at Arizona, and the newcomers were Jim Dutcher, who joined on after a successful six-year head coaching stint at Eastern Michigan; Dick Honig, elevated from the freshman program; and former U-M player Richard Carter, who replaced Honig as freshman coach.

Worst of all, Michigan fans picked the wrong year to envision a downhill coast to the Big Ten title. Defending champion Minnesota returned all five starters, and 1971–72 runner-up Ohio State had four regulars back. In all, eight of the Big Ten teams returned at least four starters, with a whopping 39 of the 50 starters from 1971–72 back, including MVP Jim Brewer of Minnesota and four other first-team all-conference picks. In addition, freshmen now were eligible for varsity play, and Indiana's Quinn Buckner was among those rookies to step in and make an immediate impact. Michigan's nonconference schedule was challenging, too, with Notre Dame, Oregon State and Brigham Young at home; road games at Dayton and Detroit to start the season; and a rugged holiday tournament in New York.

Starting to play

The season started well by some measures, but shaky by Michigan's sky's-the-limit standards. The Wolverines beat Notre Dame by nine and Oregon State by 11 at home to start 2-0, although Campy looked human in going 0-for-8 in shooting from the field in a scoreless outing against the Beavers. The Wolverines then lost a six-point decision on a neutral floor to Brigham Young, which outrebounded Michigan 47-31. BYU received 27 points and 15 rebounds from 6-foot-11-inch center Kresimir Cosic, the Yugoslavian Olympic team center. Following the 2-1 start, Johnny admitted that the preseason hope and hype had left his team tight. "I've never been in a situation like this. I've never seen a team under the pressure we've had," Johnny told reporters. "We've had it from magazines, newspaper articles, everything. I don't think we've been loose like we should be. And I can't pinpoint why. Everyone thinks we should win every time. But we aren't that good."

It was uncertain whether Johnny really had serious doubts or, like a typical coach, was trying to slam the brakes on the runaway bandwagon. Michigan rebounded from the BYU loss with solid though unspectacular wins at Dayton, by three points, and at Detroit, by nine. They returned home for the four-team Michigan Invitational and climbed to 5-1 with a 16-point victory over Western Michigan, despite being "as flat as could be," according to Johnny. Brady had 23 points and 15 rebounds, but according to writer Jerry Zimmerman's account in the *Huron Valley Advisor*, the big man was "the only bright spot in a lackluster performance that continued to inspire 'Dump Orr' chants and considerable booing."

The Wolverines responded 24 hours later with their best outing yet, a 101-65 demolition of Toledo, a team that had played Michigan State to a 98-96 loss earlier in the month. Campy scored 30 points and Wilmore added 28. Brady's and Kupec's defense helped hold Toledo All-American candidate Tom Kozelko to 11 points as Michigan climbed to 6-1.

Detroit Free Press columnist Jack Berg filed this account:

Johnny Orr could hardly contain himself. "That's the night we should have played UCLA," Orr said. His smile was as wide as Michigan's margin over Toledo in the championship game of the third-annual Michigan Invitational, and that smile was about as wide as the Grand Canyon. 101-65. It was never close.

With his "Gawsh darns" and "Gawsh, they were great" spoken in twangy, downstate Illinois accent, Orr sounds as if he's just jumped off the farm wagon and is in town for a big night of watching haircuts. There have been some critics who have said he coached like a farmer, too, that Michigan couldn't play defense. Michigan couldn't do this or that. Presumably, though, the only coach in the country who hasn't been criticized lately is UCLA's Johnny Wooden, with six straight NCAA championships and eight in the last nine years . . .

(The) victory had to be a great confidence builder for Russell, the 6-foot-8 forward from Pontiac who had been quite ordinary in the first six games. "There was a fantastic amount of pressure on Campanella," Johnny said. "Here he was on the cover of *Sports Illustrated* and he'd played two bad games and hadn't done anything. Wherever we went, fans were yelling '*Sports Illustrated, Sports Illustrated*' at him . . . Then there was that stuff about three balls, one for Henry, one for Campy and one for the rest of the team. The kids read that and it affects them. Gawsh darn, they're young players. Campanella is only 19 years old."

Michigan, rated 17th nationally, came back from Christmas break and jetted to New York's Madison Square Garden for the East Coast Athletic Conference Holiday Festival tournament. The Wolverines advanced to the semifinals with an 88-70 victory over Boston College, but their inconsistency resurfaced and they stumbled through the rest of the tournament. In an indicator of things to come in the rugged Big Ten, the 7-1 Wolverines lost to eventual champion St. John's in the semifinals, 85-83. While that didn't necessarily cost them their Top 20 ranking, the subsequent 84-79 consolation-round defeat to Manhattan did.

Similar close losses and a lack of a take-charge leader would make the upcoming Big Ten season a nightmare for Johnny. Michigan started the conference with a 68-62 road victory at Ohio State, its first win in Columbus in seven years. The Wolverines then topped Iowa at home, 71-59. Next came a road trek to East Lansing, where the Wolverines went to 3-0 with a 78-71 win over Michigan State. The 3-0 start in the conference rekindled optimism and lifted Michigan to a 10-3 overall record, but the Wolverines followed that with a 1-4 stretch that knocked them out of the title race and seemed to unravel any confidence they had built.

Purdue popped the Michigan bubble as it rallied from a 13-point first-half deficit to notch a 64-63 win in Ann Arbor. The Boilermakers hit the winning basket with :04 to play, then Brady's amazing 40-foot hook shot that swished through the net was waved off because it was released a fraction after the horn sounded. Michigan came back to post an 80-79 win at Northwestern to move to 4-1 in conference play, but a 79-73 loss at home to eventual Big Ten champion Indiana, followed by an emotional 75-68 loss to Iowa in Iowa City, dropped the Big Blue to 4-3.

If only the players had the coach's competitive fire: Johnny's frustrations spilled out in the defeat at Iowa. He received a technical foul for throwing a towel at an official and had to be restrained by his assistant coaches during a jawing match with another official late in the game. Johnny was livid with calls that left Michigan with 27 fouls and Iowa with only 13. The Hawks, then coached by current NCAA executive director Dick Schultz, scored their last 11 points at the free-throw line as four Wolverines fouled out in the final six minutes. A bench-clearing brawl, started by a frustrated Michigan player, ended the game with :01 to go.

Home to critics

Michigan returned home to play Michigan State, and instead of a lift from the home crowd, the team was greeted by a "Dump Orr" banner unfurled by students. The Wolverines nevertheless posted a 97-81 victory over the Spartans, fueled by Wilmore's 34 points and 13 rebounds, to momentarily stop the criticism. Now 5-3 in the Big Ten and 12-6 overall, Michigan traveled to Illinois for a must-win game. The Illini escaped with a crucial 76-75 decision, though, ending Michigan's hopes for a conference championship.

Johnny admitted he was bothered by the "Dump Orr" banners and chants. He responded to the criticism by saying that the Wolverine talent was overrated, the Big Ten talent vastly underrated. "No one likes to be criticized," Johnny told reporters. "How would you like to be told you're bad every day? Would you like that? I've seen it (the banner) before; they had it up there last year . . . You learn to live with it . . . People might have overrated our talent in comparison to the other teams in the conference. We've only had one player on our team make All–Big Ten, and that was Henry Wilmore. I don't think our talent is any better than a lot of other teams, or any worse. It seems that the general impression is that all our guys have to do is go out on the floor and we're going to win. It's just not so. There's not a bad coach in our league." Johnny acknowledged that criticism of his players' effort "is justified in certain instances—going for a loose ball and sometimes getting back on defense."

Michigan would lose its last four Big Ten games, closing 6-8 in the conference and 13-11 overall, the identical record posted by Iowa and Michigan State. Wilmore finished fifth in Big Ten scoring at 21 ppg, and what was considered a disappointing season for Campy still netted averages of 18.4 points and 9.6 rebounds a game. The manner in which the Wolverines fizzled out to a second-division Big Ten finish meant it was open season on Johnny down the stretch and into the off-season. Among the pit bulls was *Detroit News* columnist Joe Falls, who wrote:

> So much was expected of the University of Michigan basketball team and they have produced so little. Maybe some of this is Orr's fault—for painting such a bright picture in all of his preseason comments and analysis. But the truth is the Wolverines have been a big disappointment . . . The tough thing even talking about Orr's future is that Big John is such a nice guy, such a decent person, that you'd like him to stay around for a thousand years. But they don't pay off on personality . . . A look at the records shows John has not exactly rewritten the record books in his five years at U-M . . . Of this stuff NCAA titles aren't made and, like it or not, some people at U-M think basketball has become an important sport, one that can produce revenue and also championships . . . In other words, basketball at U-M no longer is a sport merely to fill in the blank days between football seasons. It can be an exciting and vibrant sport—when played right and when you win.

Canham repeatedly said Johnny's job was safe. He told John Papanek of the *Michigan Daily:*

> I don't give a damn if all those people boo. They certainly have a right to. But my personal opinion is that those people don't know anything about basketball. For one thing, anybody who thinks that Michigan has the best talent in the Big Ten is dead wrong . . . I never worry about a one-year situation anyway. Winning and losing is not the only thing we're concerned about at the University of Michigan. We're not like those wild places where they hire a guy for two years, then fire him because he didn't get a championship. You should see the stack of letters I got that said "Fire Bo Schembechler" because Bo didn't kick the field goal in the Ohio State game. I can't listen to all those nuts . . . John Orr, in my estimation, has done a good job. I wouldn't say I'm happy with the way the season has gone so far, but, hell, I'm not going to blame the coach for that.

After the closing four losses dropped Michigan out of NIT tournament consideration to a final 13-11 record, Wilmore told Jeff Mortimer of the Ann Arbor *News:* "This was said to be one of Michigan's best teams in history before it even stepped on the court. There was some undue pressure. People didn't have a chance to show what they could do before they were judged . . . There'll be some good players left on this team. I hope there's enough patience to let them develop."

Johnny said in a post season interview with the *Michigan Daily* that while some of the press and fan criticism was justified, some was unfair:

> I think the news media, as a whole today, have to write something sensational or critical in order to get recognized. I think Michigan fans should be behind the team, not against us. But these things change. If UCLA loses (in pursuit of its seventh straight national title), they'll hear it, too . . . Nobody likes criticism. Most of the coaches I talked to at the national convention last week are in the same situation. It's a sign of the times. The last six weeks of the season I didn't feel well, and I couldn't sleep at night because I was so upset . . . In coaching they say that as you become more experienced, you get dumber. I think I'm a better coach now than I've ever been.

Canham again reiterated his patience and support of Johnny by announcing at season's end that there would be no coaching change. "I think we're all disappointed," Canham said, "but John Orr is a good coach, and I'm not going to fire a guy because his team had one bad year. I think this team was a much greater problem to coach than most people realize. They're all good players and good kids, but none of them is the inspirational type to direct our team on the floor. They're all quiet."

The criticism and frustration of 1972–73 left Johnny seriously pondering a career change. He later would admit that he decided in early March of 1973 to quit his Michigan job but explained that wife Romie told him to wait a couple of weeks until April before he made such a rash decision. "I would go to bed at night," Johnny said, "and pray that the Lord would come through the window and either tell me to get the hell out of there or say, 'Orr, you're all right, stay.' One morning, before April 1, I awoke with a new feeling. I decided to stay."

• 1973–74 Season

The 46-year-old Orr came into 1973–74 knowing his job probably was on the line, and he would start his most challenging season in coaching with four seniors gone from the top six, and no players taller than 6-foot-8-inches. One change in his coaching staff brought Bill Frieder on board to replace the re-signed Dick Honig. Frieder, a tireless recruiter and basketball junkie, had guided teams to consecutive Michigan state high school championships at Flint Northern, and he would continue some of the dynamic recruiting established by Fred Snowden.

With only one senior, the Wolverine team promptly voted juniors Campy and Kupec as co-captains. "Having juniors as co-captains was unprecedented in Michigan history," Johnny said. "We told them whatever the team did would be next to their names on the record book. We gave them a pretty good talking to."

After Campy and Kupec, both 6-foot-8-inches, Johnny would fill the other forward spot with 6-foot-2-inch Wayman Britt, a sophomore who played for Frieder at Flint Northern but played sparingly in 1972–73 as a Wolverine freshman. Steve Grote, a 6-foot-2-inch guard from Cincinnati, received the distinction of being the first freshman to start for an Orr team. The freshman joined 5-foot-10-inch junior Joe Johnson in a starting backcourt that at first glance looked anemic by Big Ten standards. In fact, one cynical preseason story called Johnny's 1973–74 team "Campy Russell and a bunch of nobodies." Michigan was picked to finish anywhere from fifth to ninth in the Big Ten race.

What this team lacked in height and pure talent, it would make up for in hustle and chemistry. Campy showed his commitment to winning by dropping 20 pounds from his frame over the off-season, in part by eliminating red meat from his diet. Kupec and Grote displayed signs that they would fill the leadership void lacking at Michigan the previous year. Just ask Grote's father, Hal, about his son's spirit. "Steve's aggressive," the elder Grote told reporters after his son signed with Michigan. "He'd just as soon pop you as look at you." Nobody could beat Cincinnati's Elder High in basketball when Grote was a senior. He led the team to a state championship and was named MVP of the Ohio state tournament. He was selected all-state in football, too, and personally was recruited by a prominent local gent named Woody Hayes. Yet Grote chose to play basketball, despite minimal recruiting interest: Only Michigan and Ohio State in the Big

Ten offered basketball scholarships. "People all along said I wasn't good enough," Grote said.

Johnny's preseason analysis for the pivotal 1973–74 season? "We'll be small, and we don't jump very well, and we throw the ball everywhere. But we've got good speed, and Russell has all the tools to be great," he told reporters. Not exactly a reason for Romie to throw away the phone number of the moving company, but Orr's optimism would be borne out.

Early games

The season began with an 86-74 victory over Southern Illinois and a small crowd of 5,707 fans watching at the 13,000-seat Crisler Arena. Even in victory, and with the new and improved Campy playing so crisply (29 points and 16 rebounds), the boos came out with four minutes remaining and Michigan leading by 11 when Orr's team went into a delay game, spreading out the defense in hopes of getting some back-door layups.

Next up was the first road game in a season that would present many interesting trips. Michigan rode a 24-4 late-first-half surge to post a 75-65 win at Toledo, on the strength of Campy's 21 points and 9 rebounds. Then came an emotional road game with neighbor Detroit, coached by Dick Vitale, who was trying to rejuvenate a Detroit program that once boasted greats like Dave DeBusschere and Spencer Haywood. The Titans took a step in that direction this night with a 70-59 victory over the Wolverines, paced by Owen "Magic" Wells' 38 points. In his elation in beating the in-state Goliath, Vitale breached normal protocol as he launched into his victory dance with 1:21 to go to celebrate Detroit's third win ever in 10 meetings with Michigan.

Michigan rebounded at home with a 77-61 victory over Xavier, before 4,113 fans, as Grote scored 15 first-half points. Then another revved-up in-state foe, Western Michigan, got the chance to play the Wolverines on its home floor. Michigan shot just 38 percent from the field but used a 31-10 edge in free-throw scoring to outlast the Eldon Miller–coached Broncos, 83-76, in three overtimes. Orr would have several good battles against Eldon Miller's teams in later years as Miller moved on to Ohio State and then Northern Iowa.

Michigan returned home to yet another sparse Crisler Arena crowd of 4,352 and ripped Dayton, 76-54. (This victory would look more impressive later when Dayton would lose in the NCAA tournament in three overtimes to the dynasty team from UCLA.) The Wolverines, playing their fourth game in eight days, were starting to earn respect for their defensive play. They allowed

62.5 ppg in regulation time during their 5-1 start. The stingy defense eased a bit in the next outing, a 101-88 victory over Yale in the first round of the Michigan Invitational, but the pressure returned in a 70-66 triumph over previously unbeaten Bowling Green in the championship game.

Next came a slightly tougher tournament, this one in Los Angeles hosted by the mighty UCLA Bruins. Michigan's first-round foe, San Francisco, was an NCAA tournament qualifier the previous season and was ranked in the Top 10 in the preseason. But the Dons, struggling this season with a 2-5 record, couldn't handle Michigan's balance in an 88-66 loss. Michigan improved to 8-1 and earned a shot at John Wooden's UCLA wonders, now 7-0 and the winners of 82 straight games. For Johnny O, it was his first head-to-head coaching matchup with the legendary Johnny W, although Orr had played at Beloit against Wooden's Indiana State team.

Even with the terrific trio of Bill Walton, Keith Wilkes and David Meyers leading the Bruins, Orr's gang showed some spunk early. Kupec and teammates held Walton scoreless over the first 11 minutes, and Michigan used an early 9-0 run to build a 14-8 lead. It was a 20-20 game before Britt sat down with his fourth foul with eight minutes to go in the first half. The Wolverines still were within 11 points when Britt fouled out with 13 minutes to play in the game, and Britt's absence was too much for Michigan to overcome. Campy limped off with a sprained knee with seven minutes to go, and by then the outcome was already decided as Michigan became victim No. 83 in a 90-70 loss. Walton had 20 points, 21 rebounds and, according to Orr, "15 intimidations." Johnny told Falls of the *Detroit News:* "There's no question about it, that's the best team I've ever seen. They're relentless. They keep coming at you . . . It was an honor just to play them. They make you play hard. I'll say this: If we continue to play that hard, we'll be a contender in our conference this season."

Big Ten opener

Michigan immediately gained another chance to prove its ability against a nationally ranked team. The Wolverines came home to Crisler to start their 1973–74 Big Ten season against defending champion Indiana. Coach Bob Knight's squad, widely considered the team to beat in the Big Ten, was ranked seventh nationally after a third-place national finish in 1973. Despite trailing by as much as 15 points in the second half, Michigan stunned the Hoosiers, 73-71, before a Crisler crowd of 10,165. Amazingly, the comeback was completed in the end without

Campy and Britt, who each fouled out in the final five minutes. Michigan shot 60 percent from the field in the second half, and Campy led with 20 points and 14 rebounds. A basket with 1:17 to go by freshman sub Lionel Worrell put the Wolverines ahead to stay.

The victory was a tremendous confidence builder for the Wolverines, who zoomed into the No. 18 spot in the national rankings at 9-2. The two teams to beat Michigan, UCLA and Detroit, were a combined 19-1 at this point, and losers to Michigan that were playing well included 8-1 Southern Illinois and 9-2 Toledo. Michigan's play left Orr beaming, and he was quoted in *Sports Illustrated* the next week: "Our guys weren't supposed to win any and we've won nine already."

Knight spoke up for Johnny in the postgame press conference. "A lot of people up here have been on John Orr's ass who don't know a damn thing about college basketball," Knight told reporters. "John is doing a heck of a job because Michigan never quit out there. It's easy for a coach when he's lost a game like this to come out and say, 'We played poorly,' but that's not the case. Michigan really deserved a lot of credit because they just beat us."

Indiana's defeat signaled that an interesting Big Ten race was ahead, although Johnny slyly maintained, "I don't know that we're contenders. I think we'll have a lot to say about who wins, but Indiana is a very fine team and they'll be right in there." The coach credited the season's resurgence to defense, noting: "We're about 250,000 percent better than last year." Campy added, "Our team was so tall last year we kind of took things for granted. We didn't have real desire. This year, we knew we were small and we knew we would have to hustle and play defense to win."

Next up was a road trip to Minnesota, and a chance to avenge a 98-80 loss in Minneapolis in 1972–73 that started the season-ending four-game losing streak. Coach Bill Musselman had an entire new lineup, but the atmosphere in the old barn the Gophers called home gave visitors fits and, usually, losses. The aged Williams Arena actually burned the Gophers, though, in a 66-65 Michigan win. A scoreboard bulb facing the Minnesota bench was burned out, and the Gophers admitted after the game that during the final minute they thought the score was 65-63 instead of the actual 66-63 count. Thus, Minnesota's last-second tip-in didn't tie the game at 65-65 as Musselman and folks on the east side of the arena momentarily thought, leaving some confusion and frustration for the home folks.

That victory helped Michigan climb to 14th in the national rankings, but another tough test awaited at home. Michigan State brought a 2-1 conference record to Ann Arbor, and in another dinger, Johnny's club beat the Spartans, 84-82. Kupec nailed a 17-foot jumper with one second left for the Wolverines, who outscored State 25-12 in the final 8:34. Campy was sharp again with 27 points and 10 rebounds, and Britt had 10 second-half points. This victory continued a trend developing in 1973–74: in games decided in overtime or by four or fewer points, Michigan was 5-0. In 1972–73, the Wolverines had finished 3-6 in games decided by six or fewer points.

Now 3-0 in the Big Ten and 11-2 overall, Michigan had a chance two days later to move into sole possession of first place if it could beat 4-0 Purdue on the Boilermakers' home floor. Game day started on a sour note. Foggy conditions canceled its flight so the team embarked on a five-hour bus ride. The Wolverines arrived just hours before tip-off, and went on to lose a frustrating 85-84 overtime decision to the Boilermakers.

Yet another perilous road trip came next, this time to Iowa City. Iowa was only 4-10 on the year, but Johnny knew another cliff-hanger was possible. He was right. Michigan overcame a 13-point first-half deficit and needed two breaks to force overtime: Campy's basket with 13 seconds left; and Iowa's missed 1-and-1 free-throw with six seconds left in regulation. After falling behind by four points in overtime, the Wolverines rallied for an 86-84 victory. Grote matched his career high with 27 points, and Michigan moved to 4-1 in the conference, one-half game out of first place.

Next foe Wisconsin was enjoying one of its best seasons in years, and the 19th-ranked Badgers brought a 3-1 conference record and an 11-2 overall mark to Ann Arbor. Another fickle turnout at Crisler, with just 8,230 on hand on a cold January night, saw Michigan finally avoid a nail-biter in securing a 83-75 victory. All five Wolverine starters scored in double figures, led by Campy's 25 points and 11 rebounds.

Michigan had established that it was for real, and it was suggested that the previous season's collapse was a fluke. Campy was atop the Big Ten in scoring, and the "bunch of nobodies" around him were bunched between 10 and 14 ppg. The Wolverines' rebirth played well in the media. Falls of the *Detroit News*, who had called for Johnny's firing the previous year, now wrote:

> Somebody should say something nice about Johnny Orr, the Michigan basketball coach. Like me. I questioned his ability last

year, saying he'd had enough time to put together a winning program at U-M, but hadn't done so. Your friendly correspondent left the broad hint they'd be better off hiring a new man. Well, the Wolverines are 11-3, and Orr has to get some of the credit. He took all the criticism and in the face of it put together a sound team. Good. I liked the man last year and I like him even better now. Like I've been saying, John: Win some games and we'll all love you.

Sensing something great in the making, Johnny told United Press International's Richard Shook: "I certainly was on the spot before the season, there's no question about that. Certainly, this is one of my favorite teams . . . This team started out with nobody but the coaches and the kids believing in them, and I'm not sure about the coaches' and assistant coaches' beliefs. Now it's on the verge of becoming the greatest team in the history of Michigan basketball."

Next up was a road trek to Illinois to face a team that had lost six straight and was 4-10. Not only did Michigan's 101-77 victory mark the first blowout of the Big Ten season for the Wolverines, it let them move into a tie for the conference lead as Purdue dropped to 6-1 with a two-point loss to Michigan State. Michigan shot 55 percent from the field and rode an 18-point, 17-rebound performance by Kupec.

Halfway point

Michigan returned home at the halfway point in the Big Ten season and kept up the pressure with a 91-68 win over Ohio State. The Wolverines, now 7-1 and 15-3, had all five starters score in double figures for the third straight game. The surprisingly easy one-sided game was called a "leg crosser" for the coaches. "We're 7-1 (in Big 10) and that's unbelievable," Orr said.

The only negative part of Michigan's easy win over Ohio State was the still modest home attendance (9,132), unimpressive for a school that was the Big Ten co-leader. It even was worse the next outing as only 6,042 spectators were on hand for what turned out to be a thrilling 50-48 escape over Northwestern. Kupec's 16 rebounds helped offset the Wildcats' slowdown tactics. The win, coupled with Purdue's 112-111 loss to Iowa, put Michigan alone in first place, one-half game ahead of Indiana.

Michigan climbed to 15th in the national poll and faced a big rematch against Indiana, which had won seven straight since its opening loss in Ann Arbor. A record crowd of 17,521 crammed into Assembly Hall and helped the Hoosiers slow Michigan's title express with a 93-81 victory. Campy's 30 points and 11 rebounds and Britt's 24 points weren't enough as the Wolverines allowed a season-high 93 points. Indiana, led by Steve Green's career-high 37 points, climbed to 8-1, a notch better than Michigan's 8-2 in the 14-game conference race. "All we can hope for now is that we continue to play well," Johnny said following the loss. "We won't fold up, because we have too good a group of kids."

The Wolverines returned home for a critical game against Purdue and didn't fold. The diminutive Joe Johnson scored a career-high 22 points and Kupec added 21 points and 12 rebounds to lead Michigan to a convincing 111-84 win over the Boilermakers. Michigan hit 19 of its first 21 shots and raced to a 55-30 halftime lead. Grote didn't practice all week due to illness, but the fiery freshman came out and tallied 22 points. "I've been coaching 25 years, and I've never had a team perform like this one," Johnny said after the blowout. "I deserve one of these." Orr's club shot 58 percent from the field before 11,732 fans, the largest Crisler crowd of the season. Michigan improved to 11-0 at home, 17-4 overall and 9-2 in the conference, one game behind first-place Indiana's 10-1 record. Purdue coach Fred Schaus called Michigan "the best team we've seen in the Big Ten. They rebound, shoot, and have great quickness, and they have Campy Russell. Campy is the best college basketball player I've seen in two years."

Another big road trip loomed as Michigan rolled into Madison to face the Badgers. Campy felt dizzy before the game, but a sniff of ammonia did the trick, and soon he had his old nose for the basket. He exploded for a career-high 36 points and 11 rebounds as the Wolverines posted a 78-74 victory and kept pace with Indiana, which topped Michigan State by six points. "We really worked hard and made a lot of great passes," Johnny said. "This was Campy's best game by far. He was simply brilliant. They couldn't stop him." Michigan avoided foul trouble, too, accumulating only 14, and Wisconsin was outscored 12-4 at the free-throw line.

With a subsequent 79-56 triumph over visiting Minnesota, Orr's team completed a 12-0 home record to become just the second Michigan team in history to finish its home schedule unbeaten. Campy's 28 points and 15 rebounds helped the 19-4 Wolverines move into a share of the Big Ten lead. Indiana lost an 85-77 decision to Ohio State in Columbus to forge a first-place deadlock between the Wolverines and Hoosiers, both 11-2 with one game left. There was more at stake, too. In these pre-expansion days of the NCAA tournament, only the conference champion was NCAA-bound, with the runner-up going to the inaugural (and long since canceled) Conference Commissioners Tournament. Indiana would close its Big Ten season at home against 10-3 Purdue, which still had an outside chance to tie for first. Michigan faced a tough test by closing at Michigan State. The Spartans needed a win to place fourth and keep alive slim hopes for an NIT berth.

Trying for tournament

The trek to East Lansing would provide some interesting sidelights. First, Johnny would try to clinch a share of his first conference championship, and clinch Michigan's first conference championship in eight years. Second, Johnny was trying to clinch his first 20-win season as a college head coach and get Michigan's third 20-win campaign in history. Third, the coach hoped to extend his excellent record against Michigan State, which now stood at 7-2 in six seasons. Fourth, Campy (23.1 ppg) would try to hold onto his lead and claim the Big Ten scoring title. Spartan guard Mike Robinson (21.1 ppg) needed to outscore Campy by 16 points in this game to become the fourth player in Big Ten history to win three consecutive scoring titles.

Before a sellout crowd of 12,500 at Jenison Field House, the Wolverines raced to a 51-28 halftime lead and shot 59 percent on the game to coast to a 103-87 victory over Michigan State. Campy won the scoring crown with his 36 points, 16 rebounds and seven assists, all game highs. Meanwhile, Indiana used two John Laskowski free throws with :08 left to escape with an 80-79 win over Purdue. That denied the Wolverines the outright title and forced a one-game playoff between Michigan and Indiana to determine the conference's NCAA representative. "This is the greatest team I've ever had," Orr exclaimed. "This is one of the greatest Michigan teams ever."

The playoff with Indiana was held two days later on a neutral floor in Champaign, Ill. A newspaper poll of six other Big Ten coaches turned out 5-0 (with one abstention) in favor of an Indiana victory. "Sure, we'll be underdogs," Orr said. "We've been underdogs all 24 games this season."

In a testament to this Michigan team's great balance and composure, the Wolverines posted a 75-67 victory over the favored Hoosiers to claim the NCAA tournament berth, despite playing the final 4:48 with Campy on the bench with five fouls. Indiana whittled an 11-point deficit to one with 3:27 left, but Orr's delay game—the one that was booed at home way back in the season opener—worked to perfection to stifle the Hoosier charge. "It shows what a great team we have when we lose Russell and still win," Orr said. "That's the way it's been with us all year. Someone has always come through for us." Kupec, who led all scorers with 22 points and 15 rebounds, gained a measure of personal revenge. His Oak Lawn (Ill.) team lost to Buckner's Dolton Thornridge team three years earlier in the Illinois state high school finals, 52-50, on the same Assembly Hall floor. Johnny was tossed into the shower by his jubilant players, and that drew this comment from Roy Damer of the *Chicago Tribune:*

> Orr is one of the real nice guys in sports and his job was on the line this season. Even he admits had this season been a failure, he would have left Michigan. He was a proud man (today) as he faced the press with the lights beaming off his bald head and his shirt soaked because his players had thrown him into the shower. But those who were all wet were those who had underestimated his Wolverines.

Knight stuck his head into the Michigan locker-room celebration and offered the following praise: "You deserved this game. You'll be a hell of a representative for the Big Ten." Later, unsmiling, Knight opened his press conference with a question: "Would the Michigan writers who have been on John Orr's ass please stand up? I think we've seen a pretty good coaching job by a darn good coach . . . This is a game of quickness, and Michigan is strong, aggressive, quick and smart." Among the congratulatory calls Johnny received after the Indiana win was one from UCLA's Johnny Wooden. "I got a call from John Wooden and (UCLA athletic director) J. D. Morgan," Orr said. "He (Wooden) said the way we played against Indiana, we'd be very successful. I don't think John Wooden and J. D. Morgan call everybody."

Regional

Michigan advanced to a date with Notre Dame three nights later in the NCAA Mideast Regional at Tuscaloosa, Ala. Campy Russell told reporters following the Indiana win: "I don't care what people say about Coach Orr. He's a hell of a coach. He's the same coach as last year. Our team just didn't jell last year. It was all 10 or 15 guys. We didn't play hard. We didn't dive for the loose balls. Last year they said (Orr) was a bad coach, this year they're saying he's the greatest coach in the country. We played this season for Coach Orr, for all the coaches, and for ourselves. We're just a bunch of little guys who couldn't play basketball . . . Now we're Big Ten champions. If Notre Dame underestimates us, we'll beat them. If they don't underestimate us, we'll beat them anyway."

Notre Dame, 25-2 and rated third nationally, had ended UCLA's 88-game winning streak earlier in the year and was considered one of the three favorites, along with UCLA and North Carolina State, to win the elite 25-team NCAA tourney. Coach Digger Phelps' Irish, led by John Shumate and freshman phenom Adrian Dantley, would try to accomplish an unprecedented double national championship for the school, as two months earlier Notre Dame claimed the national championship in football with a 24-23 win over Alabama in the 1974 Sugar Bowl. "We're probably about an eight-point underdog," said a grinning Orr. "That's about average, I'd say."

Playing its third road game in its third state in a six-day span, Michigan reached up and handed Notre Dame a 77-68 defeat, as Campy scored 24 of his 36 points in the second half and had 18 rebounds. "Russell is the greatest all-around player in the United States," Orr said. "Bill Walton is the best big man, but Russell plays guard, forward and center for us. I didn't teach him a thing. He's just a great player." The Irish, who missed 11 straight shots early and fell behind 28-8, forged a 54-52 lead early in the second half before Campy pushed Michigan ahead to stay.

Beating Notre Dame provided a particular sense of irony for Johnny, who was under fire just one year earlier. Recall the quote attributed to Phelps that Orr's idea of defense is scoring 91 and holding foes to 89. "A *Sports Illustrated* fellow wrote a very bad article about me last year that wasn't warranted," Johnny said following the Notre Dame win. "He said my team couldn't play defense . . . That article fired us up. We had it on our bulletin board tonight . . . All I know is Digger (Phelps) put his arms around my shoulder tonight and said, 'John, I never said that about your ability to coach defense.' Boy, was I proud."

One reason for Orr's pride was that the 6-foot-2-inch, 175-pound Britt guarded the 6-foot-5-inch, 225-pound Dantley and held the future All-American to two points, miles under his 18.5 ppg average. Britt contributed 18 points, 7 rebounds and 4 steals. Johnny joked that despite Britt's tiny frame, "He can jump. We taught him that."

Meeting Marquette

Now just one win away from the Final Four, Michigan (22-4) faced Coach Al McGuire's tough Marquette team (25-4). The Warriors, ranked seventh nationally, were led by All-American Maurice Lucas and reached the NCAA quarterfinals with wins over Ohio (85-59) and Vanderbilt (69-61). McGuire wouldn't underestimate Michigan, though; he told reporters about a previous meeting with an Orr-coached Michigan team. "Our biggest thing is not to get into a running game with them," McGuire said. "We played at Michigan a few years ago with a good team and I decided to run with them (and Michigan won, 86-78). After the game I told the reporters to get me a psychiatrist. You don't run against John Orr's teams."

The fatigue of the fourth crucial game in eight days might have been a contributing factor as Marquette edged Michigan, 72-70, to end the Wolverines' magical season. Campy had 21 points and 14 rebounds but missed two shots in the final seven seconds that could have forced overtime. The Warriors, who topped Michigan in bench scoring, 11-2, later would beat Kansas by 13 points in the NCAA semifinals but lose to North Carolina State in the championship game, 76-64. The Wolfpack, who finished 30-1, had ended UCLA's seven-year championship reign with a win in the semifinals.

Tournament aftermath

With a 22-5 final record and No. 6 ranking in the final Associated Press poll, the pride was back in Michigan basketball. Johnny was voted Big Ten Coach of the Year, Campy was picked second-team All-American. The Wolverines had met virtually all their preseason goals: go unbeaten at home; win the Big Ten; reach the NCAAs. The only goal they missed was to beat all the Michigan and Ohio foes: the early loss at Detroit left them 8-1 in that category.

Chicago sportswriter David Israel joined in the parade of stories on Michigan's—and Orr's—great revival from 1973 to 1974, and wrote of Orr's reaction to the criticism:

> "It was the first time in all these years that my coaching had ever been criticized," Orr said. "I think I became a changed person because of that. That really hurt me personally. That hurt our recruiting. I didn't want to go out anywhere. I didn't want to see anybody. At a party, I felt people were saying things about me. And I'm sure sometimes they were. I really felt sorry for my family. I was embarrassed when I went out and spoke at banquets. My first line was that I was the most unpopular coach in Michigan. I think I was a changed person completely . . . (but) they could fire me now and it wouldn't bother me. Now, I'm contented. No one will ever say again I can't coach or that my teams don't know how to play defense."

Orr was named one of six regional coaches of the year. He

told John Hannen of the Toledo *Blade* of the joy this 1973–74 Wolverine team had given him: "I'm not saying I'm going to coach forever. As a matter of fact I might not be in it too much longer. I will tell you one thing, though: When you get a group of kids like this, when you go through a season like we did, and see the love they have for one another, then you know why you're in this business."

Then there was student critic Jim Barahal, the mouth that in the previous year roared his way to election in the Michigan student government on a "Dump Orr" platform. After the 22-5 finish to the 1973–74 season, Barahal acknowledged: "I'll tell you frankly, the guy (Johnny Orr) made me look like a donkey. But to see Michigan win after all those awful years, it was worth it. And who knows, maybe in some demented way I had something to do with it." (The "demented" contribution never garnered Jimbo an invitation to the Michigan postseason banquet. It's just as well. It's hard to eat with your foot in your mouth.)

Johnny Orr probably learned more about his own character and the unpredictiblity of coaching during this 1972–74 stretch than he did at any other time in his career. From that point on, whenever he told a player to keep battling through tough times, he could speak from experience. The ball finally bounced Orr's way, and he would enjoy even more success throughout the 1970s as Michigan head coach. After the pivotal 1973–74 season, his next six Michigan teams averaged 20 wins a season and had three top-two Big Ten finishes.

• Subsequent Seasons

In 1974–75, Orr and his team overcame many setbacks. All-American Campy Russell passed up his senior season and turned pro, the sixth man from the previous year transferred and two others were ineligible. Yet Michigan broke to a 9-1 start and eventually took second in the Big Ten. The Wolverines finished with a 19-8 record, including a berth in the NCAA tournament, where they suffered a first-round overtime loss to eventual national champion UCLA.

In 1975–76, C. J. Kupec and Joe Johnson had graduated, but junior transfer Rickey Green and freshman Phil Hubbard stepped in and helped the Wolverines to a 25-7 record and another runner-up finish in the Big Ten. Michigan won 11 of 12 games late in the season, including NCAA tourney wins over Wichita State (74-73), Notre Dame (80-76), Missouri (95-88) and

Rutgers (86-70), to reach the NCAA finals. With a national championship ring at stake, Michigan played 31-0 Indiana for the third time that season. Orr's gang broke to a 35-29 halftime lead, thanks to 60-percent shooting from the field. The Hoosiers rallied to tie the game with 10 minutes left, though, and outscored Michigan 23-9 over the last six minutes as they secured the first of three NCAA titles under Bob Knight. Indiana's 57-point second half still stands as a championship game record for most points in a half. The final score was Indiana 86, Michigan 68, and the Hoosiers capped a rare unbeaten season.

Michigan garnered a No. 1 national ranking and a Big Ten title during the 1976–77 season. Johnny was named National Coach of the Year in both 1976 and 1977 by separate selectors.

"It was kind of a strange deal. I got a call from (athletic director) Lou McCullough at Iowa State, and he said he was looking for a basketball coach and asked if I have any guys to recommend. I told him, yeah, my top assistant, Bill Frieder. Lou knew he was a pretty good assistant coach, but he needed somebody that people could associate with as a proven head coach. He started telling me about Hilton Coliseum, and he asked if I'd come out and take a look at the place and see what I thought. I came out, he showed me Hilton, and I told them all the things you'd have to do to get a guy that was known nationally."

"They asked me if I'd be interested, and I said, hell, no. At the time, I only was going to coach three more years at Michigan and then retire. I wanted to coach 15 years in the Big Ten, and that was plenty. I had interviewed one time for a job at Stanford, and talked to the athletic director at Florida but never went down there to pursue it. I wasn't serious about coaching anywhere but Michigan."

"Lou McCullough called me back three or four days later and asked me that if they would do the same things for me that I suggested, would I be interested? He asked me if I would bring my wife back and look things over."

"The more I thought about it, I liked the security I'd have at Iowa State. I liked the challenge. Certainly money was involved. But the bigger thing was the fringe benefits, and the fact the people here were so nice. I got to meet (Iowa State University President W. Robert) Parks. They kept saying, 'He's not going to go for this,' but he greeted me and said, 'Welcome to Iowa State, Johnny. I'd sure like you to come and be my basketball coach. We've never had a great basketball team, and I'm not going to be here much longer.' I told him that if we could get a few things worked out, I'd come. And Dr. Parks turned to Lou and said, 'Whatever Johnny wants, you give him.' And I heard that and said, 'Dr. Parks, I'm going to be your coach.' Lou said, 'But you want more money than I'm getting.' So I told Lou, 'Well, give yourself a raise.'"

• Coming to Ames

Lou McCullough deserved a pay raise, and perhaps some therapy, after a trying 15 months from January 1979 through March 1980. During that unsettling stretch, McCullough had to fill his two most visible coaching jobs in his athletic department—football and men's basketball.

Lou's personnel problems began in the fourth quarter of a bowl game involving his alma mater and his old boss. At the 1978 Gator Bowl, fiery Ohio State coach Woody Hayes slugged Clemson University noseguard Charlie Bauman, who had intercepted a pass from Buckeye quarterback Art Schlichter in the final minute to douse Ohio State's last comeback bid in a 17-15 loss. After inflicting the Buckeye black eye that was the talk of the national sports world, Hayes was fired the next day after he refused to resign. Ohio State's search was greeted with the usual coaching vacancy speculation involving Lou Holtz, then of Arkansas, which never came to pass. The Buckeyes eventually plucked Iowa State Cyclone head coach Earle Bruce to take Woody's whistle.

Bruce, an Ohio State alumnus and former Buckeye assistant coach, had struggled through three consecutive 4-7 seasons to start his Iowa State career, then broke through with three straight eight-win football seasons in Cyclone country from 1976 through 1978. After Bruce's teams beat Nebraska two straight seasons in 1976–77, and earned back-to-back bowl trips in 1977–78, his visibility was greatly enhanced on the national scene.

"Earle Bruce is the best all-around coach I've ever been associated with," McCullough now says. "It really hurts when you lose a football coach because you have nine assistants out recruiting, and they build up relationships and contacts. When you bring in a new coach with new assistants, you lose that continuity in recruiting."

Bruce's departure for one of college football's elite jobs left McCullough looking for a new head coach during the heart of the 1979 recruiting season. Lou's search ended with the selection of Donnie Duncan, an assistant coach for the flashy Oklahoma Sooners.

• Ames Basketball Legacy

Cyclone basketball presented its own problems for McCullough. To appreciate the impact of this job hire and the long-term benefits of bringing someone of Johnny Orr's caliber to Ames, recall the basketball environment during the previous decades. Iowa State, which turns out scores of respected engineers, veterinarians, and agriculture specialists, wasn't synonymous with top-notch basketball in the pre-Orr era. Its last national tournament berth in basketball came in 1944. Skeptics even joked back then that if basketball inventor James Naismith had fooled around with his famed peach basket in Ames, he would have created a new harvesting method instead. Students quizzed on the productivity of Hercle Ivy would assume the subject is horticulture, not a former Cyclone basketball great.

By the late 1970s, Iowa State was regarded as a football school in a football conference. Even before Earle Bruce's gang made a national breakthrough in 1976 and earned bowl bids in 1977 and 1978, Iowa State was attracting fans to the bright new football stadium. Cardinal and gold people still crow about beating the mighty Nebraska Cornhuskers back-to-back in 1976 and 1977. For the big games, students from Greek Row and dormitory floors started camping out at noon Friday to reserve the best student seats for Saturday.

For visibility, basketball wasn't even a clear-cut No. 2 on the Ames campus. By the late 1970s, Iowa State's wrestling and gymnastics teams had enough national championship banners and Olympic-caliber athletes to share the winter spotlight with roundball. For all its beauty, Hilton Coliseum often resembled a museum, as noise rarely was a problem for an opposing team. On average during the 1970s, nearly half the arena's 14,000 seats were empty when the Cyclones took the court. The biggest roars at Hilton during Iowa State basketball season occurred on nights when Coach Ed Gagnier's gymnastics team performed its halftime clown routine. The closest thing to a running style in Hilton came when Coach Bill Bergan's Cyclone trackmen used the outer concourse for indoor track practice.

Throughout the 1970s, Cyclone basketball had four different head coaches plus three separate stints with interim co-coaches. This revolving door in leadership contributed to a lack of enthusiasm and did nothing to establish a winning tradition. Mediocre basketball wasn't limited to the Ames campus. As college basketball was moving rapidly into the TV age, Big Eight basketball in general could be characterized as the Not Ready for Prime Time players.

• Maury John Era

There was a brief period in the early 1970s when Cyclone basketball seemed to be ready to explode onto the national scene, under Iowa State's first head coach of the decade, Maury John, another guy with theme-song potential. Maury was Iowa State's Johnny Orr of the 1970s—in fact, his birthday falls in the same week of June as Orr's, though he was born eight years earlier. His renowned "belly-button" defense helped him gain national respect while serving as Drake's head coach, especially when his Bulldogs scared the Alcindor out of John Wooden and another of his awesome UCLA teams in the NCAA national semifinals in 1969 in a one-point loss. A TV announcer billed Drake's tenacious pressure against the mighty Bruins the "belly-button defense," and a slogan was born. Maury later used the catchy phrase as the title of the book he wrote on his trademark man-to-man defense.

Drake's impressive showing en route to its third-place finish in that 1969 Final Four propelled Maury to the National Coach of the Year award in voting of the U.S. Basketball Writers' Association. It was another in a series of big-time accomplishments by Maury. He proved his ability in Division I by taking Drake to three straight Missouri Valley Conference championships. With that record of success, it was widely regarded as a brilliant move when Iowa State hired Maury away from Drake in 1971 to replace retiring coach Glen Anderson. According to newspaper accounts, Maury's salary even was bumped from $18,000 to "$20,000 or more."

Maury's complemented a talented Cyclone coaching staff that included legendary leaders like Harold Nichols in wrestling, Cap Timm in baseball and Jack McGuire in swimming, plus up-and-coming young coaches like Johnny Majors and Jackie Sherrill in football, Ed Gagnier in gymnastics and Bill Bergan in cross country. Best of all, Maury's arrival coincided with Iowa State basketball's 1971 move from the Armory into the stylish Hilton Coliseum. The timing seemed perfect for Iowa State basketball to soar: a big-time coach, a showy arena. Hilton, named after the university's only graduate to serve as its president, was built for $8 million, without tax funds. It compared favorably with any college arena in the nation. Cyclone basketball rarely filled the previous home for hoops, the 6,000-seat Armory, but with the new building and with Maury's arrival, the 1971–72 season saw Iowa State's average attendance mushroom to 13,000. That crowd average slipped a tad to just under 11,000 in year two and to 9,300 in year three, but those still were encouraging crowds.

Maury, who inherited a team that had lost 12 of its last 13 games in a 5-21 finish of 1970–71, was hungry to play well immediately, and he brought in four junior-college transfers for his first Cyclone team. That 1971–72 club pumped up the volume but still lost six games by five or fewer points and finished 12-14. Iowa State came back to post records of 16-10 and 15-11 in Maury's second (1972–73) and third (1973–74) campaigns, although the latter season typified the Cyclones' basketball frustration of the decade.

The 1973–74 Cyclone team started out 4-0, matching its best start since 1957, but Maury was ill. A trip to the doctor in December 1973 revealed an inoperable tumor on his esophagus. "Talk about the irony of it," said Eric Heft, now a Cyclone radio color analyst who played three seasons for Maury. "He found out about (the tumor) the day we played Drake, his old team. We went down there that night and lost on a last-second shot (61-60). The team didn't know at the time what was going on, but he was not at practice the next day. It was at least a week before they told us what was happening." Maury's top assistant coach, Gus Guydon, a former Drake player under Maury, joined fellow assistant Tom Smith in taking over interim co-coaching duties when Maury began cancer therapy.

Iowa State pulled together and compiled a 9-3 non-conference record, including a convincing win over Iowa, but later finished just 6-8 in Big Eight play. Maury, who made an occasional appearance at practice or a game for a pep talk that winter, announced his resignation in July 1974 due to his health problems, and he eventually lost the battle with cancer and died later that year. He was 54. "I watched Maury go from 190 pounds to 130 pounds," Lou McCullough said. "Even down to his last breath, he still had hope. They don't make them any better than Maury John. He was a wonderful coach and a wonderful person."

• A Trickey Replacement

McCullough, in one of his first acts as Iowa State athletic director after succeeding Clay Stapleton, hired Oral Roberts head coach Ken Trickey as Maury's replacement in August 1974. Trickey had recorded a 118-23 record the previous five seasons at Oral Roberts, and his 1971–72 team averaged 105.1 ppg, after scoring 100 or more points 20 times—quite a feat in the pre-three-point goal era. That team also set an NCAA record with 126 field-goal attempts in a game. The up-tempo basketball style improved Oral Roberts' attendance from under 1,000 a game in his first year to nearly 9,000 his final season. Trickey was the third head basketball coach hired in Iowa in 1974 at the state's "Big Three" universities: The University of Iowa had hired Lute Olson and Drake had chosen Bob Ortegel. Trickey called Cyclone basketball "a slumbering giant on the verge of big things" when he was introduced in Ames on August 23, 1974.

Trickey's first Cyclone team started 8-9 before losing seven of its last nine games to close with a 10-16 record. The highlight of the season was the remarkable scoring of sophomore Hercle Ivy, appropriately nicknamed "Poison." Ivy, the best player to come out of St. Louis Northwestern High since former Boston Celtics ace Jo Jo White, had seven 30-point outings and finished fifth nationally in scoring at 28.3 ppg with an amazing 29.9 ppg average in Big Eight games. Not even the explosive Ivy could jump start the Iowa State basketball program, though, and soon Trickey found himself floating down Ames' Skunk River without a paddle. The coach's second season (1975–76) was a certifiable nightmare. Trickey's troops lost their first 13 games, the worst start in school history. Eleven days after the unlucky 13th loss, Trickey agreed under fire to resign as Iowa State's head coach and accept a buyout of his contract. The Cyclones went on to finish 3-24, matching the worst winning percentage in a season since Iowa State started fielding teams in 1909. Guydon, a hold-over from Maury John's staff, joined fellow assistant coach Jack Sutter as the Cyclones' interim co-head coaches for the final 12 games.

• Lynn Nance Gets a Chance

McCullough gambled in his choice to replace Trickey in 1976 by hiring Lynn Nance, a former FBI agent and an assistant coach at Kentucky. If Nance wasn't superstitious before becoming Iowa State's 13th head basketball coach, he probably exuded such paranoia once in the job. Just 33 years old when hired, Nance was one of the younger major-college head coaches in history, and he faced the unenviable task of becoming the Cyclones' third head coach in four seasons. Ask former Iowa State players like Steve Burgason about continuity: The Ames native was recruited by Maury John and played on his final team, then played for Trickey, had two sets of interim co-coaches, and ended his career in Nance's debut season.

That first Iowa State team under Nance in 1976–77 finished 8-19 while attracting an average of 5,642 fans at home. The Hilton attendance surged to an average of 9,075 in 1977–78, though, when Nance's second team started 6-1 in the Big Eight en route to a 9-5, second-place finish and a rare home-court advantage in the first round of the Big Eight postseason tournament. The Cyclones subsequently lost to Missouri, 65-63, to miss a trip to the tournament semifinals in Kansas City. They still finished over .500 at 14-13, which would stand as Iowa State's only winning basketball record from 1974 through 1983. The 9-5 record in Big Eight play also was Iowa State's best conference showing in 15 years, and Floridian Andrew Parker of Iowa State led the Big Eight in scoring.

Talk of a Big Eight title was prevalent in 1978 prior to Nance's third season. One national preseason poll even picked

Johnny was a Navy man who served most of his tour at a base in Mare Island, Calif. [*right*] Romie Robinson caught Johnny's eye at Beloit, and even though she later transferred to the University of Missouri, the couple ended up getting married shortly after graduation in 1949.

Johnny spent 15 months in the Navy, although the atomic bomb was dropped and World War II ended a few months after he enlisted.

While serving as athletic director and player-coach of basketball and baseball at Mare Island, Johnny became good friends with a couple of southern Illinois natives—brothers Mel and El Tappe, who went on to play pro baseball for the Cubs. [*right*] Johnny put his lanky frame to good use as a first baseman on his Navy team.

After being discharged from the Navy, Orr continued his
college career with Dolph Stanley at Beloit College. For
three consecutive years, Orr led the small Wisconsin school
to berths in the 32-team NAIB tournament in Kansas City,
and twice was named All-American. He scored 1,347 points
in three seasons and drew the attention of pro scouts in his
final season.

Move over George Bush, there's another prominent guy with a good history as a first baseman. After his senior year in high school, Orr turned down a chance to sign a minor-league pro contract with the Chicago Cubs. [*right*] Johnny's eloquent speech upon receiving his All-American honors for Beloit at the national tournament prompted a Beloit sportswriter to note: "Most of the players sputtered acknowledgement to the plaudits, with at least one exception—Johnny Orr. Orr speaks freely and is completely at ease before an audience, and without a trace of braggadocio." [*below*] Orr had a reputation at Beloit as both a skilled shooter and a deft passer.

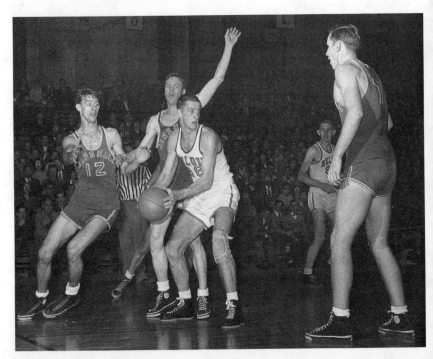

Johnny and Romie met at Beloit while taking an educational psychology class. Johnny says the thing that impressed him when he met Romie was that "she had that confidence in herself. She was a cheerleader and was very active in all kinds of student organizations. You'd see her picture in the yearbook all the time." [below] Johnny and Romie were married in Kansas City on June 18, 1949, just two weeks after they graduated from college. Four daughters and one grandchild later, the Orrs are going strong after 43 years of marriage.

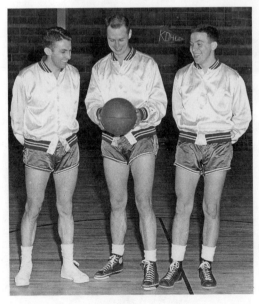

Johnny played one NBA season, the first part with the St. Louis Bombers and the last stretch with the Waterloo Hawks. Johnny clearly missed Dolph Stanley's up-tempo style, though, and never felt comfortable in the Bombers' deliberate style of offense. (Buzz Taylor photo, St. Louis, Mo.) [*left*] Johnny made an attractive sum of money for several years in Wisconsin when playing on several semipro teams on nights and weekends after his day job as a teacher and coach. (Hein-Foto, Fond du Lac, Wis.)

Johnny's first coaching job was at Milton, Wisconsin, and his team went 15-7, the most victories for Milton in 15 seasons. (*Janesville Gazette* photo) [*below*] Johnny had many successful seasons in basketball at Dubuque Senior and took his first team there to the state tournament. (*Des Moines Register* photo by Tony Cordaro)

[*above*] Johnny said he enjoyed coaching high school football so much he nearly pushed his career that direction. His best season in football at Dubuque was in 1958, when the Rams finished third in the state polls. (Dubuque *Telegraph-Herald* photo)

While in Dubuque in the 1950s, the Orrs were introduced to the joy and chaos of raising children. With young daughters (*from left*) Jenny, Robin and Leslie, there never were dull moments.

Orr posed with fellow Wisconsin football coaches, said he made some great friends coaching in Wisconsin. He left Dubuque in 1959 to be assistant basketball coach with the Badgers, where Orr is believed to be the last person to coach both football and basketball in the Big Ten Conference. (University of Wisconsin photo)

Long before there were shoe contracts, Orr and his young family appeared in a Madison newspaper advertisement to promote a local business.

Orr was 35 years old when hired as
Massachusetts head basketball coach in
1963. (University of Massachusetts photo)
[*below*] Johnny, shown visiting with then
Massachusetts governor Endicott Peabody,
expresses fond memories of his years in
Amherst.

The entire Orr family made the trip to Hawaii in November of 1990 for the Maui Classic. [*left*] Johnny said his grandson John Henry "looks like he's going to be a center on the football team. He's a chunky guy, but I was chunky as a toddler, too." [*below*] Johnny and some family members share fun at the Johnny Orr Roast in Des Moines in April 1992. (*from left*) Son-in-law Craig Boylan and daughter Leslie, who with their son John Henry live near Des Moines; Romie and Johnny; daughter Becky, who lives in Ames, and her fiancé John Montgomery; daughter Robin, who also lives in Ames. (Photo by Gene McGivern)

Romie Orr is the most loyal Cyclone fan at Hilton Coliseum. "Most people don't know how important my mother is to my father," Robin Orr said. "My mother is the optimistic one. She always makes you look for the best in people." (Ames *Daily Tribune* photo by Jim Percival)

Iowa State as high as ninth. The enthusiasm was boosted by a school-record 129-69 win over Northeastern Illinois in the season opener. The Cyclones went on to lose one-point road decisions to Iowa and Creighton, though, and never had the spark of the previous season as they finished 11-16. The Hilton hex that surfaced with Maury John's passing seemed to kick in again.

Meanwhile, the relationship between Nance and McCullough was eroding. The coach was irked that he occasionally had to shift practice sites, moving from Hilton across campus to the aged State Gym, to accommodate public and student ice skating in the Coliseum. Nance's woes intensified, and during that third season he sent criticism McCullough's direction during a WHO radio postgame show. Following a loss at Colorado, his team's fifth straight defeat after a 3-1 Big Eight start, Nance said he was puzzled that his boss wouldn't step up and say, " 'We know you've faced some adversity and are behind you 100 percent . . .' This is a good time for people to stand up and be counted. If they think someone else can do a better job, let them say so. It worries me a little bit that we aren't hearing anything."

Ralph Olsen, a prominent Iowa State donor for whom the Cyclones' main athletic administration building was named, was a close friend of Nance's. His lobbying helped Nance receive a two-year contract extension in 1979, despite the losing record and a slight dip in attendance to 8,083 per game. Nance came to the Big Eight basketball tip-off luncheon the next fall and boldly said the Cyclones could win the conference championship. When asked if he was nervous about his job security given the public feud with his boss, Nance told reporters, "No, I'm not nervous. I just signed a two-year contract this spring. I can say about what I want to now. If we're not better, it will cost them $70,000 to fire me next spring. And I'll just go down to Florida and play a lot of golf for a year and see what turns up." Although Nance later said the comments were made in jest, the statement did nothing to heal the rift between the coach and the athletic director.

Part of the rap on Iowa State basketball of the 1970s was its soft non-conference schedule, with several teams that did little to inspire a run on ticket sales. Nance's bold dreams for 1979–80 were buoyed by a school-record-margin 65-point victory over Roosevelt—the Chicago college, not the Des Moines high school. But reality returned in the Cyclones' overtime loss at Hilton to Division II Nebraska-Omaha, and a three-point escape against Division II Eastern Montana.

The abrupt end of the Nance era perhaps set the tone for McCullough's bizarre coaching search. Iowa State took a 1-3 Big

Eight record and 7-10 overall mark into the Saturday, January 26, 1980, match with Oklahoma State. It was Nance's 99th game as the Cyclones head coach, but he wouldn't be around for No. 100. Following the 69-60 victory over the Cowboys, Nance told his players he was resigning. Bob Fowler, a player who had followed Nance to Iowa State from the University of Kentucky, apparently knew what was unfolding. When Fowler fouled out late in the game, he left the court, peeled off his jersey and flung it into the stands, then beelined for the locker room. In a brief postgame television interview on the TVS Network, Nance didn't reveal his plans but hinted his days as Iowa State coach were numbered. Announcer Gary Thompson closed the interview by saying, "Well, Lynn, we're running short of time." To which Nance responded, "I think we are, too." The Ames *Daily Tribune* broke the story the following Monday, revealing that Nance told his players following the Saturday game he would resign. The *Tribune* noted that Nance would accept a settlement for the remaining two years of his contract. Assistants Reggie Warford and Rick Samuels were named interim co-coaches, and attendance would average just 6,470 during that season of turmoil.

(Nance's coaching resurrection through the 1980s and into the 1990s was impressive. If the Iowa State experience at all haunted him or created skeptics, Nance vindicated himself when he took Central Missouri State to a national championship in NCAA Division II and had a five-year record of 114-35 with the Mules. He was an assistant coach again for one season in Division I at Fresno State, then went 61-27 in three seasons as head coach at St. Mary's of California. He landed a more prominent Division I job as head coach of the University of Washington in 1989, and his career record sits just under .500 overall after his first three seasons.)

• The Search Is On

McCullough began his search for the ninth guy in 10 years to hold the title of head or interim head coach for Iowa State basketball. Perhaps it's more than a coincidence that in this era, the university's residence halls had started using Hilton Coliseum for temporary housing at the start of the school year. "When you add up all the pluses, this is a damn good job here," McCullough said in announcing a national search for Nance's replacement. "To what extent is ice (time) a problem at Hilton? When you're losing, it's 9 on a 10-point scale. When you're winning, it's about a 2 . . .

The committee will comb the United States for the best coaches and bring several in for interviews. Whether that takes two, three or four weeks, whatever. The sooner the better, but there is no timetable."

McCullough later revealed that approximately 100 coaches applied for the vacancy, with 81 sending in formal applications. He estimated that his nine-week search resulted in 2,000 phone calls, and he sought the advice of people like Bob Knight, who was called more than a dozen times, Wooden, and then-NFL head coaches Bart Starr and Dick Vermeil. The search took McCullough to games and meetings in California, Texas, Mississippi, Alabama and Georgia, and he said that 10 candidates were brought to Ames for interviews. McCullough later told the *Des Moines Tribune*, "I hope I don't have to go through this again in my lifetime."

Knight pushed for his former player and graduate assistant coach, Mike Krzyzewski of Army. A *Des Moines Register* story March 16, 1980, speculated that Krzyzewski "appears to be the front-runner . . . although he's also in consideration for the Duke post, which could leave ISU in the cold." Indeed, Duke offered its job to Krzyzewski, who accepted, and the famed Coach K is now in his 13th year with the Blue Devils, with two NCAA titles to his credit and six Final Four appearances in the last seven years. It was a busy time nationally for coaching vacancies, and that movement also would affect the Cyclone search. North Carolina State soon would hire Iona's Jim Valvano as its head coach, and Oklahoma would woo Billy Tubbs away from Lamar University.

Other top candidates at Iowa State were Gerald Myers of Texas Tech, Bob Weltlich of Mississippi and Tony McAndrews, then a fifth-year Iowa assistant coach. Myers and Weltlich turned down the job, and McAndrews said he was offered the job and was prepared to accept but got into a disagreement with McCullough over the timing of the announcement. McAndrews, whose Iowa Hawkeye team was playing Louisville in the national semifinals, wanted to delay an announcement until after Iowa was finished in the tournament. "I didn't want to go into Indianapolis as the Iowa State coach and take away from what (Iowa Hawkeye players) were trying to do," a puzzled McAndrews said the following week. McAndrews said he was offered a four-year contract after interviewing in Ames on Thursday, March 20, but he refused the condition that it be announced immediately. "I tried to call McCullough Sunday (March 23, after Iowa's NCAA semifinal loss), but didn't hear anything," McAndrews said. McAndrews added that word of an Iowa State job offer to him had spread to the point that "I was already receiving calls from other coaches interested in assistant jobs."

• Along Came John

Orr's involvement was at first behind the scenes. Iowa State assistant athletic director Dave Cox, in his first year on the job, was assigned to escort Orr from the Des Moines airport when he came in as a consultant in mid-March. "I think Johnny was at Creighton to speak, and on the way home he was going to stop in and look our place over and see the facilities," Cox said. "Lou sent me to the Des Moines airport to pick him up, but he didn't want anyone in the press to know he was coming. So we had him come in at night. In the 40-minute ride I was convinced in my mind that the best person for our job was Johnny Orr. In listening to him talk about Michigan, I had a very distinct feeling John didn't feel appreciated. I kept talking about our great fans and how hungry they were in the winter for a winner. They support wrestling well, but they're really hungry for exciting basketball. He had not seen Iowa State's facilities in quite some time. We kind of got excited together standing in a darkened Hilton Coliseum. You could see it in his eye, that sparkle was there. I told (associate athletic director) Max Urick I really think Johnny Orr will come here if everything fell into place. I thought he'd be fantastic for Iowa State University, and we'd be good for him. I wasn't in on Orr's conversations with Lou, but John told me he'd call me that night when he got back to Michigan."

Cox recalls feeling surprised when he didn't hear from Orr by 11 p.m. "I thought, 'How could I have missed on this?' Well, about midnight he finally called," Cox said. "I told him he should come. He said, 'I just can't. I'm not as interested in the money as I am being respected. But money was one way of showing it, and Lou can't come up with what it would take.' So I said, 'If we would come up with the money, would you come?' And he said, 'It would be hard to say no.' "

Cox and Urick both felt there was a chance to get Orr, but they worried that McCullough had closed the door on that idea. "Lou didn't like it when things didn't go smoothly," Cox said. "We thought Lou felt, 'Hey, we made our shot, we were a little short, and that was it.' We went to Lou, and to our delight he told us to call him again. Well, then we couldn't reach Johnny. We couldn't find him all morning. He was on his way to the Final Four in Indianapolis. Max even called the Atlanta airport and had him paged, thinking he'd be stranded there if the weather was bad. It dawned on me that one guy who might know where he was was (Bill) Frieder. I called him in Indianapolis and he went down to the lobby and got Orr so he could talk to Lou."

McCullough persuaded Orr to return to Ames with Romie that weekend to meet President Parks and look over the community and some potential houses. Orr flew back to Ann Arbor from Indianapolis, and after attending the Michigan state high school finals Saturday night, he flew to Ames with his wife. They were shown most of the prime homes in Ames—some of which weren't even for sale. In fact, the $175,000 house the Orrs eventually chose was the residence of Ames realtors Lee and Barb Matsen.

The best sales job, though, came in Parks' direct plea to Johnny. Orr told a reporter later, "It's nice to feel wanted." Orr noted that "In 13 years at Michigan, I only met the (university) president three times." The offer was made and Johnny knew it was right the next day when on the ride to the airport, Romie said, "Let's come here." Orr said later, "I've been married to her for 30 years. I knew better than to argue with her."

After hearing Orr's salary request, the dollar-conscious McCullough wasn't sure if he could afford to hire Johnny. In the end, Lou knew he couldn't afford not to. Iowa State wanted to make sure that Orr didn't have a change of heart, so they sent Cox to Ann Arbor Monday to personally escort Johnny back to Ames for a Tuesday, March 25, press conference. "Max got the idea that somebody should be there, so I flew out to bring him back," Cox said. "It was very emotional for him." In fact, Orr cried when telling close friends of his decision. Michigan athletic director Don Canham was vacationing in the Bahamas at the time, and when Orr finally reached him by phone, the Michigan boss advised him to take a day and think it over. Orr said, "They've got a guy here right now, and I'm getting on a plane in 15 minutes and going. I told him what they're doing for me, and he just said, 'Just make sure they do all of that.' " Canham and Orr were close friends and still are close, but Orr said he was irked that a couple of weeks earlier, Canham had shown up 45 minutes late for an appointment to discuss Orr's salary, then laughed when Johnny proposed a raise.

Cox said he had Orr sleep in his son's bed that night, "Because we wanted to hide him from all the media guys." If that sounds a bit paranoid, note that in the competition to break the story on a new coach, Ames *Daily Tribune* sports editor Dave Reynolds spent part of the previous week staking out McCullough's west Ames house, watching for potential interviewees, from his car parked down the street. When Reynolds saw McAndrews, who at the time was walking with a cane after a recent airplane crash, enter Lou's house, he knew he was a serious candidate.

By Monday night, March 24, the rumor of Orr's imminent hiring at Iowa State was sweeping Ames. Some thought it was a hoax and speculated that McAndrews would be introduced as the new coach. The *Des Moines Register*'s Tuesday, March 25, morning story stopped short of confirming Orr and still mentioned McAndrews as a possibility. The *Des Moines Tribune*, it its Tuesday afternoon edition, quoted McAndrews as saying, "I hope it (Orr's hiring) isn't true. I am very much interested in it. I don't know why he would want to start another program at his age (52)."

• He's Our Man

At a lively Tuesday press conference at the Iowa State Center's Fisher Theater, McCullough introduced Orr as the Cyclones' 14th head coach and proclaimed March 25, 1980, "a great day for Iowa State and our fans." Here's an account from an Ames *Daily Tribune* story by sportswriter John Akers:

> The announcement was made Monday that a press conference at Fisher Theater was to follow an Iowa State athletic council meeting. The meeting would announce the naming of former Michigan coach Johnny Orr as the new ISU head coach, though nobody was telling the latter. This press conference was nothing like the one held for present football coach Donnie Duncan, which was less ceremonious and meant mostly for reporters . . . This was a media event, complete with the blaring of trumpets, the ruffle of pompons, the presence of Cy, a huge banner proclaiming Iowa State is Orr Right and bumper stickers . . . It was the type of event reserved for big names. It was the proper way to greet the biggest name in ISU basketball since Maury John traveled about 30 miles north in 1971. When the band started playing the Iowa State fight song cheerleaders hit the theater floor, and soon the new head coach entered through a side door. Loud cheers followed, as Orr made a couple of tight-fisted jabs near his chest. He was ready to go. The man was simply dressed in a woolen suit with a small Cy stitched to his lapel. It didn't take long for his backhills charm, slang and humor to dominate the event.

Even Iowa Governor Robert Ray was part of the welcoming

committee. Ray sent the following telegram to Orr on the day of his hiring:

> DEAR JOHNNY
>
> I WAS DELIGHTED TO LEARN OF YOUR DECISION TO RETURN TO THE STATE OF IOWA WHERE YOU HAD SOME OF YOUR EARLY SUCCESSES IN YOUR REMARKABLE COACHING CAREER. WE HAVE A LOT OF PRIDE HERE AT IOWA—IN OUR STATE, IN OUR STRONG UNIVERSITIES, IN OUR BRIGHT AND TALENTED STUDENTS, AND IN OUR EXCELLENT FACILITIES SUCH AS THE IOWA STATE CENTER. WE ALSO ARE A PEOPLE WHO ARE THRILLED BY WINNING BASKETBALL—AND BY THE POTENTIAL YOU BRING WITH YOU TO CYCLONE COUNTRY. I LOOK FORWARD TO WATCHING YOU AND IOWA STATE NEXT SEASON, AND I WELCOME YOU TO AMES AND TO THE STATE OF IOWA.
>
> BEST REGARDS
>
> ROBERT D. RAY
> GOVERNOR OF IOWA

Almost as newsworthy as Orr's hiring were the eye-opening salary and perks in his contract. While fat salaries for pro athletes and college coaches are the rule in the 1990s, Orr's lucrative 1980 contract was among the first attractive package deals that would become standard for the high-visibility jobs in major-college sports. It was another signal that college sports were becoming as much entertainment and business as a campustown diversion. True to his capitalist philosophy, Orr did nothing to downplay his $45,000 annual salary—a raise of nearly $12,000 from his wage at Michigan—or the six-year guarantee, or the perks like radio and TV shows, and basketball camp income that figured to push the package well over $100,000. In fact, he even bragged it up. "When I was a kid starting out, I wanted to be the best paid," Orr said.

"Got a calculator?" McCullough told reporters. "The $45,000 is just the beginning. We wouldn't have offered a six-year contract to anybody but him. If Johnny Orr isn't qualified, who is?"

The 52-year-old Orr came to Ames with a 209-113 record in

12 seasons at Michigan, including 10 straight winning seasons, two Big Ten titles and two conference runner-up finishes. He was just four years removed from playing in the national finals, and twice was selected National Coach of the Year. Orr was the dean of Big Ten basketball coaches then, and was the only Big Ten coach at the time ever to lead a team to four consecutive NCAA berths. That was no easy feat in the NCAA tournament's 1970s pre-expansion days when the field was half the size of today's. Orr's Wolverine teams also received two NIT berths, including one just weeks earlier. That 17-13 Michigan finish in 1979–80 was accomplished with an all-underclassmen starting five, too.

Orr used his first Iowa State public appearance to pledge, "We're going to make ISU successful and a national power, and do it within the letter of the law. I've been coaching 28–29 years, and have never been on probation and never been fired. Someday we're going to a national tournament. I love Ann Arbor, and I love Michigan, and I hate to leave, but I feel this is a new challenge and it's a great opportunity again." When asked if Iowa State was a coaching graveyard, he replied, "I think if you get the right guy in a graveyard, he can get out."

Orr's Michigan teams were 10-2 in games against the University of Iowa's Lute Olson, a fact that played well at Iowa State, a school trying to escape from the Hawkeyes' shadow. Iowa newspapers had their readers swimming in black and gold ink the previous weeks, after Dan Gable's wrestlers won their third straight national title—once again beating out the Cyclones—and Lute and his Hawkeye players became instant celebrities by reaching the Final Four. But Orr's surprise hiring left the Iowa fans so quiet you could hear Hawk broadcaster Jim Zabel's jaw drop.

• Media Reaction

The banner headline in the March 26 *Des Moines Register* read: "ISU stunner: Orr is new coach," and the Page 2 jump headline read: "Orr vows to make ISU national power." *Register* staff writer Bob Dyer wrote that ISU "dropped a blockbuster on the college athletics scene" with its hiring of Orr. It even was a Page One sports story in the *Chicago Tribune,* whose headline read, "Iowa St. gives Orr 'everything.'" Reporter Roy Damer began the *Tribune* story: "Johnny Orr left Michigan to become Iowa State's basketball coach Tuesday because, by his own calculation, 'This job is going to make me the highest paid coach in America, and that's great.' "

Back home in Michigan, Frieder told the Ann Arbor *News* that Orr's departure was "The most shocking sports news of the decade . . . John and Romie loved Michigan and they loved Ann Arbor, and it was incredible that they left." Michigan State coach Jud Heathcote told the Ann Arbor *News* that he was "just as shocked as anyone . . . I'm also disappointed because the Big Eight's gain is the Big Ten's loss. I feel that John is an exceptional coach and, in my opinion, I've never felt he has received the recognition in his home area that he has received nationwide." Canham told the *Detroit News*, "It was an outstanding package for his security and his family. I think it was strictly a financial decision. Johnny is one of my closest friends, but we couldn't get into a bidding war with them. To his credit, Johnny never tried to use this as leverage."

Ironically, writer John Viges of the Ann Arbor *News* had interviewed Orr during the previous week. Among Johnny's comments—made prior to agreeing to come back to Ames to reconsider the job offer—was this statement: "I'll be here (at Michigan), there's no question about it. I hope to be here at least five more years." Viges wrote after Orr's departure: "When I first heard the rumor of Orr and Iowa State, my first reaction was 'Nah, you must be kidding. Why would Orr go there?' " Orr's response: "It seems strange, but if you knew all the details it wouldn't seem so strange."

Detroit News columnist Joe Falls, a writer with whom Orr often feuded, soon thereafter scolded Michigan for its compensation of Orr, writing:

> What's this business of Michigan, mighty Michigan, paying Johnny Orr only $33,655 to head up its basketball program? That's shameful. Maybe you can say it was Orr's fault for living with it so long, but you would also think a matter of pride would be involved and they would give the man a more decent wage . . . If nothing else, they had to know Orr was making less than Jud Heathcote at Michigan State ($39,200) and has been on the job 10 years longer. These things get around among the coaches and had to hurt Orr, a man who is very sensitive about himself. You can't blame him for leaving.

Here's a sampling of other sportswriter reactions to Orr's move to Ames:

Waterloo *Courier* sports editor Russ Smith

There may not have been a dozen basketball coaches in the country Iowa State could have hired who would, even for a few days, have diverted the attention of the state's fans from (National Basketball Coaches' Association) Coach of the Year Lute Olson and his Iowa Hawkeyes. But the Cyclones came up with one who would rank high among the dozen when they plucked Johnny Orr off the University of Michigan campus Tuesday.

Ames *Tribune* sports editor Dave Reynolds

The announcement today of Johnny Orr as head coach at Iowa State comes as a big surprise to most folks. After its three top candidates withdrew from consideration, it appeared Iowa State would have to be content settling on an assistant coach or a head man who originally may have been a fourth or fifth choice. But ISU pulled out its checkbook and decided to finally make a strong commitment to a program which has received second billing to football in recent years. As one former ISU cager said about that situation today, "It's about time."

Cedar Rapids *Gazette* writer Mark Dukes

Iowa State has provided 52-year-old Johnny Orr with a nice, comfortable security blanket—with the understanding, of course, he gives Cyclone basketball fans something to sink their teeth into. Orr, a veteran of 15 collegiate seasons with a mile-long list of credentials, Tuesday agreed to guide the Iowa State basketball program.

Detroit *News* columnist Joe Falls

In his time at Michigan, Orr became one of the fixtures in college basketball. He was one of the clan. Ray Meyer, Bobby Knight, Digger Phelps, Dean Smith, Frank McGuire, Al McGuire and Johnny Orr. Only a few are left. But everybody knew Big John of Michigan. He had a sense of humor and that down-home way of titillating audiences in hotel lobbies or high school gyms. He was never more fun than on the charity golf circuit in the summertime. He'd bang one a mile and keep you in stitches all afternoon.

But there also was a bitter side to this man and it surfaced in ways he probably wasn't even aware of. You could meet him almost anywhere, in a bar, on a plane, in the corner of a high school gym, and he'd be putting somebody down. It might be another coach or another team, but he'd be knocking somebody, and it seemed so unnecessary. Didn't he know that he was John

Orr of Michigan . . . Big John had a lot of problems with his role at Michigan. He never really liked the pressure. For one thing, he hated it when people expected him to win. He wanted to play the role of country bumpkin. The thing is, he was a pretty good coach and he didn't have to resort to any of those tricks . . . Now he's got the gold, but you wonder if he'll ever get the glory. Johnny Orr will find out if money can buy peace of mind.

The emphasis on Orr's salary seems almost trivial a decade later, but it received a lot of play at the time. *Des Moines Register* sportswriters Buck Turnbull and Bob Dyer each wrote analysis stories that were printed the day after Orr's hiring ("pure coincidence," according to Dyer) under a headline "Johnny Orr: Is he worth more than Hawks' Olson?" Turnbull questioned the propriety of the unusual salary, but Dyer argued that Orr was worth it. Here's an excerpt from Turnbull's column:

Can Iowa State afford to pay a basketball coach more than its football coach? Can the Cyclones justify hiring a basketball coach at a larger salary than Iowa is paying Lute Olson? What set of priorities is involved here when Iowa State jumps the salary scale for a basketball coach to $45,000, making the job pay more than the athletic director's job at Iowa and equal to the athletic director's position at Iowa State?

Certainly, there should be no argument with Orr's qualifications as an outstanding basketball coach. He's a proven winner. The Cyclones should feel most fortunate to land a man of his caliber . . . Only time will tell if he's worth the high salary, plus all the fringe benefits supposedly promised him, but there seems little doubt that Iowa State is leaving itself wide open for criticism of its financial dealings. The Cyclones are already paying off $81,000 in contract obligations to former basketball coaches, first Ken Trickey, and then Lynn Nance, while entering into a six-year agreement with Orr.

It's one thing to keep up with the Joneses, and inflation has made that more difficult by the month, but Iowa State is inviting a taxpayers' revolt by continuing to operate its athletic department at such a huge deficit. State appropriations to help defray the deficit now are running close to a million dollars a year, counting salaries from the merger of the women's athletic program last summer, and this isn't exactly an opportune time to offer someone the moon.

Here's an excerpt from Bob Dyer's viewpoint:

Orr is just the tonic Iowa State needed to revive a program that in recent years often has been in a shambles. That his price tag came high is no surprise. Orr can sit down with this country's coaching giants and not feel out of place. Such men do not come cheaply.

Johnny Orr cost Iowa State $45,000 a year, plus numerous fringe benefits. He was a bargain. Iowa Coach Lute Olson, who is revered in most parts of this state, makes $42,500 a year and is worth every penny of it. But if another university hired away Olson, you can bet he would be making quite a bit more at his new station . . .

Last year, Iowa State season ticket sales were off 900 as attendance dipped from an average of 8,083 in 1979 to 6,430 this (1980) season. It doesn't take a mathematical whiz to realize that if Orr's presence increases season ticket sales by 1,000, at $52 a pop he will easily pay for himself. What price tag, however, can be put on Orr's name, which secures national publicity for a program that has had an image problem? No, at $45,000, Orr was a steal.

Even Governor Ray was queried at his weekly press conference about the propriety of Orr's salary. "This is a person who could demand a higher salary," Ray said. "He got it, and I think it will be money well spent."

Time has proven former Governor Ray's, Lou McCullough's and Bob Dyer's viewpoints to be correct. Johnny Orr was worth the investment. Johnny has outlasted Ray, McCullough, two ISU women's basketball coaches, two Iowa State head football coaches, a couple of ISU presidents and two head basketball coaches at both Iowa and Drake.

"I've known John Orr for many years, and I want to advise you this: If you need a friend [*pause*] get a dog."

—GEORGE RAVELING

". . . and George, when he was coaching at Iowa, I remember playing him and I looked down the bench and he was hyperventilating. I said, 'Hell, I think we're going to win this game.' "

—JOHNNY ORR

"I never really had any second thoughts about coming here to Iowa State. A lot of people said I came here to retire (in a few seasons), but I had no intention of doing that. But I really didn't think it would be this hard getting the players. Recruiting in the Big Ten area has been difficult because Iowa State didn't have the exposure there. If Iowa State had been in the Big Ten, we'd have gotten many more great players."

"Getting Barry Stevens was big—he was a big guy for us because he was our first great player from Michigan. (Assistant coaches) Gary Cook and Charlie Harrison got us established in recruiting in Illinois. A big regret is that they worked so damn hard to help us get it going, by the time we finally got it going they were gone to other jobs. I've had good guys who have worked with me here."

"I enjoyed my first (1980–81) team very much. That was a hard-working team. They would try to do what I asked and never questioned what we told them. Whoo, Lefty Moore did a great job for me, and Ron Harris, what a freshman year he had. Big old (Ron) Falenschek had some good games. And Robert Estes, man oh man, he was only 6-foot-5-inches and he played center for us some and did a hell of a job. Jonny Ness, (John) Kunnert, (Doug) Jones, Mal Warrick, Bill Buchanan, Charles Harris, Derrick Thomas, Terrence Allen. We went out there and won that tournament (Elm City Classic) in New Haven. That team never gave up, they hung in there right until the end even though we had some very difficult things happen."

• It's Going to Take Some Time

Johnny Orr's hallmark quote from the early years at Iowa State summed up the paradox of his situation: "I've got a great job at Iowa State. I've got a great contract, the people at Iowa State are great, we have a beautiful basketball arena. Now if we just didn't have to play the damn games, it would really be great."

Welcome to Orr's first Cyclone season. An optimist would say Iowa State was only a couple of players away from being national contenders. A realist would note that those two missing players were Magic Johnson and Julius Erving. When people held up "John: 3-16" signs back then, the reference probably wasn't Biblical but rather a prediction of the win-loss expectation for Orr's first Cyclone teams.

Johnny joked that he never was more popular among his coaching peers nationally than in the months following his hiring at Iowa State. Orr kidded that Notre Dame's Digger Phelps, who never beat Johnny's Michigan teams, suddenly wanted to get the Cyclones on his schedule. "Digger wants to play me now. So do about 500 other teams," Orr said.

Every coaching move brings challenges, but Orr's challenges were magnified by the fact he left a perennial Top 20 program at Michigan and moved to Iowa State, whose budget for basketball trophy cases was miniscule. The Cyclones had only one winning season in the previous six years. They had four different head coaches in the previous 10 years. They hadn't played in a national tournament since 1944. They hadn't surpassed 16 wins in a season since 1956. Johnny inherited a program that didn't enjoy top billing in its home state and even had to share the spotlight in its immediate area. The Cyclones were in a visibility battle with Lewis Lloyd and his Drake Bulldogs to establish their program as No. 2 in Iowa. Both were chasing Lute Olson and the Hawks.

Thus, after all the talk of the contract, the cars, the country clubs, and the comfort subsided, Orr had plenty of reason for doubt. Iowa State lacked basketball tradition. Iowa State lacked national exposure. Iowa State lacked a significant in-state recruiting pool, compared with nearby states like Illinois, Michigan and Missouri. Most prominent coaches wouldn't touch this job with a 10-foot pole or a 7-foot Bol, even if Manute was thrown in the deal. After some rough days, and after a lot of work, Orr gradually saw his vision for Iowa State come to pass. It didn't happen overnight, and it didn't come easily. In fact, after Johnny's first Cyclone team dropped under .500 with an 8-9 record, it took him six seasons—until Feb. 12, 1986—before his Iowa State career record climbed back above .500 (at 84-83).

Perhaps the most recognizable photo in Orr's first year at Iowa State was a shot of him visiting a campus fraternity house, Sigma Chi, the greek letters he wore as a fraternity man at Illinois and Beloit. Johnny, surrounded by amused students, was photographed bouncing on a trampoline at a Sigma Chi Derby Days fundraiser. Johnny's early Iowa State years were like the trampoline ride. Certainly, he felt queasy in the stomach at times, and no doubt had some days where he felt a bit out of his element. Orr's program sank deep into the canvas but kept springing up, a little higher each year. Many say Johnny's pinnacle at Iowa State came with his 1986 or 1988 National Collegiate Athletic Association (NCAA) tournament teams, when current National Basketball Association (NBA) players Jeff Hornacek and Jeff Grayer bounced the trampoline to new heights. The optimists hope that the current Fred Hoiberg era will produce another great ride. It already has returned the Cyclones to the NCAA tourney. The most crucial work, though, was done from 1980 through 1983, in laying the foundation for Orr's basketball program to grow.

"Johnny worked out even better than I expected," recalls former athletic director Lou McCullough. "I coached in the Big Ten at both Ohio State and Indiana, and I just didn't want this to be a letdown for John. But he came right in with enthusiasm, like it was his first job. That was what was so pleasing."

There were distractions, though. Orr recalled a visit at his office from the Story Country Sheriff. "He came up to my office and served these papers," Orr said. "He said I was being sued for $15 million. I thought that was funny as hell. I didn't have any money." A young player for Detroit Northwestern High, Curtis Jones, had been recruited by Orr for Michigan. Because Jones didn't qualify academically, and he eventually had problems in junior college, Jones filed suit, trying to collect damages from everyone remotely related to his experience. "It seemed funny at first," Orr said, " but I had to get a lawyer and give a deposition, and I eventually had to go to Detroit on the deal. It ended up costing me $4,000. I didn't really remember much about the guy at all. We were trying to recruit him but he couldn't pass the entrance test. So we called a coach at Southern Idaho Junior College and told him about this player. Curtis went there, but he had a lot of problems. So he came back later and said we ruined his pro career by not letting him in school, and he sued everybody." Given the challenge of building the Iowa State program, it would not be the first time in those early years that Johnny would try to avoid a court of law or a basketball court.

• Finding Assistants and Players

Johnny's first action at Iowa State came in filling out his coaching staff, and with the 1980 recruiting season dwindling away, he moved quickly. He said more than 175 applied for his assistant jobs, including 8 to 10 head coaches of major universities. Since Orr knew the first couple of seasons would be tough, he appropriately brought in a guy with a reputation as a survivor. Just five days after his hiring, Johnny tabbed Charlie Harrison to be an assistant. Harrison overcame a childhood bout with polio and two subsequent operations on his legs to have a high school athletics career. Harrison had a stint as a graduate coach for Bobby Knight at Indiana and was an assistant on Oklahoma's 1978–79 Big Eight championship squad. He distinguished himself in 1979–80 as a 30-year-old assistant coach at New Mexico who abruptly was elevated to interim head coach the first week of the season. Harrison's boss and another Lobo assistant coach were fired and several players were declared ineligible in a scandal over forged transcripts. Harrison had only four legitimate scholarship players, and it actually deteriorated further when three of those four were ruled academically ineligible at midseason. New Mexico finished 6-22 that season with one remaining scholarship player and a cast of walk-ons recruited from the student body.

Nine days after Harrison's hiring, Johnny selected his other full-time assistant, this time from the Chicago area. Gary Cook, 39, who had a 97-18 record in four seasons at Barrington (Illinois) High, had coached in seven different prep conferences in the Chicago area and would help the Cyclones establish firm roots that would eventually make Chicago the strongest recruiting base for Orr. From Michigan, Johnny brought in a former Wolverine player, John Robinson, as a part-time coach, and a former Central Michigan player, Ric Wesley, as a graduate coach. (Wesley was elevated to full-time assistant in 1983 and is the only coach to stay with Johnny from the first year to the present.)

Cook was influential in attracting Iowa State's first signee, Ron Harris, an underrated small forward from Chicago-area Rich Central High. Harris led his high school team to a 29-1 record as a senior and eventually played much bigger than his 6-foot-3-inch frame for Johnny. He would go on to start all 111 games in his four-year career and help the Cyclones reach the National Invitation Tournament (NIT) and defeat Iowa during his final year in 1983–84. Harris probably would have been signed by a more prominent major college, but his modest height and some academic problems he encountered as a high school junior diminished interest. Johnny's second prep recruit from that late spring was Terrence Allen, a slender 6-foot-1-inch, 150-pound point guard from Florida. Allen also would emerge as a pivotal player in the Cyclones posting a winning record by Orr's fourth season.

The 1980–81 Cyclone team was perhaps the most geographically diverse in school history. There were players from Florida (Allen); Georgia (senior guard Charles Harris); Kentucky (senior forward Bill Buchanan); California (freshman Tony Rasheed); Illinois (freshman Ron Harris); Missouri (juniors Malvin Warrick and

Robert Estes); Minnesota (sophs Ron Falenschek and Doug Jones); and junior colleges in Texas (senior guard Lefty Moore) and Idaho (junior forward Derrick Thomas)—along with two Iowans (senior guard Jon Ness and junior forward John Kunnert). At a school that once produced a gritty, outmanned championship football team known as the Dirty 30, this band of Cyclones looked like the Green 13, considering their sparse major-college basketball experience. Warrick was the heady, dependable player that Orr liked in the lineup, and his was the most unusual journey. The valedictorian of his senior class at Kansas City Lincoln High, Warrick went to Purdue, played for two different coaches there, then transferred to Iowa State to pursue his engineering and basketball careers. He practiced but was ineligible to play as a transfer during 1979–80, and in that time saw three more coaches come and go: head coach Lynn Nance and interim co-coaches Reggie Warford and Rick Samuels. With the arrival of Johnny, Warrick had worked with seven coaches in five years.

Johnny's presence added an air of excitement and promise in that first season, yet it still qualified as a season on the brink. The brink of insanity, that is. The first bad break occurred late in the fall when the Czechoslovakian National Team cancelled its U.S. tour, including an exhibition game with the Cyclones set for Hilton. Because Iowa State couldn't arrange a replacement game on short notice, it did without an exhibition tuneup and had to open its season on the road against Southeastern Conference contender Vanderbilt. Another setback came the week before the opener when potential starter Kunnert sprained his ankle in practice.

That left Johnny relying on a starting cast that included two returners (Estes and Moore), an unproven center (Falenschek), a freshman (Ron Harris) and a transfer (Warrick), to open on the road against Vanderbilt, which already had a 2-0 record.

• First Season, 1980–81

With a sellout crowd of 15,545 on hand in Nashville, Orr's first game brought a respectable 97-87 defeat. Some odd developments that night, however, were indicative of the frustrations the coach would face in his rebuilding process. Iowa State was outscored 33-15 at the free-throw line, was whistled for 34 fouls and had a player, Estes, ejected for an alleged flagrant foul. Both Estes and Orr said after the game that the objectionable contact was accidental, but this was the kind of luck this team would incur over and over that winter. The bright spot was Harris' 25-point Cyclone debut, including a 12-of-16 field-goal shooting performance.

Johnny and his team returned to Ames for their Hilton Coliseum debut, but again there was no cakewalk. The Cyclones had to face All-American Lewis Lloyd and the Drake Bulldogs, who had won the previous two meetings with the Cyclones and would beat Georgetown later in the month. Johnny said later, "I was excited, as excited as I've ever been before a game." Before a crowd of 13,200—a rouser by Hilton standards in those days—Iowa State rode Harris' 28 points to a 74-72 win. Maybe this was the night when the Hilton hex started to lift. It didn't hurt that the fabulous Lloyd was slowly coming back from a broken leg, but how else do you explain Sweet Lew's 8-of-24 shooting and modest 18 points? Johnny was at a postgame party when he received a congratulatory call from his former Michigan assistant coach and replacement, Bill Frieder. Johnny was awakened at 7 a.m. the next day with another congratulatory call, this one from Indiana's Bob Knight. That was no surprise, because Orr said Knight was the first coach to call him when he announced plans to accept the Iowa State job.

Drake came into 1992–93 3-9 against Orr's Cyclone teams, and 0-6 in Hilton Coliseum, but its biggest loss to Johnny may have been in ticket sales and boosters. Many observers today say that Orr's arrival and gradual success redirected hundreds of central Iowa fans away from the Bulldogs in Vets Auditorium and sent them north to Hilton. In 1980–81, the Lewis Lloyd–led Bulldogs averaged 9,444 fans, Drake's best gate since the one that came to see the 1968–69 NCAA Final Four team. But Lloyd's departure the next year started a gradual overall decline—7,408 in 1982–83 attendance and annual averages of 5,156 in 1984, 4,075 in 1985, 6,441 in 1986, 5,971 in 1987, and 4,861 in 1988. At the same time, Iowa State basketball ticket sales were climbing, from an average of 6,470 in Lynn Nance's final year, to 9,171 in Orr's first year, to 12,675 by his fourth year. "There were a lot of fence-sitters in Des Moines that just wanted to see good basketball," said former Des Moines sportswriter Bob Dyer. "John's popularity in Des Moines is evident in his TV show—all of his major sponsors are from Des Moines. He just sucked Des Moines dry."

The Cyclones followed the Drake victory with an 83-69 win over Northern Iowa, fueled by Ron Harris' 21 points. Now 2-1, Iowa State next traveled to Dallas to play Southern Methodist. The Cyclones built a 10-point first-half lead but ended up dropping a 58-55 decision to the Mustangs before only 3,106 spectators in what Orr called "our poorest game so far." Iowa State returned home to play 5-0 Creighton, and the Cyclone fans saw the feisty side of their new coach. A bizarre double technical foul whistled on both Falenschek and Orr in the final five minutes led to a five-point play that helped Creighton escape with a 77-73 victory. Iowa State had pulled within 57-55 with 4:10 left when Estes was called for his fifth foul. Falenschek was trying to untangle his body after a collision and was slapped with a technical when his arm hit a Bluejay player. Johnny received what he said was an undeserved two-shot bench technical foul simply for asking what happened. "The referee said, 'Did you see what he (Falenschek) did?' " Orr said after the game. "All I said was 'no,' and he called a technical. Ask him. If he says differently, he's a liar. I'll punch him right in the mouth."

The Iowa game

Iowa State had a week off for final exams before its next game against Iowa in Iowa City. The Hawks, coming off their Final Four appearance in 1980, were 5-1 and ranked 15th nationally. "I told Charlie Harrison (his assistant coach), 'Iowa sure looks a lot different now that I'm not coaching at Michigan,' " Orr said prior to the game. "When I was up there, I'd say, 'They're not so good.' Now, I've completely changed my mind." Orr's Michigan success in Iowa City's Fieldhouse (8-3), overall against the Hawks (16-5) and all-time against coach Lute Olson (10-2) were mentioned frequently during the pregame coverage that week. Johnny had joked on the summer banquet tour it was like a "picnic" going to Iowa City to play, but he dreaded having to take this inexperienced team to play the solid Hawks. An Iowa fan spread out a picnic blanket in front of the Cyclone bench moments before Iowa State returned from the locker room, giving the crowd at the old Fieldhouse a laugh and even drawing a smile from Johnny when he saw it.

Orr later explained the source of the "picnic" comments: "I was in here with one of my Michigan teams one afternoon several years ago warming up before our game that night, and the Fieldhouse was full of people playing badminton, volleyball, running all over the place. My kids were down at one end of the floor shooting, and all of the sudden this lady walks out on the floor, spreads a blanket and sets up a picnic. I didn't see her right away, but my assistant coach (Bill Frieder) did and he told me about it. I told him to ask her to move, he told our manager and the manager went over and tried. He came back and said she didn't speak very good English and either didn't understand or didn't agree to move. I told Frieder to go down and tell her, and he came back with the same answer. So I walked over there and said, 'Lady, I'm going to be nice to you about this. We'd like you to move. Pick up your blanket and your picnic things and leave the floor. Otherwise, I'm going to have my players run over your ass.' She seemed to understand that, because she picked up and left. And that's how this picnic business got started."

Iowa jumped to a 16-point halftime lead en route to an 85-59 decision, aided by a 25-11 edge in free-throw scoring and a 61-34 rebounding advantage. Lute said later, "If we had left our regulars in, we might have won by 50." Johnny knew days like this were part of the growing pains his program would endure, and it would make it sweeter when he would win three straight over the Hawks later in the decade.

Winning streak

At 2-4, the Cyclones would uncork a five-game winning streak prior to conference play. They edged Coach Gene Bartow's 7-2 Alabama-Birmingham team, 71-70, at Hilton, despite some shaky free-throw shooting down the stretch. Iowa State missed the front end of five one-and-ones and both ends of a two-shot foul, yet still escaped with a win. Johnny was irked at the blown chances but later said, "I really shouldn't criticize this team. I try not to get mad at them and keep telling myself it takes time. But I'm impatient." Johnny's irritation was mild compared to Bartow's—the Alabama-Birmingham coach chased the officials off the floor at the conclusion.

Trip from hell

The Cyclones broke for Christmas with their families, then headed east to New Haven, Conn., for the Elm City Classic. This four-team tournament was a good fit for a young team like Iowa State's, thanks to beatable opponents Fairfield and East Carolina. However, the excursion turned into a nightmare for the Cyclones. First, Falenschek was felled by the flu on the eve of the trip, and Johnny himself became ill the same day. Both eventually made it to Connecticut, but the misadventures were just starting. A power failure at the 11,000-seat New Haven Coliseum melted the ice rink and forced tournament officials to move the games 25 miles away to the 3,000-seat Fairfield gymnasium. When Orr took his team to Fairfield to practice, there was no one to greet them and only a janitor on hand to open the building. "We had to give the janitor a tip to let us in," Johnny said later.

"When I saw the gym, I told (assistant athletic director) Dave Cox, 'Tell Lou McCullough I want to renegotiate.' " The trip also would include a memorable bus ride: "This bus driver was the king of the CBs, that's all he did," Orr explained. "It was a two-minute bus ride (to the restaurant), and 40 minutes later we got there. We tried to get under three bridges but couldn't fit, and had to back up three times." To top it off, Iowa State's hotel in Fairfield recently had been damaged by fire. "The top four floors were condemned," Orr said. His team eventually moved to a hotel in Bridgeport.

The Cyclones beat East Carolina in the first game, 80-73, but the day was marred by the death of Lefty Moore's mother, Minnie Moore, 52, who was stricken by a heart attack at home in Detroit. Lefty would play both the East Carolina and Fairfield games with a combined 30 points, including 12-of-12 free throws, before returning home for the funeral. His scoring and poise helped the Cyclones shade Fairfield for the title, 47-46. Robert Estes sank a short jump shot with 12 seconds left for the winning margin. Ron Harris scored 19 against East Carolina but was scoreless against Fairfield. Orr knew that such inconsistency was typical for a freshman in major-college basketball.

The Cyclones returned home and escaped an upset bid by Wisconsin-Parkside, a National Association of Intercollegiate Athletes (NAIA) team. The Cyclones trailed 49-46 with 8:08 left but rallied for a 67-58 victory. Jon Ness, a senior guard and crowd favorite from nearby Story City, canned three long baskets to spark the comeback. (Ness clearly was ahead of his time: he'd have been a terrific three-point scorer had the bonus shot been part of the college game back in 1977–81.) Ness would get more minutes as the season progressed, and his attitude in accepting his reserve role is one example of why Johnny is so fond of this first team. Iowa State closed its non-conference season with a 94-72 win over Western Illinois, fueled by Robert Estes's 27 points.

Big Eight action

Johnny's first Big Eight game was in Lawrence, Kansas, a place that has haunted him during his Iowa State career. (The Cyclones were 1-11 at Kansas University's Allen Fieldhouse under Orr through 1992, including four straight blowouts during 1989–92.) In the first trip, which produced a frustrating 70-58 defeat, the Cyclones pulled within five points with less than three minutes left in the game. They appeared to cut it to three, but a basket by Estes was negated by a goaltending call. The Darnell Valentine–led Jayhawks, who entered with a 10-2 non-conference record, outscored the Cyclones in free throws, 20-4, continuing another trend of Johnny's debut season.

Next up in the three-game road trip were weekend games at conference favorite Missouri and nonleague foe St. Louis University. "Whoever made this schedule sure tried to get rid of Lynn Nance," Orr joked. Johnny was dealt a giant setback when Falenschek hurt his foot at practice the day before the Mizzou game. It later was diagnosed as a stress fracture that would sideline him for the next 10 games. The 6-foot-11-inch center was coming off a career-best 15-point, 9-rebound outing, and in his absence at Columbia, the Cyclones lost 92-69. Tiger Steve Stipanovich had as many rebounds (15) as Orr's entire starting five. The trek to St. Louis brought more frustration as the 6-7 Billikens, coming off an upset of Memphis State, rallied for a 61-59 victory on a basket with :06 remaining. The Cyclones, outscored at the line 15-7, received 17 points and 15 rebounds from Estes. Adding to Orr's woes at St. Louis was a knee injury incurred by Kunnert, Falenschek's replacement. Kunnert had 14 points and 8 rebounds before going down.

Now 7-7 overall and 0-2 in the conference, the Cyclones returned home to play Oklahoma and its first-year coach Billy Tubbs. The Sooners were struggling with a 5-9 record. True to the bizarre developments of the season, Iowa State jumped to a 20-0 lead en route to an 88-67 victory. The game marked the first start for freshman Terrence Allen, a guy who would make his mark by the time he left Iowa State.

At 8-7, Orr probably should have canceled the rest of the season at this point. Do you remember March 1980 when the newly hired coach proclaimed he felt 20 years younger in coming to Iowa State? He appeared to gain back all 20 years during the next five weeks of 1981, a stretch that produced a 10-game losing streak. It started with a respectable six-point loss in Stillwater to Big Eight co-leader Oklahoma State. The Cowboys improved to 14-3 overall and 4-0 in the Big Eight by outscoring the Cyclones at the line, 21-7.

The Cyclones dropped below .500 for good in a Hilton loss to Nebraska, 61-56. If Johnny hadn't second-guessed himself on leaving Michigan before now, he might have wondered on this night. The tip-off was delayed for 25 minutes when a search was on for Iowa State's white uniforms. Through a mix-up, the Cyclones came dressed in red uniforms, which matched Nebraska's red and created plenty of confusion for the officials. Iowa State's Campus Security was called in to dispatch a vehicle across campus to Beyer Hall in search of the white uniforms, but they still weren't found. Finally some three-year-old white jerseys were uncovered. The Cyclone gang looked a bit like basketball Orr-phans on this night, decked out in red shorts and aged jerseys. "I've never heard of anything like it in my life," Johnny said following the game. "They couldn't find our white ones any-where."

As the beat went on and the losing streak rolled along like an odometer, Johnny turned philosophical. He told Buck Turnbull of the *Des Moines Register:* "Some years ago, Dean Smith was so down that he turned in his resignation at North Carolina, but the president wouldn't accept it, and now he's one of the top coaches in the country. Heck, it took Johnny Wooden 10 years at UCLA before he ever got into the NCAA tournament . . . I have to think about things like that to keep my spirits up."

Johnny courts exposure

Then came the Missouri contest and Johnny's famed dash onto the court during the game to protest what he perceived as a flagrant foul by Mizzou's Stipanovich. Johnny got plenty of na-tional exposure in the next day's newspapers as the Associated Press photo of Orr waving his arms on the court made papers from coast to coast. (In-state television viewers didn't see the game, however, because WHO-TV in Des Moines had replaced the Iowa State–Missouri Big Eight Game of the Week with the Iowa-Illinois game.) Johnny was hit with two technical fouls for the Missouri march and his ensuing tirade. Orr said Stipanovich not only slammed the ball on the face of 5-foot-9-inch Lefty Moore twice during the game, but also was swearing at the officials. "I couldn't take it anymore," Orr said. "I couldn't sit there and take it. I'm not going to sit by and watch one of my players get hit in the face with the ball. If anyone thinks that, they're crazy. I won't stand for it . . . I have no use for those two referees at all. They can say what they want to say in that Big Eight office. They can reprimand me and do whatever they want to do. But if they think I'm going to sit by and watch that, they're crazy." Missouri coach Norm Stewart wisecracked, "I thought if John had cut left and gone in, he was open from the free-throw line. He certainly got everyone's attention."

Ron Harris recalled that Orr apologized to his team after the game for going onto the court. "He told us he doesn't want us to ever to do anything like that," he said.

However confusing or amusing Johnny's charge onto the court was, in retrospect it accomplished two things: it further dispelled the notion that Orr was in Ames for the money and merely coasting into retirement; and it sent notice to the players and fans that he hated losing and was hungry to quickly build a winner. Few coaches at Iowa State could have displayed such behavior without drawing a reprimand, but Orr escaped without any school action. Johnny already had people in his corner, and that loyalty and support in turn motivated him even more to bring winning basketball to Iowa State.

Ten years later, Orr's Missouri march has been elevated to inclusion in the entertainment archives, yet he says it wasn't a premeditated move, like a baseball manager kicking dirt on an umpire as a motivational ploy. Johnny also says he's not sorry he did it. "Hell, no, I don't regret it," Orr says. "I was so mad, I can't believe those guys (officials) didn't see that. I was so mad I didn't even realize what I was doing, but I'm not sorry."

At Norman, Okla., the next week, before a crowd of only 2,038, the Sooners and the Cyclones played for last place. After Oklahoma won 78-66, Coach Billy Tubbs joked about the officiating: "I don't understand some of those calls. Usually they try to stick it to me or Johnny, so tonight they had a hard time figuring what to do."

The low point of the losing streak for Orr came against Oklahoma State. By now, the Cyclones had eight consecutive losses and had bottomed out in last place, somewhere Johnny had never been as a player or a coach. Cox, the administrator who oversaw men's basketball operations, remembers going back to check on Orr before tip-off, as the Cyclone pep band was poised to play the familiar "Here's Johnny" welcome. Cox found the coach slumped against a wall, wearing a pained look. "Oh, Coxie, they're going to play that song," Johnny said. "You don't know how hard it is to go out there to that song when you're losing." Cox told Orr, "But John, they love you." Orr found the strength to make the grand entrance, even though Iowa State would lose again.

The next game at Hilton was the regular-season finale, and the losing streak finally ended with a 67-56 win over Colorado. Ironically, the game was played during winter quarter break, so the Iowa State student pep band was absent. Filling in was the West Marshall High School band, which didn't know the Carson theme song, to Johnny's delight. Orr entered the Hilton floor to the theme from "Hogan's Heroes," perhaps a fitting way to remember the strange season that was 1980–81.

There were positive signs in that 9-18 season finish: Robert Estes was named second-team All–Big Eight after leading the team in scoring at 15 ppg; Ron Harris made the Big Eight's All-

Freshmen team and gained valuable experience; and the team rarely folded, as just four of the 18 losses came by more than 14 points. The best development of 1981 came in recruiting a few weeks after the season when Orr signed Michigan all-stater Barry Stevens from Flint Northwestern, a 27.3 ppg scorer. Orr also brought in some steady players in year two who would help the Cyclones get over and stay over the .500 mark, including Fort Dodge's Tom Peterson and Chicagoan Raynal Harris.

• The Building Years, 1981–1985

Orr's growing pains hung over to year two, though, as he weathered a 10-17 record. A 2-7 start and an eventual 1-11 road record hurt the Cyclones, but there was optimism after the Cyclones finished the season with three straight Big Eight victories. Included in that final run was Johnny's only victory in Lawrence, and a respectable four-point defeat to Oklahoma in Norman in the quarterfinals of the Big Eight tournament. Stevens averaged 13 ppg, and like Ron Harris the previous year, was another sign that Orr would attract quality players in time.

The 1982 recruiting efforts of assistant Gary Cook netted a solid group from Chicago. Sam Hill, David Moss, Ron Virgil and Paul Beene all signed that spring from the Windy City. Although Hill would sit out the 1982–83 year while establishing academic eligibility, another Chicago kid, Jeff Hornacek, quietly stepped into the picture during that third season. A walk-on who enrolled for the spring semester of 1982, the slender Hornacek showed promise during practice while sitting out as a redshirt. (He later would become a key player in Johnny's rise to national acclaim with the Cyclones and since has risen to all-star status in the NBA.)

The 1982–83 season also marked the arrival of Jim Hallihan as an assistant coach, replacing Harrison, who left to take a head coaching position at East Carolina. Hallihan, like Orr, was a native of southern Illinois. He was head coach the previous three seasons at East Tennessee State, and that bench and practice-planning experience would play an important role in Iowa State's success the rest of the 1980s. The following year, Orr hired another former head coach, Steve Antrim, to join his coaching staff. Antrim stayed four seasons but left in 1987 to became head coach at Wisconsin-Milwaukee.

The first huge victory of the Orr era came early in the third season. A tall and talented Minnesota team led by future NBA standouts Kevin McHale and Randy Breuer came into Hilton and lost to a scrappy Cyclone team in overtime, 80-78. Tom Peterson came off the bench to hit two free throws with five seconds left to force the extra session. The enthusiasm surrounding Cyclone hoops mushroomed as Iowa State started 5-0, but the team cooled off to finish 8-5 in non-conference play, falling victim to its lack of height.

The Cyclones won five out of seven games during an early stretch of conference play, though, to start out 5-4 in the Big Eight, their first time over the .500 mark in Big Eight play in Orr's three seasons. The pivotal game in that stretch was a 73-72 overtime win at Hilton against top ten–ranked Missouri, won on Stevens's last-second shot and witnessed by a regional TV audience. At 13-9, a winning season and NIT bid seemed possible, but Orr's gang of overachievers wore out down the stretch. They lost their final six games to close with a 13-15 record.

The 1983–84 team finally took the magic trampoline ride to a winning record. Orr's fourth Cyclone team finished 16-13 and garnered an NIT bid, the school's first postseason basketball tournament berth in 40 years. The Cyclones bolted to an 11-3 start, including a 4-0 record in overtime games. Undoubtedly the biggest victory was the 76-72 double-overtime defeat of Iowa in Hilton, which was the first of three straight wins over the Hawkeyes during the mid-1980s. The Cyclones also beat Oklahoma and Kansas at Hilton that year and earned their first-ever home game in the Big Eight tournament with a top-four finish. The Cyclones, relying on quickness to overcome height disadvantages, again tired out down the stretch and lost six of their last nine regular-season games. They did receive an NIT bid and were awarded a home game based on their tremendous fan support, but they lost a 20-point decision to a taller and more physical Marquette team.

Orr said goodbye to Ron Harris and Terrence Allen but for the next season welcomed another impact player in Michigan all-stater Jeff Grayer, who hailed from the same Flint, Mich., high school as Stevens. Orr also brought in guard Gary Thompkins from Jackson, Mich. Those recruits let the Cyclones take another large step toward national respect. Grayer didn't disappoint, showing signs from game one in 1984–85 that he would become the school's most complete player ever in scoring, rebounding and defense. The future All-American, Olympian and NBA player complemented the explosive Stevens and new playmaking whiz Hornacek. Johnny's fifth Cyclone team added a few more firsts in a 21-13 season. It started 5-0, including a 54-50 victory over Iowa in the new Carver-Hawkeye Arena. That marked the first Cyclone basketball victory in Iowa City since 1921. Iowa State also escaped with a one-point victory over Drake, and played Indiana to a 69-67 loss at home, adding to the promise of exciting basketball at Hilton. The Cyclones later would surprise Missouri in Columbia, and upset Kansas and heralded frosh Danny Manning twice: in Hilton, 72-70, and in the Big Eight tournament semifinals in Kansas City, 75-59. The latter win gave Iowa State a school-record 21 victories and gave Orr's team its best dose of national visibility. The Cyclones then took nationally ranked Oklahoma and Wayman Tisdale down to the final seconds in the Big Eight tournament finals before losing, 73-71, to earn more respect and gain an NCAA tournament berth.

The Cyclones had the misfortune in their first-round tourney draw to face an athletic Ohio State team, whose quick guards presented matchup problems and neutralized Iowa State's strength. The Buckeyes of Coach Eldon Miller made the Cyclones' first NCAA tournament appearance in 41 years a brief one with a 75-64 victory in Tulsa.

Barry Stevens, Tom Peterson and Ray Harris completed their eligibility, and the Cyclones had another key defection after the season on the recruiting trail. Flint Northwestern's Glen Rice, a national blue chipper who was on the verge of signing with the Cyclones in November, held off a decision until spring, then signed with Michigan, passing up a chance to play with former prep teammate Grayer. Earlier, Illinois had signed Chicagoan Lowell Hamilton, another prominent player who strongly considered the Cyclones. But Iowa State would add two more Illinois natives in 1985, Elmer Robinson and University of Illinois transfer Tom Schafer, to bolster its depth and continue the program's rise. Despite the inability to sign future NBA star Rice, Johnny rolled into the 1985–86 season brimming with hope, and he and thousands of Cyclone fans wouldn't be disappointed.

"That '86 team was a good team. We had some dynamic players. Of course (Jeff) Hornacek and (Jeff) Grayer have gone on to become great players. And we had guys like (David) Moss, Sammy Hill, Elmer (Robinson), Gary Thompkins, (Tom) Schafer. And Ron Virgil—he was out of sight. What a great year he had. For his size, I can't even believe he played for us. I wish we could find another one like him."

"What was good about that team is that physically we didn't look particularly good, with small guys like Virgil. We had no big guys, so we knew we had to play like hell. Mentally, that really helped us. That team really jelled together. We could bring Elmer or David Moss off the bench, and they'd be tremendous."

"The fans were so loyal, too. We were walking off the court at halftime of the Miami game in the NCAA tournament, and this guy says, 'I know we're not playing well, I know it doesn't look good, but Johnny, we're not worried, because we have you. You're our savior.' I felt like looking at him and telling him, 'You're full of it. If they don't play well, there's nothing I can do, man.' "

• Dream Season

Johnny's sixth season at Michigan was his breakthrough year there, with a Big Ten title, a 22-5 record and advancement to the National Collegiate Athletic Association (NCAA) tournament quarterfinals. The 1985–86 season at Iowa State was Orr's sixth season in Ames, and another storybook year was realized. The Cyclones gained national respect and were a treat to follow. Some highlights:

- A school-record 22 victories and a berth in the final 16 of the NCAA tournament, highlighted by an upset of No. 5 Michigan, Johnny's former school.
- A frenzied fan atmosphere at Hilton Coliseum, where the vocal spectators spurred the Cyclones to an unprecedented 13-0 home record. The attendance average of 14,024 also set a school record, up from the previous high average of 13,259 in the 1984–85 season.
- A rising pool of talent in the Big Eight, with an unprecedented five teams (Oklahoma, Missouri, Kansas, Iowa State and Nebraska) earning NCAA bids, and one, Kansas, reaching the Final Four. Only three Big Eight teams reached the Final Four

from 1960 through 1985, but the 1986 Kansas team was the first of four Big Eight teams to make the national semifinals in a six-year span from 1986 through 1991.

- The stiffest non-conference schedule in school history with NCAA qualifiers Indiana, Iowa, Illinois and Michigan State, and NCAA tournament games against Miami of Ohio, Michigan and North Carolina State. All seven averaged 20-plus wins.

- Opposing rosters that featured a star parade of individuals, including more than two dozen future National Basketball Association (NBA) players, including four of the 10 players selected to the consensus All-American teams: Indiana's Steve Alford, KU's Danny Manning, Miami's Ron Harper and Michigan State's Scott Skiles.

- A 13-point victory over Iowa, the third straight triumph over the solid Hawkeyes.

- A berth in the Big Eight tournament finals for the second straight year, and a two-point championship game loss to eventual Final Four team Kansas.

- Exciting games in general, with 12 of the 23 games decided by four or fewer points.

- A fast-starting team, which finished 20-0 in games it led at halftime.

- A slump-resistent bunch that on 9 of 10 occasions immediately rebounded from losses with a victory.

• Recruiting

Ironically, the greatest season in Iowa State basketball had a sour start during the previous spring's recruiting chase. Johnny's task in 1985–86 and beyond would have been different if he had won the recruiting battle for Glen Rice, who would carry Michigan to the national title in 1989 and go on to NBA success with the Miami Heat. There was a time when Johnny and the Cyclones were sitting pretty in the pursuit of Rice, who played at the same high school as Barry Stevens, Jeff Grayer and NBA player Trent Tucker. Rice was close to signing with the Cyclones during the November recruiting period. But Flint Northwestern coach Grover Kirkland, an influential advisor, steered Rice away from an early signing, primarily so complacency wouldn't set in on his star senior's game. Rice was anything but complacent that winter. He played so well as a senior that Johnny's former assistant, Michigan's Bill Frieder, who didn't rate Rice as a blue-chip prospect prior to his final year, started recruiting the Flint player heavily. The home-state push nosed out the Cyclones, and Rice eventually signed with the Wolverines in April.

Johnny didn't dwell on losing Rice. He stayed positive as he approached 1985–86, and focused on his main task of replacing Barry Stevens, who had compiled 2,190 points in the previous four seasons and was the chief scoring weapon. Grayer, who as a freshman had averaged 12.2 ppg and 6.5 rpg and made the Big Eight's All-Defensive team, would absorb most of Stevens's 21.7 ppg average. Although only a sophomore and standing just 6-foot-5-inches, Grayer would play this season like a miniature version of NBA all-star power forward Karl Malone. Grayer averaged 20.7 ppg and 6.3 rpg and consistently displayed the unselfish skills that earned him a reputation as the greatest all-around player in Iowa State history.

Jeff Hornacek

The other superstar of this season was senior Jeff Hornacek. It's easy to forget Hornacek's climb from complete obscurity upon arrival at Iowa State, given his later NBA success and his million-dollar annual income with the Phoenix Suns and the Philadelphia 76ers. At some point, people even started pronouncing his name correctly ("that's *Horn-a-SEK,* not *CHEK*"). He came to Ames without a scholarship in January 1983. He arrived with the body of a cross-country runner and the patience of a cross-country trucker, fresh off a fall semester job driving a fork-lift at a paper-cup company. He evolved into a wizard of a play-maker and outside shooter by the time he finished in Ames in 1986. He became Iowa State's all-time leader in assists with 665 and surpassed Kansas' Darnell Valentine's Big Eight career record in the process. (The record since has been broken by Nebraska's Brian Carr.) Hornacek also set the Cyclone career record for steals with 209. Particularly impressive was how Hornacek never changed his personality when he attained his fame on campus. He still was a regular guy who wheeled around Ames in a 1974 Ford Grenada.

Hornacek's father, John, coached NBA star Isiah Thomas's freshman team at Westchester St. Joseph's High near Chicago, and Isiah often was a shootaround partner for Jeff as a teenager. Orr's recruiting coordinator, assistant coach Gary Cook, knew the elder Hornacek, and that connection helped Iowa State avoid the kind of miscalculation that virtually every other midwestern college made. Hornacek averaged 19 ppg as a senior shooting guard at Lyons Township High in LaGrange and was named

Player of the Year in his conference, but his team didn't run an up-tempo offense. Lyons' deliberate offensive style didn't showcase Hornacek at his best. Illinois State, where John Hornacek played basketball decades earlier, was interested in Jeff as a baseball shortstop but didn't think he was prime-time basketball material. Basketball coaches from Western Michigan and Wisconsin-Green Bay looked but didn't offer a scholarship. Tex Winter, who at the time was coaching at Long Beach State, recalled that he inquired about Hornacek. "I had some interest, but every Big Ten coach I talked to told me he couldn't play," Winter said.

Hornacek sat out the fall semester of his freshman year and took a factory job while trying to sort out his options. He wanted to play at prestigious Cornell University, but there was doubt whether he'd be admitted under the Ivy League school's strict academic standards. "Jeff was convinced he could play major-college basketball, he just wanted someone to give him a chance. And Coach Orr was that person," said John Hornacek. So Jeff Hornacek decided to quit waiting on Cornell and give Iowa State a try. On a miserable January day, his dad drove him to Ames to enroll for the spring semester. "It was a Sunday morning, 27 below zero, and blowing snow so bad you couldn't see," said the elder Hornacek. "They closed most of the highways, and we were the only ones on the road. But Gary (Cook) had said we had to get there to get registered for school the next day, so we kept driving. It took us about 7½ hours to get there."

Hornacek enrolled and joined the team as an invited walk-on. He practiced with the team but didn't suit up for the final seven weeks of the 1981–82 season to retain four years of eligibility. Hornacek says Johnny treated him as well as any scholarship player from day one, even though this was a raw freshman on first sight. Iowa State trainer Frank Randall recalls that Hornacek hardly looked like a future NBA standout when he arrived. "I saw this skinny, little kid and thought, 'What's Cook bringing this guy in for?' " said Randall, who quickly became a Hornacek admirer. "The coaches had guys ahead of him (on the depth chart) the first couple of years, but every year as soon as they started playing, he was in there."

In 1985–86, Grayer and Hornacek formed the nucleus of Iowa State's most athletic team ever. Guard Gary Thompkins added quickness, outside shooting and solid defense on the perimeter; junior center Sam Hill could rebound, shoot from the outside and run the break better than most centers; small 6-foot-4-inch forward Ron Virgil could shoot well and was a clutch player. This also was the Cyclones' deepest team, with muscular

6-foot-5-inch freshman Elmer Robinson able to score, run and rebound; 6-foot-8-inch senior center David Moss a capable sub for Hill; 6-foot-7-inch midseason transfer Tom Schafer providing scoring and rebounding help on the front line; and 6-foot-8-inch sophomore Lafester Rhodes also having scoring prowess.

• Preseason Predictions

The Cyclones faced an uphill run in the search of the school's first Big Eight basketball title, though. There was a potent team brewing in Lawrence, where Kansas coach Larry Brown returned all five starters from his 28-6 team of 1984–85. As it turned out, Danny Manning and teammates surpassed the lofty expectations that winter and would become one of the great teams in Big Eight history. On the bright side, Oklahoma wouldn't have All-American Wayman Tisdale looting the lanes for the first time in three years. The Sooners were 84-20 with Wayman in uniform and won two Big Eight titles, so few tears were shed in Big Eight country when Tisdale passed up his final year for the NBA.

At the 1985 Big Eight preseason media day, the conference's best depth in memory was on display, and Johnny and his players were upbeat about their team's chances. "This is the best chance since I've been here to make a run at the title," Orr said. Hornacek added, "We'd like to be known as one of the best teams in the league, but if they want to rank us low, we'll surprise them."

Johnny accurately predicted a big year for Hornacek, who in the previous season shot 84 percent from the line, averaged 12 ppg and established himself as a savvy playmaker. "He's one of the smartest players I've ever had," Johnny said. "He's the most valuable player to a team I've ever had. I think (Jeff's) one of the best players, not only in our league, but in the country." Hornacek responded, "It feels good to know he's behind me. But that's Coach Orr: he's behind all of his players. It's nice when you have the confidence of the coach. It gives you confidence in your abilities."

Orr told the Big Eight reporters that a rugged schedule would make it difficult to match the 21-13 record of 1984–85, but he said the 1985–86 Cyclones actually would be better than the previous team. "If we would have known the NCAA tournament was going to expand to 64 teams (in 1985), we wouldn't be playing all those teams," Johnny said. "It's dumb on my part. Now the NCAA sees that you lost, and they don't think you're any good.

But go out and beat those weak teams that are dogs, and they say, 'Whoooee, they must be good.' But we're capable of competing with almost anyone in the country, and that's exciting. This team will be fun to watch." The team even was fun to watch in the preseason: an exhibition game at West Des Moines Dowling High ended prematurely when Moss shattered a backboard with a slam dunk.

• The Season Opens

The Cyclones remained hungry when they opened the regular season a couple of weeks later at Hilton. Before 14,233 fans, Iowa State demolished South Dakota State, holding the Jackrabbits under 40 points with an 83-39 triumph. The 39 points were the fewest allowed by an Iowa State team in 19 seasons and would be the fewest ever allowed by an Orr-coached Cyclone team (at the time this book was published, at least). To illustrate how far Johnny had taken this program by this sixth season, this game wouldn't have been a blowout for Iowa State during the 1970s or early 1980s. South Dakota State, while no Indiana, had two starters back from a 26-7 team that was the 1985 NCAA Division II national runner-up. Hornacek, who was instructed by the coaches to take more outside shots this season, scored the team's first eight points and closed with 24, including a 9-for-14 day in field-goal shooting.

Next came a trip to Illinois State to play a team that reached the NCAA tournament the previous three seasons, including a 22-8 record in 1984–85. Johnny's 1984–85 team had posted an improved 4-5 record on the road, compared to Iowa State's combined 6-41 away record from 1980 through 1984, and Orr stressed that it was imperative to show even further gains on the road. The Cyclones responded in their first road test with a 55-52 victory in Normal, Ill., as Hornacek converted a three-point play with 10 seconds left to give the Cyclones a 2-0 record. "Boy, he made a fantastic basket," Orr said following the game. "It was unreal, wasn't it?" The Cyclones committed only nine turnovers.

However, the exciting victory was overshadowed by a tragedy on the eve of the game that numbed the entire Iowa State community. An Iowa State University plane returning from the NCAA Cross Country Championships in Wisconsin crashed in a Des Moines neighborhood on a foggy Monday night just three days before Thanksgiving. Seven people perished in the flaming wreckage: Iowa State women's cross-country runners Sheryl

Maahs, Julie Rose and Sue Baxter, trainer Stephanie Streit, head women's CC coach Ron Renko, assistant track coach Pat Moynihan and pilot Burt Watkins. Adding to Johnny's own heartache was the knowledge that his team had been scheduled to travel in that ill-fated university plane for its trip to Normal. When the planes were delayed in the ice and fog, Orr's team switched plans and boarded a bus, and didn't learn about the plane crash until later Monday night while on the road to Illinois. "It's a very empty feeling," Johnny said following the Illinois State game. "I feel so bad about it. I feel terrible. It really hit me today. I must have flown 40–50 times in those planes." The accident prompted the Cyclone team to wear a black band on the shoulder strap of their jerseys the remainder of the season in memory of the crash victims. Over the next couple of months, the success and effort of Johnny's team helped provide moments of joy to a campus and a community trying to deal with the tragedy and get on with life.

San Francisco State was up next following a brief Thanksgiving break, and the Cyclones made it 3-0 behind Grayer's 24 points in 29 minutes of play, 90-53. Gary Thompkins added 16 points. The Division II Gators had played Minnesota Friday night in Minneapolis, arrived in Ames at 3:30 a.m. following the game and met the Cyclones less than 10 hours later at 1 p.m.

Northern Iowa was next at Hilton, and another strong defensive effort aided the Cyclones' 83-60 triumph. Thompkins, who had a season-high 10 assists, held UNI standout Randy Kraayenbrink to nine points, 16 under his early-season average. Panther coach Jim Berry sang a familiar song in the postgame remarks at Hilton. "They're easily the quickest team we'll face," Berry said. "It's like they have bullwhips in their hands and they're whipping us all the time." The win was the seventh in a row for Orr's teams against in-state foes.

The 4-0 Cyclones next headed south to Veterans Auditorium to play Drake, a trip that had produced a 1-6 record in Iowa State's previous seven Des Moines excursions. The beat went on, too, as Johnny's winning streak against in-state foes was snapped in a 77-69 defeat. This game pointed out one Iowa State vulnerability that would haunt it throughout the season—a height disadvantage which invariably led to foul trouble. (In fact, this 1985–86 team would set a school season record with 678 fouls.) Grayer picked up three fouls during the first 10 minutes, and three Cyclones eventually fouled out. "I think we got screwed on a couple of calls tonight, but that's going to happen to you on the road," said Iowa State's Sam Hill, who fouled out. It was one of 28 times during Hill's career he'd make an early exit via fouls. Coupled with a Drake win over Iowa State that school year in football, this marked Drake's first sweep of Iowa State in football and basketball in 35 years. It marked the last sweep, too, because Drake dropped down to Division III status in football shortly thereafter.

Fun at home

The Cyclones had little time to dwell on the loss. Three nights later they were back in Hilton, and who better to help erase the memories of a rare in-state stumble than the invading Iowa Hawkeyes, a team that boasted future NBA players Roy Marble, B. J. Armstrong, Brad Lohaus and Ed Horton. Although the Hawks raced to an 8-0 lead to temporarily defy the Hilton magic, Iowa State answered with a 20-3 surge en route to a 74-61 victory. The 61 points by Iowa followed its 50 against the Cyclones the previous year, and those were Iowa's lowest outputs against the Cyclones since resuming the annual series in 1971. Grayer scored 22 points and Thompkins had 14 as Hilton was at its rockin' best. "That's the sixth man," said Iowa State's Ron Virgil of the home crowd. "It makes you jump higher, run faster, play harder, everything." The Hawks shot 53 percent from the field but self-destructed with 26 turnovers against the Cyclone pressure. Iowa coach George Raveling said, "Iowa State is an opportunistic team. When you make mistakes, they make you pay for them." Johnny added, "I said it was going to be a great game, and it was a great game. We showed more poise tonight."

The Hilton edge resurfaced four days later against unbeaten Michigan State, a Scott Skiles–led team that eventually would win 20-plus games and join the Cyclones in the NCAA Sweet Sixteen. Johnny's friend and rival, Jud Heathcote, the Spartans' head coach, had scouted the Iowa State–Iowa game in person and declared, "This is our first game on the road, and Iowa State looks almost unbeatable in here. Their crowd really gets into it." Johnny was concerned that Michigan State would neutralize the Cyclones' quickness. "Michigan State is like us. They're not a team we like to play. I don't think we can press them. They're too quick." Virgil hit 18 points in the first half, and Iowa State won a beauty in overtime, 82-80. Elmer Robinson's lay-in—his only basket of the game—with two seconds left in overtime was the deciding play. The Cyclones had only nine turnovers to offset the Spartans' 25-3 advantage in bench scoring. "Man, that was exciting," Johnny said. "We were lucky. Both teams were terrific."

Two days later, Iowa State made it 6-0 at Hilton and 7-1 overall with a 95-58 victory over South Dakota. Not only did Iowa

State have bragging rights in Iowa, it now claimed the mythical state championship of the Dakotas. Grayer scored 23 points, Hornacek had 14 points and 10 assists, Hill had 10 rebounds, and Rhodes came off the bench to score 14.

Johnny joked that his team is "leading the Big Ten Conference" following wins over Iowa and Michigan State. That boast was dashed the next weekend after an 86-65 loss to No. 17 Indiana in Bloomington, the Saturday after final-exam week. The Cyclones fell behind 19-4 and never could recover, despite Grayer's career-high 30 points. Hornacek became the 12th Cyclone to surpass 1,000 career points and also became the school's career leader in steals.

On the road

Iowa State returned after Christmas and flew to Nashville, the city where five years earlier Johnny made his Cyclone coaching debut. The Cyclones ruled the Music City Invitational with impressive wins over Rice, 94-60, and host Vanderbilt, 80-79. Orr's team held Rice to 19 first-half points and rode Grayer's 20 points and Hill's 10 points and 12 rebounds. The Cyclones improved to 9-2 the next night by stopping Vandy on its home court. Grayer, who earned MVP honors of the tourney, netted a career-high 33 points, and Hornacek chipped in 22 points and 7 assists.

Johnny's team left Nashville on a roll and hoped to use an upcoming swing to Chicago and Michigan to get some valuable exposure in prime recruiting territory. The Cyclones failed to make a giant splash in either outing and came home with their lone two-game losing streak of the season. The Cyclones played in Chicago against NCAA tournament–bound Illinois and lost a 64-62 decision. They followed that up four days later with a 77-67 loss at Detroit, despite Grayer's 25 points. The Cyclones cut a 13-point halftime deficit to one point during the final half but couldn't get over the hump against the Titans.

Next, Iowa State played its first game in Hilton in three weeks, an exhibition encounter against outmanned Canadian foe Windsor University. Grayer's 25 points led six Cyclones in double figures in the 114-61 romp. This was one of nine times in 14 pre–Big Eight games that Iowa State would allow less than 65 points. The Windsor victory didn't count on the record, so the Cyclones closed the non-conference portion of their schedule at 9-4.

• Big Eight Season

Johnny was happy to be at Hilton to open the Big Eight season, especially since potent Missouri was the foe. Another of Norm Stewart's tall and talented teams invaded Ames, but the story of the game would be Iowa State's depth. Fueled by an 18-0 edge in bench scoring, the Cyclones rolled to a 92-84 victory over the Tigers. Grayer's 24 points led six Iowa State players scoring in double figures, and Hornacek contributed 12 assists. Missouri lost despite posting a Hilton record .674 shooting percentage from the field. The 92 Iowa State points—achieved prior to the NCAA's implementation of the three-point field goal—was the most ever by an Orr-coached Cyclone team against a conference foe.

Next, Iowa State climbed to 11-4 overall and 2-0 in the conference with a 77-73 road win against Kansas State. It was Johnny's first win at Ahearn Fieldhouse and just the second victory there by a Cyclone team in 20 years. Iowa State zipped to a 47-32 halftime lead behind Hornacek's 17 first-half points and held off a late Kansas State charge fueled by Norris Coleman's 32 points.

Not only had the Cyclones never won the Big Eight title in modern times, they hadn't started 4-0 against league competition since 1944. Orr's team couldn't pull it off this season, either. An Iowa State road trip to Norman, Okla., saw the Oklahoma Sooners extend their home-floor win streak to 43 as they outmuscled the Cyclones, 95-83. Tisdale was gone to the NBA, but Darryl "Choo" Kennedy's 30 points powered the Sooners and offset Grayer's 29 points. "We never could shake them," OU coach Billy Tubbs said.

A return home was the right tonic for the Cyclones, and a new color scoreboard was unveiled in the arena during the clash with Colorado. The Cyclones lit up both the scoreboard and the Buffaloes, 90-62, and their 28-point winning margin was the school's largest in Big Eight play in 27 years. Grayer's 23 points, Hornacek's 18 points and the team's 65 percent field-goal shooting were keys. Iowa State had just 12 turnovers and raced to a 10-0 lead to set the tone. Johnny still got a good workout, though, as he was hit with a pair of technical fouls and chased official Woody Mayfield off the floor. When asked to rate the officials on a scale of 1–10, Johnny replied, "Zero."

Orr's frustration was only beginning. A trip to Lincoln, Neb., was next, a stop that wasn't one of Johnny's favorites, anyway. His five previous Cyclone teams were 1-4 in Huskerville and had averaged just 60 ppg there. This time would be no different.

Grayer and Nebraska's Chris Logan were ejected with eight minutes left in the first half after a scuffle, and Iowa State eventually lost, 75-58. Johnny called the skirmish "absolutely bizarre," and said the officials overreacted. "That's the first time in 34 years of coaching that I had a player thrown out for fighting," Orr said. Logan said he punched Hornacek in retaliation for an elbow, only to be greeted by a fist from Grayer, who was protecting his teammate. "The next thing I know, the Iowa State players were all over me like honeybees," Logan said later. With Grayer on the bench and Sam Hill fouling out, it was the second-lowest scoring output of the season for the Cyclones. Nebraska's Dave Hoppen, who seemed to own Iowa State throughout his career, had another big night against the Cyclones with 24 points and 13 rebounds. This would be the last time he would inflict such damage, though, because later that month Big Dave incurred a season-ending knee injury and watched from the sidelines in two subsequent games with the Cyclones.

Next up was a return to Hilton and a mighty challenge against a fifth-rated Kansas team that would lose just four times all season and bow only once to a Big Eight foe. Larry Brown's team, 19-2 and ranked fourth nationally, was coming off a week in which it beat Missouri, Oklahoma and Louisville. This was one of those rare Kansas stumbles, though, as Iowa State held off the Jayhawks for a 77-74 victory. The Cyclones had just two first-half turnovers and only six on the game, and shot 59 percent from the field. Hornacek hit six free throws in the final 59 seconds to hold off KU's late run. Grayer scored 19 and Hornacek contributed 16 points and 12 assists, but it was Virgil's unexpected 5-of-7 shooting night from the field that deflated Brown and the Jayhawks. "I'm disappointed, but Iowa State played a great game," a gracious Brown said. "Hopefully, now they'll get some respect, and our conference will get some respect." Johnny was beaming afterwards: "Our crowd was on the ball. They were wild. This is the biggest victory we've had since I've been here. If we get hot at a certain time, we can beat just about anybody."

Iowa State then traveled to Stillwater, hoping to finish the first half of the conference at 5-2. This was a pesky Cowboy team that included a 7-foot-4-inch Englishman, Alan Bannister, and Andre Ivy, the brother of former Iowa State star Hercle Ivy. Poor free-throw shooting dunked the Cyclones in a 67-65 overtime defeat. Iowa State missed 12 of 20 attempts at the line, and Jason Manuel's free throw for Oklahoma State with seven seconds left in regulation forced the key overtime period that was ruled by the Cowboys.

Next up was the return match with Oklahoma, and coming on the heels of the disappointment in Stillwater, it seemed like a prime chance for the start of a Cyclone slump. But the Hilton magic kicked in, and Johnny's team escaped with a 73-70 victory over the No. 6 Sooners. Grayer sank 21 points and Hornacek had 16 points and 13 assists. The Cyclones now were 5-3 in the Big Eight and 14-7 overall.

Iowa State hit 15 wins by posting a 26-point victory in its next outing at Colorado, a place where Cyclone teams had lost seven of the previous eight games. The 26-point margin, accomplished before a sparse crowd of 3,203, marked the largest conference road win by an Iowa State team since 1969. The victory also was significant because it gave Johnny an 84-83 career record over six seasons at Iowa State, the first time his combined Cyclone record was above .500 since the middle of his inaugural 1980–81 season. The victory also clinched a third-straight winning season, the first such string by a Cyclone team since 1960–1963.

The Cyclones made it three victories in a row with an 84-74 win over Kansas State the following Saturday. Hornacek broke Valentine's Big Eight career assist record with 12 and also scored 21 points, and Grayer's 29 points offset Coleman's 30 for the Wildcats. "Records don't mean anything unless you're winning," Hornacek said following the game. "It might be nice personally, but it's much nicer if the team is winning, too." This also marked the first time since 1945 that Iowa State swept the season games against Kansas State.

Johnny's teams had never won four consecutive Big Eight games, and only one Iowa State team had done it since 1973. These Cyclones couldn't pull it off, either, as they traveled to Columbia and lost 71-62 to Missouri. Grayer led with 19 points but the Cyclones shot only 36 percent from the field. "It's absolutely amazing that we only lost by nine points (given the way we shot)," Johnny said after the game. "I guess that shows we're a pretty good team." Second-semester transfer Tom Schafer from Illinois had his best game to date with 12 points and seven rebounds in 22 minutes off the bench.

By now once-beaten Kansas was running away with the Big Eight regular-season title, but Iowa State still had a strong shot at second place. The Cyclones returned home and moved into a second-place tie with Oklahoma by beating the Hoppen-less Nebraska Cornhuskers, 81-73, behind 20 points from Grayer and 16 from Robinson. That left the Cyclones 8-4 in the Big Eight and 17-8 overall. They climbed to 9-4 and 18-8 the next outing and capped an unbeaten season at Hilton with a 76-61 revenge victory over Oklahoma State. Grayer scored 25 points and Virgil hit 6-of-7 from the field as Iowa State finished the month with a 5-2 record. That marked the school's best February since the 1956 team went 5-2, and was surpassed only by the 1945 team's 5-0 February slate.

The final game of the regular season brought an unenviable trip to play No. 2–ranked Kansas in the home finale for the KU seniors. The game produced another Allen Fieldhouse blowout by the Jayhawks to the tune of 90-70, KU's 33rd straight win at home. Grayer scored 26 points and moved to 999 points in 61 career games, with tournament games to come. "Maybe we'll get a chance to play them again," Johnny said. Even in defeat, the Cyclones finished second in the rugged Big Eight standings. Oklahoma State later upset Oklahoma to give Iowa State the second-place finish outright.

Big Eight tournament

A couple of breaks fell the Cyclones' way during the seeding for the Big Eight tournament. A dangerous Kansas State team would have been Iowa State's first-round foe, but star Norris Coleman's eligibility was in question. The league said the Wildcats must forfeit their regular-season games, dropping them to No. 8 seed and bumping lowly Colorado up to No. 7. So for the third straight season, the Cyclones faced Colorado in the Big Eight tournament quarterfinals, and a second-half surge allowed the Cyclones to pull away to a 78-60 victory. An estimated 4,000 Iowa State fans made the trip to Kansas City and saw Grayer score 16 points, Hill add 15 points and a season-high 14 rebounds, and Virgil contribute 14 points, 11 rebounds, a tourney-record 6 steals and 4 assists. "I feel pretty good because we didn't shoot well and we still won by 18 points," Johnny said. "I can remember a few years ago when we'd shoot 60 percent and couldn't win."

Iowa State rolled into the finals with a 75-58 victory over Nebraska. The game was tied 30-30 at halftime, and Grayer had just one point, but the Cyclones uncorked a 45-point second half and had just seven turnovers on the game. Hornacek, who was undergoing a mild shooting slump, hit 17 points and grabbed seven rebounds, and Moss had a season-high 12 points off the bench to lead another balanced attack. The Cyclones, now assured of their second-straight 20-win season, took a 20-9 record into the Big Eight Championship game, their second straight appearance in the finals. This year's foe was the heavily favored

Jayhawks, who survived a rugged semifinal game against Okla-homa, a contest many reporters called the real championship game. "We'll have to play almost perfect to beat Kansas," Johnny said. "But we're capable if we put it all together."

The Cyclones trailed the Jayhawks by as much as 14 points before they scrapped back into contention in the closing minutes. They pulled within 73-71 in the final minute, and Hornacek's steal with seven seconds left gave them a chance to tie the game and force overtime. Then a controversial traveling call on Hill—whistled by Orr nemesis Woody Mayfield from across the court—negated a foul being whistled against Kansas. Instead of Iowa State facing a one-and-one free-throw situation that could have forced overtime, the Jayhawks had the ball with one second left, and held on for the two-point win. Kemper Arena should have been renamed Temper Arena on this day, because Johnny lost his after Mayfield's late whistle. The coach chased Mayfield off the floor and added some postgame spice to a contest and a Big Eight tournament that needed none. There was no talk of moral victories this year, even though the Cyclones had just nine turn-overs, shot 52 percent from the field and outrebounded the taller Jayhawks, 33-32. Grayer, who scored 25 points, said after the game, "The media said the Oklahoma-Kansas (semifinal) game was the first-place game. I think we came out and proved we are in the top two, almost the top one."

• NCAA Tournament

A few hours later, the Cyclones received their second straight NCAA tournament bid and began preparing for another Inter-state 35 trek, this one to the north to the Metrodome in Minneap-olis. Their opening foe was Miami of Ohio, the alma mater of assistant coach Jim Hallihan. That wouldn't be the biggest homecoming game of the weekend, however, since Michigan and Iowa State were placed in the same bracket. The Cyclones were determined to make this NCAA appearance more than a once-and-out affair like the previous year. Miami was a more favorable draw for the Cyclones than cat-quick Ohio State was in 1985, although Ron Harper's presence and Miami's 24-6 record com-manded respect. The winner would play the survivor of the Mich-igan-Akron game in round two on Sunday, and a possible Orr matchup against Frieder and his old school had everyone salivat-ing.

"We're excited and proud to be in the tournament," Grayer

said prior to the Miami game. "But this year we're looking to take it a step farther. We want to come out and win a couple of games, really come out and play strong." Hornacek added, "When you're growing up, you always see the NCAA tournament (on TV). Maybe some of our freshmen or sophomores don't fully appreciate it now, but we older guys who didn't go to the NCAAs in our freshmen year feel good about coming to Iowa State and helping turn the program around." Virgil said, "A couple of weeks ago, we only had 17 wins, so we put our heads to it and decided we were going to win 20."

The coaches echoed the players' pre–NCAA tournament sentiments. "Last year, we didn't feel like we had much of a chance in the tourney," Johnny said. "We won 20 games again and got in the NCAA tournament for the second year in a row. I never would have dreamed of that happening before, but now we almost expect those things every year."

Hallihan said, "I feel very good about this team. We're not a one-man team. Last year at times I thought we were a one-man team. And we're not just a five-man team, we're much deeper. Last year, getting an NCAA bid was like a dream. We were happy to be in the Big Eight finals and elated to be in the NCAAs. This year, we wanted to win the Big Eight finals and win in the NCAAs."

Assistant coach Ric Wesley said, "It has surprised me we have done so well this season. We thought we'd have trouble winning as many games as last year, and our schedule was much tougher. But the kids have just come on so well. We have the guys coming off the bench that give us the equivalent of eight starters. Ever since we won (the Music City tournament over) Vanderbilt, I felt that if we played like we were capable of, we'd be (an NCAA) tournament team."

Assistant coach Steve Antrim said, "After last year, we wondered if we could win without Barry (Stevens). This year we've had more guys who have contributed. If you look through the game articles, you'll find a different hero every game for us."

An ice storm zapped travel plans for several teams trying to reach Minneapolis and caused a delay of several hours for the Cyclones. Johnny, trying to stay loose, joked with reporters about the delay. "If I was younger, I would have been mad," he said. "Hell, now I'm just glad to be here and not (crashed) in some field with people saying, 'That Orr, he was a good guy.' "

"Orr's presence prompted *Minneapolis Star and Tribune* columnist Sid Hartman to write in his column of Johnny's surprising decision to leave Michigan for Iowa State:

It was at the 1980 Final Four in Indiana when Bobby Knight offered a tip to this reporter. "John Orr is leaving Michigan to become the basketball coach at Iowa State," Knight said. Everyone at the breakfast table, including me, concluded that Knight had gotten some bad information. None of the 10 coaches on hand could believe that Orr would leave what looked like a lucrative job at Michigan to coach Iowa State. But Knight was right. In six years, Orr has done an outstanding job of building a competitive basketball team.

Miami of Ohio

Iowa State started its 1986 NCAA fun with an 81-79 overtime victory over Miami before 27,454 fans in the Metrodome. The shot that claimed the school's first NCAA triumph in 42 years was as marvelous and unexpected as the season. Hornacek rolled off a pick, took the inbounds pass, spun around and fired a 25-footer that made both the net, and Iowa State fans, dance. Besides Hornacek's heroics, the Cyclones committed only 12 turnovers during the 45-minute game and received 19 points and 11 rebounds from Grayer. Even then, Johnny conceded, "It looked like we were goners in the second half." Hornacek's 18-foot jumper with 27 seconds left in regulation got the Cyclones into overtime. Miami coach Jerry Pierson, whose 1985 team was eliminated from the NCAA tournament in a one-point loss to Maryland, was gracious in another killer defeat. "As soon as it left his hands, I knew we were done," Pierson said. "I'd rather get beat by Hornacek from 25 feet than by a defensive boo-boo, though. Hornacek's a leader. He makes things happen."

Des Moines Register columnist Marc Hansen previously had written about a mild shooting slump Hornacek endured during the Big Eight tournament. At the time Hansen quipped, "For the Cyclones to be the team of their dreams, Hornacek can't afford to walk in his sleep." Hansen's prophecy rang true on this day, and he wrote this account of the Miami finish:

> The play had no official name, but Jeff Hornacek, the lead actor, made one up off the top of his head. He called it, "Please Go In." His head, by the way, when last seen, was floating high atop the Hubert H. Humphrey Metrodome. That's what happens when you make a 25-footer with no time remaining to win an NCAA tournament game, 81-79. Your spirit soars and your head floats because this is the way you've always dreamed it would be since the basketball stopped bouncing you and you started bouncing it. As a kid in the driveway, in your bedroom, you taxed your imagination picturing the winning shot swishing through in the NCAA tournament. A daydream usually is as far as it gets.

"I made one from halfcourt once in high school," Hornacek said, "but it came at the end of the half. Other than that, I can't remember anything like this."

"I was standing under the basket," said Ron Virgil, one of Iowa State's most important supporting players. "I knew it was going in. He does that all the time in practice. He'll throw them in backwards from halfcourt sometimes."

With due respect to Hornacek, Virgil was, in this tournament and all season, the human version of a backward shot that swished in from halfcourt. Unexpected, unbelievable, unflappable. He came to Iowa State from Chicago, where he played at basketball-rich Providence-St. Mel's. The private school became Virgil's haven from his previous stop on Chicago's west side at rough-and-tumble Crane High School. Virgil was somewhat of an expert on game-winning shots, since he shot down Chicago State and Vanderbilt earlier in his career with buzzer-beating baskets. Anyway, Hornacek might not have had his opportunity to make the national highlight reel if Virgil hadn't fired in 6-of-8 field goals during the second half against Miami. Virgil started 32 of 33 games in this hallmark season of 1985–86 (the one he didn't was a Cyclone loss at Detroit). Johnny said Virgil "hasn't griped once since he's been here. He's been a great kid and a good recruiter. He's for us 1,000 percent."

Michigan

Virgil would play a key role in the second-round game, which pitted the Cyclones against Michigan, a reunion of Johnny and his former school. While Iowa State was basking in its emotional victory over Miami, both Iowa and Notre Dame were bounced out in the first round at Minneapolis, by North Carolina State and Arkansas-Little Rock, respectively. The Orr vs. Michigan angle added some flavor to the second round, and the most popular story line pursued at the Saturday press conference was the reunion of Johnny and his old assistant coach and close friend, Bill Frieder, coaching against each other for the first time.

"I tried to get (Johnny) back into the Big Ten," Frieder told reporters. "I tried to get him that Ohio State job, but they couldn't find a freezer big enough for all the free meat they're giving him in Iowa. He just makes too much money up there . . . John's special to me. He gave me my first (college coaching) job in basketball. He's my daughter's godfather. He's a good guy. The real quick teams with good athletes such as Cleveland State and Arkansas-Little Rock are the teams that have pulled the upsets in this tournament. Iowa State is like that."

Michigan, 28-4, was No. 5 nationally and the Big Ten champion. With an intimidating combination of size, quickness and strength, the Wolverines looked like they might name the score on Johnny's overachievers. When they broke to a quick lead in the first minute, CBS announcer Dick Stockton said bluntly, "It looks like the JV vs. the varsity." Yes, Iowa State would get outrebounded, 37-21. Yes, Grayer would be held scoreless the first 13 minutes of the game. Yes, Hornacek would score only seven points. Yes, Johnny would gamble by covering 6-foot-11-inch Roy Tarpley with the slender 6-foot-4-inch Virgil, who one writer said had "the body of an egret and the heart of a lion."

Virgil's previous 15 minutes of fame came in high school when President Ronald Reagan visited Providence-St. Mel's as a salute to its model educational program. Ronnie V. was selected to give Ronnie R. the customary school jacket and pose with the Prez for photographers. So after handing the President of the United States a jacket, it was nothing when the 165-pound Virgil matched up against the mammoth Tarpley and, at least on offense, handed him his lunch. Tarpley had 25 points and 14 rebounds, as expected. What wasn't expected was that Tarpley couldn't stop the quick Virgil on the other end of the floor. Virgil sank 7-of-8 field-goal tries and helped the Cyclones shoot 61 percent from field in a building that had become the Hubert H. Hilton Metrodome.

Virgil and his teammates were a step ahead all day. After taking a 40-31 halftime lead, the Cyclones continued to hold off Michigan runs. The Wolverines pulled within 64-63 with 1:19 left, but there was Hornacek with the slick inbounds pass to a wide-open Elmer Robinson, who zoomed uncontested to the hoop and slam-dunked Michigan into a three-point deficit. That dunk, and subsequent clutch free-throw shooting by the Cyclones, rocked the Wolverines out of the tournament, 72-69.

Michigan's future NBA guard Gary Grant was draped in malaise and blue on this day. He limped to a 1-for-9 shooting afternoon under defensive pressure from another Gary, Iowa State's Thompkins, a Michigan kid whose chance at scholarship to the Ann Arbor school ended when Grant signed on. "Me and the NCAAs just don't get along," Grant said later. There was Grayer, another Michigan kid, sending his postcard—and the state university—home. There was Glen Rice coming off the Michigan bench for a quiet two points. There was the Cyclone bench, which had a 16-12 advantage in bench scoring, led by Robinson's nine points and Moss's six. Believe it or not, Dick Stockton's JV was going to Kansas City for the NCAA Sweet Sixteen.

Iowa State broadcaster Pete Taylor said the game left an indelible impression on him and probably on anyone who's followed Cyclone basketball. "As I looked out there on the court and saw how badly the players wanted to win for (Johnny), well, I don't get that emotional, but I had tears in my eyes at the finish," Taylor said. Frieder refused to criticize his team and instead praised Iowa State. "We were outquicked at three positions, and that's tough," Frieder said. Tarpley added, "Iowa State played a great game and might very well be the underdog of the NCAA Tournament."

Those Iowa State wrestling championships were grand, and Earle Bruce had a couple of glorious football wins over the Huskers, but for sheer visibility and overcoming odds, this masterpiece was the high point by an Iowa State team in any sport in modern times. How else do you explain the mob scene at the Ames airport? Ames radio station KCCQ announced the team's scheduled arrival time, and the spontaneous celebration of 2,000 students and fans, who assembled without any crowd-control measures, spilled dangerously onto the runway. Two exuberant fans came perilously close to becoming roadkill when they dashed out to greet the plane as it taxied in.

Here's a sampling of the postgame comments from the media the next day and next week:

Cedar Rapids *Gazette* writer Mike Hlas

The Iowa State athletic program said hello to America Sunday. No Orange Bowls or Final Fours have included an Iowa State team. And since track and field and wrestling aren't part of the national sports imagination, Iowa State has been just another fish in the school of Division I schools. That was probably not about to change Sunday if the Cyclones didn't beat Michigan in the NCAA basketball tournament. The national television cameras which distinguish who is a national team and who plays in the sticks weren't there to see Iowa State. Michigan, the Big 10 champion and the odds-on choice to at least reach the Midwest regional final, was the reason the first-team analyst was here for CBS.

Quad City Times writer Mark Neuzil

Michigan fans, the king is not dead. He's alive and well and coaching basketball in Ames, Ia., and his team just whipped yours in the second round of the NCAA tournament. Johnny Orr, who took over a downtrodden Cyclone program six years ago after a successful, if unappreciated, 12-year run at Michigan, placed his team among college's basketball's elite 16 on Sunday by knocking off the 5th-ranked Wolverines . . . In the process, Orr and his band of speedsters, seeded seventh in the regional, earned something that has eluded them for a long time—respect.

Kansas City *Times* writer Dennis Dodd

As always, Iowa State stepped on the court looking like a pick-up team looking for a game against the guys who rule the playground.

Chicago Tribune writer Bob Logan

The look on Commissioner Wayne Duke's face told the story Sunday when he watched a last-second shot knock Illinois out of the NCAA tournament. That jolt was just a prelude to what Duke had to sit through a few hours later in the Metrodome. Michigan, expected to be the first Big Ten team to make the Final Four since Indiana in 1981, took a final dive instead. Iowa State's quickness and poise proved too much for the tense and jittery Wolverines Sunday in the second round of the Midwest Regional.

New York Times

With his Marine Corps-recruit bristle haircut, his "ooooes" and his cackling chuckle, Johnny Orr enjoys playing the rube. And what more rustic-sounding school could he coach than Iowa State, long the "other" basketball team in the Hawkeye state? But there is fire behind Orr's sparkling eyes and some acid in his remarks these days as he has become something of an anomaly among the coaches in the NCAA tournament. Although most other coaches have graduated "up" to their jobs, Orr left one of the finest programs in the United States—at the University of Michigan—to create a basketball team out of a moribund operation. Now in his sixth season and with an overall Iowa State coaching record only six games over .500, Orr brings his Grand Ole Opry act to Kansas City for a Midwest Regional semifinal game Friday night against North Carolina State. His Cyclones have gotten this far after victories in Minneapolis over Miami of Ohio—and Michigan. "I never regretted leaving," said Orr after his club's major upset over the nationally-ranked Wolverines—coached by his former assistant, Bill Frieder. Orr conceded, though, that "everyone thought I was nutty."

Johnny was so sick with the flu the entire weekend in Minneapolis that he leaned on a stool on the elevated court to keep from collapsing. But after this stunning triumph, he was floating on a cloud the size of the Metrodome's billowing white roof. Johnny showed his compassionate side in his first remarks after his greatest career win: "I feel sorry for Bill (Frieder), and I'd rather not have played him."

The animated side of Johnny re-emerged later in the week as his strength returned and the victory began to sink in. "It's been six years, that's pretty long," Orr said. "But this makes it all worth it. It seems like more and more good things are coming to this program. It's a good thing, too. I'm getting old . . . When we play those teams that are supposed to beat us, we play super. Ron Virgil is the skinniest guy in the United States. (Before the Michigan game) he kept telling us he didn't think he could go in there against the big guys, but he did."

Ric Wesley explained that Johnny's motivational approach was responsible for the Cyclones' upset victory. "Coach Orr is the master of making guys think they're as good as anybody," Wesley said. "He honestly believes if you outwork teams and hang together, you can beat teams with a lot more talent. A lot of guys say that but don't believe it. He really believes it . . . Coach Orr is making a nice living. He easily could be worried about taking care of himself, but his big concern is making you the best possible basketball player . . . He believes there are 10 great high school players every year and about 200 who are good enough to win with if they're determined. Most of the kids we get aren't recruited by the so-called major powers. They come here with something to prove."

Grayer said he was determined to make a good showing against Michigan. "Back home a lot of people treat Iowa State as if it's some small program. They ask Iowa State this, and Iowa State that. Not just Gary and me. We've got a lot of guys from Michigan on the bench, and I think we proved something." Despite that incentive, Elmer Robinson said Johnny always had the Michigan game in perspective. "Michigan was a big game for Coach Orr," Robinson said. "But I think people should know Coach Orr wanted to win it first for Iowa State, then for us, then for Coach Orr."

Johnny added, "When I coached at Massachusetts, I was happy as hell when February 27 or 28 came around because it was the end of the year. You didn't have to work anymore. You could go play golf. Now, you want to hang in there as long as you can because it gets better all the time the farther you go."

The Final Four no longer seemed like a silly dream. The way

the Cyclones were playing, they knew they could go nose-to-nose with anybody in Kansas City and conceivably could come away, with two wins, with a national semifinals berth. The Wolfpack team they would face in their first game posed two matchup problems, excellent height and athletic ability. And tournament experience might become a factor. Coach Jim Valvano had an 11-2 NCAA tourney record with the Wolfpack and one national title, and his team was coming off a double-overtime victory over Arkansas-Little Rock in Minneapolis.

The Cyclones were loose, though, on the heels of their upset of Michigan. Thompkins recalls a practical joke pulled by Orr. "We were about to go to Kansas City for the second round of the NCAA. Channel 5 was there to interview me and Jeff Grayer. We sat down and we were waiting for them to start the interview. So I took the microphone and I acted like I was Johnny Orr, and Jeff played Mark Mathew and started interviewing me. We didn't know they were rolling the cameras, and they played the tape of us on TV that night. So the next morning Coach Orr calls me into his office and tells me he wants to pull a joke on Grayer and he wants me to go along with it. When Jeff comes in, he tells him he saw the tape and because of it he can't start in the game against North Carolina State. Right away Jeff says, 'No, it was all Gary's fault.' We all had a good laugh about it later."

North Carolina State

Another great pack of Iowa State fans made another I-35 trek to cheer on its team, but the dream season came to an end against Valvano's Wolfpack. The Cyclones had a 20-0 record on the season when they led at halftime, but they trailed 40-29 this time at the break after they managed to shoot only 32 percent in the opening half to NC State's 65 percent. Hornacek had just six points on the game, but his basket with 13:47 left forged a 47-47 tie. Somehow, Iowa State outboarded NC State 42-30, but the Wolfpack shot 56 percent and held off the Cyclones down the stretch to post a 70-66 victory. "They were making some shots I couldn't believe," Virgil said. "That's what we usually do to the other team." Charles Shackleford had 22 points and seven rebounds to help offset Grayer's and Hill's 21 points each.

NC State lost, 75-67, to Kansas two days later to fall short of the Final Four. Ironically, this Wolfpack team would be investigated a few years later for a series of allegations, including charges of point shaving. That charge never was proven, but the fallout from the publicity led to Valvano's resignation.

Antrim said after the game that the Wolfpack's 6-foot-10-inch

Shackleford and 6-foot-11-inch Chris Washburn were intimidating. "We told our guys just to take it up straight and don't worry about it getting blocked," the Iowa State assistant coach said. "But it's easy for a 5-foot-9-inch guy on the bench to tell a 6-foot-5-inch guy that. The 6-foot-5-inch guy is the one who has to go out and do it against those giants. We all feel so empty now, but I'm sure we made some other teams feel empty this year."

Johnny addressed a festive postseason banquet and said, "I enjoyed this team more than any I've coached. They kept doing things nobody thought they could do. It's just a shame (these players) aren't all about four inches taller. Then nobody in the world would beat them."

From a 44-point win over South Dakota State in November to a four-point loss to North Carolina State in March, it was a season to remember.

• Hard to Top

The 1985–86 team's achievements—especially Hornacek's contributions—were more fully appreciated the next season. With Hornacek graduated and playing in the National Basketball Association (NBA) with the Phoenix Suns, the Cyclones struggled to a 13-15 finish and had their string of national tournament berths end at three. Even with Grayer, Thompkins, Schafer, Hill and Robinson providing a strong nucleus, the Cyclones didn't display the consistency they did in the previous season. They didn't make the big play when it was needed and lost seven games by three or less points. After a 9-5 start, Iowa State lost seven of its next nine games and eventually fell short of a national tournament bid. Grayer, a junior, averaged 22.4 ppg and Schafer closed his career by averaging 18 points and eight rebounds.

The Grayer-led Cyclones came back much hungrier in 1987–88 and immediately showed they were serious about returning to the NCAA tournament. This team made the most of its inclusion in the Big Apple NIT preseason tournament with a third-place finish, including an impressive 104-96 upset win at Purdue. The Cyclones went on to a 16-2 start, highlighted by a 102-100 overtime victory over Iowa at Hilton Coliseum. Lafester Rhodes exploded that night to score a school-record 54 points and lead the Iowa State triumph. Rhodes, who played sparingly during his first three seasons, established himself as the nation's most improved player with a 22.5 ppg average.

The Cyclones climbed to No. 10 in the national rankings before hitting a midseason slump with seven straight losses. A late-season surge never materialized, although they did receive an NCAA tourney bid. A 10-point loss to Missouri in the Big Eight tournament and a 12-point loss to Georgia Tech in the first round of the NCAA tournament ended a season of distinct highs and lows. A bright spot was the play of Grayer, who broke a school season record with 811 points and also grabbed 300 rebounds en route to second-team All-American honors. Grayer went on that year to earn a spot on the U.S. Olympic team and gain a first-round draft by the Milwaukee Bucks. He also became the second Cyclone to make All–Big Eight three times, matching the accomplishment of former NBA star Don Smith. Thompkins, a four-year contributor, closed his career as ISU's No. 2 assist man with 600.

The Cyclones of 1988–89 were expected to struggle because Grayer, Thompkins and Rhodes had completed their eligibility. In one of Orr's best coaching jobs at Iowa State, this surprising bunch finished with a bang and claimed the school's fourth NCAA tournament berth in five seasons. Johnny's team stood 11-9 overall and 2-6 in the Big Eight in early February, but exploded with five wins in its last six conference games. The Cyclones stopped Oklahoma State in the first round of the Big Eight tourney to improve to 17-10, then lost a frustrating 76-74 decision to Oklahoma in the semifinals on a last-second three-point goal. They earned a trip back to the NCAA tournament, though, and lost a first-round meeting with UCLA, 84-74.

The outlook for the Cyclones' 1989–90 team was promising, with young players like Victor Alexander, Sam Mack, Mark Baugh and Terry Woods expected to continue Orr's brand of up-tempo, competitive basketball. But Johnny again would discover that in athletics there's a fine line between a dream season and a nightmare season.

"I think so much of Johnny Orr that
if I ever get diagnosed with having a
terminal disease, I'd like to spend it
with Johnny Orr, because ladies and
gentlemen, I guarantee you, two weeks
with Johnny would seem like a lifetime."
—JUD HEATHCOTE

*"I don't have a hell of a lot to say to you.
After this roast, my sex life has been
ruined. I can no longer brag about that."*
—JOHNNY ORR

"Sam Mack's deal was one of the hardest things I've ever experienced in all my years of coaching. I never had that kind of situation before. I had never been to court, never testified. I never want to go through that again, either."

"Sam's a very likeable individual. He never caused any problems. He was a decent student. It's hard to figure him out. He just gets with the wrong guys sometimes. The toughest thing was going in after the trial and telling Sam's mother and sister and him that he couldn't come back to the team. He wanted to come back very badly. We sat there for two or three hours and talked it out, and I told them it would be better for him to leave (to Arizona State, where Orr's former colleague, Coach Bill Frieder, would offer a scholarship and a chance for a fresh start). So they agreed to it. This was so hard on his family—they're practically broke now and had to remortgage their house and everything to pay for the legal fees."

"When you talk about athletes getting in trouble or flunking out of school, that has always happened. It's just that hardly anyone knew about it 20 years ago or 10 years because of the way it was covered in the media. As far as Sam Mack's case, the thing a lot of people forget is that he was acquitted."

• Stand by Me

It's every coach's nightmare. Johnny Orr had weathered a lot of minicrises in his first 37 years of coaching, but he never faced the dismay that surfaced in the postmidnight hours of March 31, 1989. Orr was awakened in his Seattle hotel room during the NCAA Final Four weekend by an emergency telephone call from Ames. It was just two weeks after the conclusion of a 17-12 season that some say was his best coaching effort at Iowa State.

The news from home was alarming. One of Orr's basketball players, 18-year-old freshman Sam Mack, was wounded in a shootout with police after an apparent robbery attempt in downtown Ames. The gunshot wounds weren't life-threatening, but the bizarre incident inflicted pain and scars not only on this confused teenager, but on Orr, his team and the entire Iowa State campus. Just two weeks earlier, Mack had played with the Cyclones in the NCAA tournament. He started half of the games during the season and averaged 11.8 points and 6.1 rebounds a game.

Even as the hours and days passed, and more details were revealed, the incident still defied explanation. According to police and newspaper accounts, it was near the 11 p.m. closing time on March 30 when Mack and fellow Iowa State student Levin White, a member of the Cyclone football team, carried weapons into the Burger King restaurant on Lincoln Way. The restaurant, located two blocks from the Ames Police Station, has a collection of Iowa State athletic team photos on the wall, including one of Sam Mack and his 1988–89 Cyclone teammates. White, toting a semi-automatic rifle, was "yelling a mile a minute," according to a restaurant employee. Mack, who reportedly was carrying a knife, was hardly inconspicuous himself with his 6-foot-6-inch frame and his visibility as a star athlete. White allegedly demanded the cash from the safe and herded five employees and two customers into the cooler. In the confusion, White and Mack apparently failed to notice restaurant employee Amy Konek at the drive-up window. "I saw this big guy with a blue coat and a big gun and the first thing I thought was, I gotta get out of here," Konek told the Ames *Daily Tribune*. Konek squeezed her body through the narrow drive-up window and ran north on Kellogg Avenue, where she flagged down two women in a car for help. A police officer on foot patrol in the vicinity was alerted, and three other officers at the station for shift change immediately responded to the call of an armed robbery in progress.

In their haste, White and Mack missed one of the two money bags in the manager's office. And the one money bag they reportedly did grab, containing approximately $600, fell to the restaurant floor when White and Mack saw police arrive at the scene. The pair tried to flee through the east doors, and when White raised his rifle in the air, police opened fire, with bullets wounding White in the foot and striking Mack in the hip and thigh. According to police reports, three police officers then quickly surrounded the fallen suspects with guns pointed at their heads. "It was just like in the movies," Ames Police Sergeant Craig Reid told the *Daily Tribune*.

The injured White and Mack were taken to Mary Greeley Medical Center in Ames and were held under protective custody. They faced first-degree robbery charges, plus the prospect of additional charges for kidnapping and terrorism. Conviction could result in prison terms of more than 25 years for the use of a gun in the commission of a felony.

Ames, a town former Cyclone basketball player Ron Harris

once likened to "Mayberry RFD," was numbed by the incident. Ames Police Chief Dennis Ballantine told the *Daily Tribune* this was just the fourth time in his 22 years on the force that police were involved in a shooting incident. The last previous case of police gunfire came 10 years earlier at an attempted bank robbery at North Grand Mall. The involvement of two Cyclone athletes, especially the well-known Mack, heightened the drama.

A stunned Orr and his assistant coaches curtailed their weekend business in Seattle. They returned to Ames to ask the very question on everyone's mind. Why? Why would two athletes with friends, talent, fame and bright futures throw away their reputations, even risk their lives, all in an amateur attempt to heist a few hundred dollars from a fast-food restaurant? In his initial response to reporters, Orr said simply, "I'm shocked to death. Sam's mother will just be sick."

• Community Reaction

A sampling of other reactions in the Ames *Daily Tribune* reflected the entire community's bewilderment. "God only knows why these kids do these things," Chief Ballantine said.

Iowa State baseball coach Bobby Randall explained, "It's like an arrow right in your heart. It hurts everybody. It's really crazy. I've really had a hard time believing it."

Cyclone basketball player Norm Brown, Mack's dormitory roommate, said Mack didn't have financial problems. "He had plenty of money. He was on top of the world. Everything was going great for him," Brown said.

Another Cyclone player, Mike Born, questioned his teammate's role in the robbery. "Sam Mack is not going to walk into a Burger King and think people are not going to recognize him. To me, it sounds too fishy. Things just don't seem to fit. Sam is smart enough to realize he can't get away with something like that."

Iowa State student Melissa Jarrett, a friend who visited Mack in the hospital, later said, "He's just really upset and confused right now. He had so much going for him. The Sam I know wouldn't do something like this. The Sam I know is a very good kid."

The university's response was to suspend White and Mack from their athletic teams pending the outcome of their trials. Orr said Iowa State also asked the suspects to withdraw from school, although he disagreed with that request on two fronts. First, he felt it would hurt the players' chances to get fair trials; second, he feared it would make Iowa State ripe for a lawsuit if the players were acquitted. Facing the fight of their lives, Mack and White weren't worried about schoolwork and eligibility, and they agreed to withdraw for the semester.

Ames was buzzing with rumor and speculation following the arrests. The most plausible theories circulating speculated that White and Mack either were under the influence of drugs or in desperate need of cash, perhaps to pay gambling debts or to finance a drug habit. Medical tests later revealed no drugs in the suspects' bodies on the night of the robbery. Orr also said Mack had passed random drug tests given to players during the season. Testimony at the trial reintroduced the question of drugs, however. White claimed Mack and he went to the restaurant to get cash to finance a cocaine buy in Chicago. White said they planned to resell the drugs in Ames. Mack denied the charge, and ultimately the jury found his version more believable than White's.

On his return from Seattle, Orr went to the hospital to visit Mack and White and try to find some logic in their actions. He also met with Mack's mother, Willie, who came immediately from her home in suburban Chicago. Orr later saw Mack at the jail and described the cold reality of the moment. "Man, that's tough," he told the Cedar Rapids *Gazette*. "There he is. You can't even shake his hand. He's behind glass. I've been in coaching for 37 years and never have had anything happen like that." Orr said both athletes assured him they weren't on drugs at the time of the robbery. According to Orr, White told him from his hospital bed that he needed $400 and "woke up that morning and thought he was going to do something like that." Mack told Orr and his mother that he was forced by White to participate in the robbery.

With that revelation, the case took a new twist. Mack pleaded not guilty when he was arraigned on first-degree robbery charges. At the same time, White chose to plead guilty and receive a reduced sentence for agreeing to testify against Mack. This new subplot threatened to put a wedge between the Cyclone football and basketball programs and possibly divide the entire Iowa State community.

As the Burger King robbery became the talk of the state and even received national play, the public and the media waited intently for reaction from Orr and head football coach Jim Walden. This already disastrous incident put the coaches in an awkward situation: if they stuck by their athletes, some would accuse them of protecting criminals; if they weren't loyal to them or remained neutral, others would criticize them for putting their own reputation ahead of their responsibility to a player. "It makes you stop and think how vulnerable we are as coaches and as (an athletic) department," baseball coach Bobby Randall told the *Daily Tribune.* "Everybody believes coaches have complete control over athletes. It's the same way with parents. But people are accountable for their own actions. How can it be Coach Orr's fault? How can it be Coach Walden's fault? It's contrary to everything they believe."

In Walden's mind, the choice was easy, especially when White admitted his involvement and sought a plea bargain. "This is not a football-related problem," Walden told the *Daily Tribune.* "This is two young people who chose to become criminals. It was an individual act done by two people who had no regard for their teammates and families . . . I don't feel betrayed (by White's behavior). He betrayed himself, not me."

When asked if he knew White very well, Walden responded, "Apparently not very well. Everyone gets the idea that coaches know their players like they know their children, but we don't. There are certain things we don't know."

Specifically, the Cyclone football coaches didn't know when they recruited White that he was on probation on a weapons possession charge following an incident 20 months earlier at a convenience store in West Covina, Calif. White was a star defensive back at San Bernardino Valley Junior College and talented enough to earn a scholarship to the tradition-rich football program at the University of Southern California (USC). White left USC after just a few days, though, because it was learned he didn't earn enough credits at his junior college to be eligible for an athletic scholarship. He returned to junior college to fulfill his requirements and eventually accepted a scholarship at Iowa State. He enrolled for fall semester in 1988, had to sit out of competition that season due to NCAA transfer rules, but was eligible to compete in spring practice beginning the week following the robbery.

Ironically, White's on-campus recruiting visit to Ames occurred during the wild 1988 Veishea weekend. The May festival was marred that year by campus riots along Welch Avenue that received attention on national newscasts. Iowa State coaches said then that they were concerned that the negative publicity of the riots might hurt their chances to sign White, but in an interview the next week with the *Daily Tribune*, White said, "Actually, I kind of liked it. At least there was some action. I was concerned it would be too dull and just a bunch of cornfields."

It would have been easier and politically safer for Orr if he had distanced himself from Sam Mack, or at least remained neutral until the court case was resolved. Yet Orr actively stood by his player. He believed Mack's contention that White forced him at gunpoint to accompany him into the restaurant. "Sam says he was forced to do it," Orr told the Cedar Rapids *Gazette*. "Has anyone ever put a gun on you and told you, 'Hey, man, you're going to do this or I'm going to shoot you'? . . . Well, I've never had that happen to me, either, and I don't know what reaction I'd have to that. I could say, 'Go to hell,' but if he's got the gun there, and it's already gone off once, I don't know how I'd react to that."

As part of his support of Mack, Orr went so far as to predict that his player would be acquitted. He also announced that if he was cleared, Mack would be welcomed back on the team, and Orr agreed to testify at Mack's July trial as a character witness. This public declaration of support, while applauded in some circles, left the coach wide open for criticism. Those who doubted Mack's innocence believed that Orr's popularity would unfairly influence the jury. That was a major concern of prosecutor Mary Richards when she interviewed prospective jurors.

• Mack's Trial

The defense strategy at the weeklong July 1989 trial was to establish that Mack acted under duress. It was effective enough of a strategy to turn the trial into a question of credibility. Jurors interviewed later said they had to decide between the credibility of White, who had a previous police record, and the credibility of Mack, who had no previous arrests. The seven-woman, five-man jury deliberated about four hours before returning a Mack verdict of not guilty to charges of first-degree robbery and second-degree kidnapping.

The verdict surprised many Iowans, given Mack's physical involvement in the botched robbery. Orr told reporters after the acquittal, "I never had any doubts, but in a jury situation, you never know what's going to happen."

Even today, Walden disagrees with Orr's decision to publicly support Mack, although the Cyclone football coach stressed that the case hasn't affected his relationship with Orr.

"John's own strength, his caring and compassion, I think was a weakness in this case," Walden said. "He didn't have to do that. But he doesn't know how not to. His strength is his caring, almost to a fault.

"I was off the hook. My kid (Levin White) did it, and admitted it. I was more concerned about John's involvement for John's sake. A lot of people didn't think that John should have (testified), and they expressed that to me. I personally think he went too far with a kid (Sam Mack) who didn't consider him went he went through that (restaurant) door. I don't agree with the kid's defense, but I don't think Johnny had anything to do with that. The lawyers tried to make football look bad, and I didn't like that. But I can't blame Johnny Orr for that. That's what the lawyers do to get the guy off . . . Johnny didn't vote to let him go.

"I was concerned for Johnny. But there's no way any of this affected how I feel about John. It's too small a thing to worry about losing our friendship over. I understand it. I was worried for him."

Iowa State track coach Bill Bergan said Johnny's support of Mack was consistent with his record of loyalty to his players. "As a coach, I think you have to trust your athletes and you have to go to bat for them if they're in trouble," Bergan said. "They're not just things that you use and discard. They're just like your own kids. I think Johnny feels the same way. Even when a kid does get in trouble, they know they can call Johnny at 3 o'clock in the morning and he'll be there to help them. He's interested in them as a person, not just as a basketball player. In Sam Mack's case, Johnny could have divorced himself entirely from the situation, but he believes in young people and he believes in giving young people the benefit of the doubt."

Orr today maintains that his influence on Mack's acquittal was minimal and greatly exaggerated. "When I went to testify, I just told them what I thought," Orr said. "I wouldn't lie for anybody." The coach also said he wouldn't blindly go out on a limb to protect a player. He said he stuck with Mack primarily because of the player's clean slate with the basketball team.

"Usually, if you have a bad egg, you find it out pretty soon and he doesn't last," Orr said. "But if someone would have told me Sam would be involved in something like this, I never would have believed them.

"Actually, I never thought Sam was tough enough. I was always concerned that he wasn't enough of a fighter, the kind that wouldn't stand up to anybody. He's not the kind of guy to shoot someone or knife someone, he's just a nonaggressive type of individual. He came here as a Proposition 48 (academic nonqualifier) and had to qualify in the classroom his first year before he'd be eligible to play. His mother paid his way, and he understood he had to do it in the classroom to get eligible to get a scholarship. He went to class and passed."

• A Fresh Start

Orr had great hopes for Mack and the rest of the 1987 recruiting class, which included talented Mark Baugh, who eventually dropped out of the program due to academic problems. Mack's presence alone might have averted the two losing seasons from 1989 through 1991, but Johnny put his athlete and the situation ahead of his program's on-court needs. Despite his earlier statement about bringing Mack back on the team, Orr insisted that Mack get a fresh start at a new school. Orr believed Mack's departure and the passage of time would push the incident out of people's minds. He contacted Bill Frieder, his old assistant at Michigan who had taken the Arizona State head coaching job, and Frieder agreed to give Mack a scholarship and a fresh start. Orr was confident this new environment at Arizona State would let Mack resume his college studies and basketball career, which were crucial elements if Mack was ever to fully restore his reputation and fulfill his potential in his basketball career.

To Johnny's dismay, Mack encountered more problems at Arizona State. In that next season, while he was sitting out of competition as a transfer student, Mack was the subject of two police investigations in Arizona. He was accused of sexual assault by a female student at Arizona State, although charges never were filed. Later, he was arrested on suspicion of using a stolen credit card in the purchase of jewelry, although charges never were filed against him in that case, either. The publicity prompted Mack's dismissal from the Arizona State team. When word filtered back to Iowa of Mack's problems, it reinforced those who criticized Mack's acquittal and Orr's active support.

Mack relocated to Tyler, Texas, to play junior-college basketball in the 1990–91 school year, and his play there caught the attention of the University of Houston. The Cougar coaching staff mulled offering Mack a scholarship but first sought a reference from Orr. After some soul searching, Johnny responded in the manner of his father, Bert Orr, the magistrate judge in Taylorville who excused fines that people couldn't afford. Johnny recommended that Houston give Mack a final chance—under the condition that the coaches closely scrutinize his activity.

"I gave him a good recommendation, although I think if I had told them not to take him, they wouldn't have," Orr said. "I told them it's a gamble, but hopefully he's been (out of trouble) for a year and learned the hard way. I told them they've got to sit him down and say, 'This is your last chance, son.' They have to keep in constant touch with him and watch who he hangs out with.

"I know he's had enough chances. He's had more chances than the average person gets. Sam was lucky he got another chance (in 1990–91 at Tyler). But he did well in academics and was a good citizen and now (in 1991–92) has a chance to go to Houston. Hopefully he'll go down there and make up for all those problems he caused his family. I think he's good enough to play in the NBA."

Houston coach Pat Foster was quoted in *Sports Illustrated* in 1991 that Mack "has a chance to salvage his career. He's been very cooperative; he's not a problem-type player. If you threw out all the guys in college and the pros who have been in trouble, you wouldn't have a lot of players, unfortunately."

While not always a popular move, giving second and even third chances to young people is nothing new for Johnny. His record of reaching out to freshmen academic nonqualifiers is well-documented. Sam Hill, Lafester Rhodes and Elmer Robinson all made the most of their opportunities as freshmen nonqualifiers and established their academic eligibility during their idle year. Each went on contribute to some of the best seasons in the history of Iowa State basketball.

"For one Sam Mack, there have been 80 other guys that have done pretty well with their chance and have improved themselves," Orr explained. "One time we had four guys at Michigan that we dropped from the team for using drugs. We didn't take away their scholarships or take them out of school, we just dropped them from the team under our team rules. Now one of them, his life is no good. But three of them went on to graduate from college, one went on to get his master's degree. A lot of people need a second chance."

Writer Jeff Burkhead, who covered the Sam Mack ordeal for the Ames *Daily Tribune,* said his respect for Orr grew with his handling of the Mack case. "I wasn't around for some of Orr's greatest victories," Burkhead said. "But I did observe Orr during what was probably one of the lowest moments of his career. What impressed me most about Orr's conduct during the Sam Mack affair was his accessibility. While Iowa State football coach Jim Walden didn't return to Ames until several days after the robbery, Orr, who also was out of town at the time, flew back to be with his player. He also returned to a barrage of questions from the media. Orr, of course, defended Mack and the Iowa State program, but he didn't duck the media. He fielded the tough questions. Orr maintained a high profile throughout the ordeal—from the robbery through the trial—even testifying on Mack's behalf. While I believe Orr never intended for Mack to return to the team, the coach's loyalty in standing behind Mack and his family was admirable.

"The Sam Mack incident took its toll on Orr. He was emotionally drained. You could see the pain in his face. Even though Mack's subsequent problems at Arizona State cast serious doubts on the jury's not-guilty verdict, Orr's integrity stood out."

It's hard to measure whether Orr's reputation has suffered long-term damage from the whole Mack episode. The coach believes the Ames incident had negative repercussions for the entire athletic department, though. Orr said he believes the university—and the NCAA as a whole—has overreacted to cases like the bizarre Burger King robbery. While not denying it was reprehensible, Johnny said the incident should be evaluated in the proper context—as an aberration, rather than a situation created by a lack of rules or too liberal admissions standards. Orr said stricter academic standards, reducing the size of coaching staffs, tighter recruiting rules and shortening practice time—all policies being proposed in the name of reform—actually hurt rather than help the environment for student-athletes.

For example, Orr wonders whether things would have turned out differently for Mack if he'd have been eligible to play on his first day at Iowa State instead of sitting out of basketball entirely his first season due to Proposition 48 restrictions. "Here's a kid that had been going to practice every day at 2:30 for five or six years, and now they say you can't practice," Orr said. "So you've got to find something else to do." Orr argues that instead of being around motivated teammates and coaches each day who can help monitor his progress, nonqualifiers like Mack actually are worse off because they don't have the supervision and support that might keep them from running with the wrong crowd. "If they took a poll of how many college students studied between 3 and 5 p.m., there wouldn't be many," Orr said.

Mack played well at Houston in 1991–92, averaging 17.5 points and 5.8 rebounds a game while helping the Cougars to a 25-6 record and a berth in the NCAA tournament. Mack sank four three-point goals in the second half and finished with 18 points, but it wasn't enough as Houston lost its first-round game to Georgia Tech, 65-60. Mack had three 30-point scoring nights on the season. He was expected to get some attention from NBA scouts and at least have the option of playing professionally in Europe or in the Continental Basketball Association. Because he sat out two of his five college seasons, some think he might be a sleeper with long-term pro potential.

Even with the benefit of hindsight, people still disagree whether Orr was right in his unwavering support of Sam Mack. It's easy to judge coaches in good times, but it's often more revealing to judge them during a time of adversity. What this case revealed about Johnny Orr was this: when everything was on the line, he put his player's needs ahead of his own and did what he thought was right.

"The thing I remember about Romie when I met her was that she had that confidence in herself. She was a cheerleader and was very active in all kinds of student organizations. She didn't just go to college to sit around. You'd see her picture in the yearbook all the time. Meeting her was just an accident. I think some guy said I couldn't get a date with her, so I bet him I could. She agreed to go out, so we went to the student union. I asked her if she wanted something to drink, and she said she'd have a Coke. It's a good thing, because if she had ordered a milkshake, then I wouldn't have had enough money—I never had any money. I was 22 and she was 21 when we got married in 1949, and we've been married 43 years. I think it would be very difficult to have something last like that today, considering we were apart two years like that in college, and especially when you're gone so much as a coach."

"Romie has been tremendous. Just think of all the times we moved—St. Louis, to Milton, to Dubuque, Madison, Amherst, Urbana, Ann Arbor and Ames. Never once has she ever balked about going somewhere. If we thought I could advance, she'd be excited about it. I remember some of those moves. We moved from Madison to Amherst, drove all the way across the country in a Volkswagen van. We had six people and a dog, Buckets. We had three girls in the back seat, and one in the far back seat. We had a good time, though. It seemed like whenever we moved, we had fun."

"I could tell you a million stories about my daughters. I'm prejudiced, of course, but I think they're pretty talented. Three of them graduated from Michigan, one from Iowa State. I think that's pretty good. They're all very loyal. My family are all tremendous fans. Great Cyclone fans, and still Michigan fans, too."

"You get pretty attached to girls. People always ask if you'd have liked to have a boy. Sure, I guess I'd have liked to, but I never think about that. I'm just happy we had healthy kids. Besides, I think it would have been very difficult if I would have had only one son. He would have had an awful time if he wasn't an athlete of some kind."

• A Winning Team

Johnny Orr doesn't get all the bounces to go his way, but he admits to getting some great breaks in the game of life. When he counts his blessings, he doesn't think of basketball accomplishments. Instead he starts at home, praising his wife of 43 years, Romie, and their four independent, loving daughters. Orr knows this loyal support base will remain his biggest fans long after his scrapbook clippings turn yellow. Together, this family has weathered the criticism, the moving, the conflicts and the time demands that come with the coaching life. Instead of tearing them apart, these obstacles seem to have brought the Orrs closer together, which is something not all coaches' families can say.

Daughter Leslie Orr summed up the family outlook this way: "Mom and Dad are pretty Up people. When you're around them, there's always something to look forward to."

Meet the Orrs: a clan that laughs together, cheers together, golfs together and enjoys life together. They stand out in a crowd, drawing attention with their wit, charm and ambition. But when you take away the basketball, take away the celebrity status, take away the spiffy Ames home, it simply is a mom and dad and some crazy sisters. They all try to get the biggest laugh at birthdays and all try their darnedest to spoil grandson and nephew John Henry Boylan. Each is a strong individual, but blended together, it's an interesting team.

The adult Orr girls—Jenny, Robin, Leslie, Becky—are quick to tell you how lucky they are to be the daughters of such a remarkable person. They go on to say that being *Johnny* Orr's daughter is pretty great, too.

The Orr four, you see, idolize their mom, the optimistic and loyal Romie. They admire and are amused by their dad, the perpetual wiseguy, but they revere their mom, a wise woman in every respect. The girls say if their mom had a pep band parked in the Orr kitchen, it would greet everyone's morning entrance with, "Put on a Happy Face."

From their perspective, Romie had a book out—*Here's Reality*—long before Johnny's. She figuratively wrote the book, one lesson at a time, on raising a family in the fast lane. Romie the parent has the traits of a winning coach: she had a good game plan; she knew how to keep her daughters upbeat and focused; she knew how to work the clock to keep them busy and challenged; she encouraged them to create their own opportunities; she walked the fine line between being a parent and a best friend; and she assumed both parental roles in times when Johnny's job took him on the road. Is anyone surprised? After all, everyone close to Johnny Orr knows that a key to his success is his ability to surround himself with good people. And who's been at Johnny's side longer?

"Most people don't know how important my mother is to my father," Robin said. "My mother is the optimistic one. She always makes you look for the best in people." Added Jenny, "Not to discredit anything my dad has done, but my mom is the one that made it all work at home. We all know that. Mom has a very strong identity, too. That's important in the position she's in. Unless you feel good about yourself, you can get lost in it.

"If not for her, Dad probably would have been out of coaching a lot of times. At times he felt he had a family and he should be making more money, and considered being an athletic director or in business. But Mom always put it in focus for him. She wouldn't allow him to quit without him thinking it through; she said he should only quit for the right reason. He had a goal to win a national championship as a coach. She would say, 'Don't quit because of money.' She would get a job or do whatever it would take to make things work. It's ironic that now it turned out to be lucrative for them, but I think he would have stayed with it even if the money didn't go with it."

Of course, the daughters think Pops is pretty cool, too. They love him and are proud of him, and almost rank him as high as a coach as they do as a dad. But given this fearless foursome's knack for teasing the old guy, they hold out a little longer before they reveal the extent of their admiration. Just to tease Johnny, they claim Romie is a better putter on the golf course. After hearing the voices on the Walden-Orr record soundtrack, there's no question in their minds which parent is the better singer, either. On the bright side, none of the daughters make any jokes about Johnny's hair. "We tease each other constantly," Becky said. "I always say to him 'Heeeeere's Dummy.' He's able to laugh at himself."

Consider when Robin was coaching swimming one summer in Canada, and Johnny was coming up for a basketball camp. She invited him to speak to her swimmers. "They didn't know who he was," Robin said. "So I told them he cleaned belly buttons for a living."

The same banter that Johnny shares with his daughters is at the root of his relationship with Romie. "We always have done more teasing than actual communicating," Romie said. "That keeps you from ever taking yourself too seriously. I've always had a whale of a time with John and the kids. I've just never worried. It's all worked, because it had to. It's like when John's grandma raised him while he was growing up. That was a big thing, but he took it right in stride." The ever-optimistic Romie credits her ability to adapt to the bumps in the road of athletics to a simple philosophy: "Liking people, liking the sport, not minding moving around, not minding weird hours."

• The Courtship Begins

Johnny's most rewarding recruiting job of all time occurred back in the 1940s at Beloit College. It began in an educational psychology class when, as a star athlete just back from World War II, he wooed—or as Johnny might say, "whoooooed"—Romie. It was a romance that started with some double dates, eventually survived a two-year separation, but came together with a wedding ring by graduation day.

"Everyone double-dated back then, and we always had a good time," Romie said. "I took his fraternity pin shortly after we started going together. Nobody expected it to last, since we were both so socially active. His fraternity house had a pool going to guess whether it would last two weeks or three weeks before we broke up."

Johnny and Romie had more in common than their busy dance cards. Both came from small, close-knit families with modest incomes but strong work ethics. Both had a love of athletics and both aspired to teach. Both were a long way from home, yet were trained to live independently when growing up. Both fit in well on campus—Johnny eventually was elected president of the Sigma Chi fraternity, and Romie later joined Delta Delta Delta at Missouri. By most standards, they were foreign to the environment at this small, private school on the east banks of the Rock River in southern Wisconsin. "We were very different than the usual Beloiters," Romie explained. "We certainly were unusual, not coming from a wealthy family."

• Romie's Early Years

Romie and one brother were raised by hard-working parents in Kansas City. "Dad was a mechanic, and he worked in offices and on bank machines," Romie said. "He was gone a great deal. He would get home very late, because he might not be able to repair the machines until the bank was closed for the day. Mother would always be there to fix him a meal. The way I grew up provided a good background for me as a coach's wife. Dad wasn't home, and it was never perceived as a problem because he was working supporting the family. Mother accepted it." (Romie said that philosophy carried over with her children. "If John wasn't able to make the swimming meets, I'd tell the girls, 'It isn't like he doesn't care. He's gone for the right reasons. He's still thinking about you.' He was working just as hard as anybody.")

Romie attended Northeast High School in Kansas City, and her own background in athletics began in physical education and dance classes. "Northeast High School had a wonderful physical education program. The Kansas City schools in general had good phys ed programs for that era. We were very lucky to have a swimming pool in our junior high," she said.

An excellent student, Romie was inducted into the National Honor Society. While many women in the 1940s didn't attend college, Romie said her parents strongly encouraged her to get a college education. "My parents believed when you educate a woman, you educate a family," she said. "My mother insisted I have a secretarial background, too." So at 15, Romie landed a summer job at the Hallmark Card Company. She graduated from high school at 16 and chose to attend college at Beloit because "I wasn't going to go where everyone else did." She said she received a small academic scholarship but noted, with a twinkle in her eye, "I had so much fun, I didn't keep that."

Romie first came to Beloit during World War II, and only about 30 of the 300 students on campus were men. So when Johnny and the other soldiers came marching home to improve the Beloit ratio, she still was much younger than the average male student: she came to college at 16 and the men were 5 to 10 years older. Johnny also was younger than most because he entered the Navy at age 18 and came to Beloit as a sophomore at age 19.

After two years at Beloit, Romie transferred closer to home to the University of Missouri to pursue a physical education degree. "We both dated others in those two years apart," Romie said. "We'd see each other a couple of times during the school year. He'd come to visit me in the summertime. I really liked his father and grandmother, and I would go visit them a couple of times when I was at Missouri. I'd take the bus to Springfield, and one of (Johnny's dad) Bert's friends would come and pick me up and drive me back to Taylorville."

• Wedding Bells

Johnny's mother died of cancer in his first semester at Beloit, so he wasn't about to lose another great inspiration in his life. One month before his graduation in April 1949, he proposed marriage to Romie, who accepted. "I received an engagement ring in April, Johnny graduated from Beloit on June 5, 1949, I graduated from Missouri on June 7, and we were married June 18 in Kansas City," Romie said. "Johnny signed a pro contract with the St. Louis Bombers and bought a Tampico red Mercury convertible with the bonus."

Johnny's NBA connections helped Romie land a teaching job in suburban St. Louis. She continued teaching at Evansville, Wis., when Johnny started coaching at nearby Milton. She also taught two years in Dubuque at Jefferson Junior High but became a full-time homemaker for 15 years before resuming her teaching career in Ann Arbor in 1967. Romie taught 13 years of junior high physical education there and was able to retire from teaching when Johnny landed the lucrative salary package to come to Iowa State in 1980. "I knew how much my parents sacrificed to put me through school," Romie said. "When I was able to get a job, that meant the kids wouldn't have to live at home when they went to college. In the early 1970s, they were starting college. At the time, there were no scholarships, or no discounts for people on the faculty or staff. The majority of the people thought our girls could go to Michigan tuition-free."

• Daughters' Arrivals

The Orr household was introduced to the joy and chaos of child rearing in Dubuque, where oldest daughters Jenny and Robin were born in 1954 and 1955. The mix was further complicated in 1956, after Johnny's father died of a heart attack at age 56, when John's grandmother, Anna Lukach, came to live with them. Anna had raised Johnny in Taylorville when his parents worked at the state hospital in Jacksonville, so there was no question that Johnny and Romie would take her in when Bert Orr died. "We couldn't afford to send her money, she couldn't afford to go into a nursing home," Romie said. "She lived with us for six years. There were three girls (Leslie was born in 1958) in one room and Grandma in the other. Grandma loved the girls. She loved pushing them around in the stroller." Baby Becky was born in 1961 in Madison. Grandma Anna lived with the Orrs until she moved into a sanatorium in Madison in 1961, after she had a relapse of tuberculosis. She died in 1962.

Romie incorporated her teaching skills into her parenting philosophy. "Being in phys ed, I believed that in marriage, it's wise to love, honor and keep the kids tired," she said. "If they showed any interest at all in something, we'd let them take lessons. The girls had to support each other because we were too busy doing other things. We were interested in exposing them to different sports without making the decision for them."

As it turned out, oldest daughters Jenny and Robin were in highly competitive Amateur Athletic Union (AAU) swimming programs. They spent much of their youth and teen years practicing and traveling to meets, and later competed for the University of Michigan. Jenny was a member of a national championship relay unit while swimming at Michigan as a freshman; Robin made All-American in water polo there. Leslie and Becky had other opportunities with the growth of women's athletics programs in schools during the 1970s, and they competed in diving, gymnastics, softball and track. At summer camp in Canada

Johnny with his 1973–74 Michigan coaching staff (*from left*) Richard Carter, Jim Dutcher and Bill Frieder. Seven of Orr's former assistant coaches went on to become head coaches. (University of Michigan photo) [*right*] Orr and Bill Frieder made a great pair at Michigan, and Frieder succeeded Johnny as head coach when Orr left for Iowa State in 1980. "I can't think of a better person for a guy to work for," says Frieder, now head coach at Arizona State. (Photo by Bob Kalmbach)

Johnny has been a hit in Ames since his first press conference there, March 25, 1980, announcing his surprise hiring. (Ames *Daily Tribune* photo by Gary Clarke)

Through his busy speaking calendar, Johnny has rubbed elbows with many celebrities. This Ohio State Fair appearance with Bob Hope brought together a group that included Johnny and then Notre Dame coach Digger Phelps (*far right*). (Conrad Photographers, Columbus, Ohio)

Even Carson would love this: Johnny lights up Hilton Coliseum with his pregame entrance, made to the band's rendition of the "Tonight Show" theme. "I still get chills when they play 'Here's Johnny,' even when I'm coaching the other team," said Tom Abatemarco, former Drake head coach and now a Colorado assistant coach. (Ames *Daily Tribune* photo by Jim Percival)

Even though the early seasons at Iowa State produced
losing records, Orr said he fondly remembers his first few
Cyclone teams. Ron Harris (*right*), Malvin Warrick (*34*),
(*front, from left*) John Kunnert, Doug Jones and Robert
Estes share a laugh with Johnny. Orr said, "They really
were excited about playing for me." (United Press
International photo by Tom Peterson)

Ron Virgil (*left*), shown with Orr and assistant coach Jim
Hallihan, was a classic overachiever who played a large role
in the Cyclones reaching the final 16 of the 1986 NCAA
tournament. (Ames *Daily Tribune* photo)

While Johnny has recruited some excellent Iowa players, he's had great success with recruits from Illinois and Michigan. His 1986–87 team was keyed by Illinois natives Elmer Robinson (25), Tom Schafer (55) and Sam Hill (33), and Michigan natives Jeff Grayer (44) and Gary Thompkins (3). (Ames *Daily Tribune* photo by Tom Wallace) [left] One of Johnny's biggest victories in the early years at Iowa State was an overtime upset of nationally ranked Missouri. With Ames businessman and broadcaster Gary Thompson conducting a postgame interview, Johnny congratulates Barry Stevens on his last-second shot as fans mobbed the court. (Ames *Daily Tribune* photo by Jim Percival)

Johnny has had his run-ins with referees, including Woody Mayfield (*right*), who is now working games in the NBA. "I made Woody Mayfield famous for all the problems we've had," Orr joked. "I got him hired into the NBA—they wouldn't have known who he was otherwise." (Ames *Daily Tribune* photo)

Orr has had some long nights on the road in the Big Eight. While the conference has emerged as a national power in recent years, Orr has been singing the Big Eight's praises for nearly a decade. (Ames *Daily Tribune* photo) [*left*] Orr was tickled to receive a plaque from Iowa State associate athletic director Dave Cox after his 300th career win in December of 1984. (Ames *Daily Tribune* photo by Gary Clarke)

Orr and assistants Steve Antrim (*left*) and Jim Hallihan
embrace after a stunning 72-69 victory over No. 5-ranked
Michigan in the second round of the 1986 NCAA
tournament. Orr has called this upset of his former school
his greatest win in coaching. (Ames *Daily Tribune* photo by
Jim Percival)

Johnny says the coaching life is more stressful today. "It just seems like everything today is going against the coaches." (Ames *Daily Tribune* photo) [*below*] Johnny, here with ISU athletic director Max Urick, never gets tired of watching the NCAA selection show in March and seeing his team in the elite 64-team field. Johnny's Iowa State teams have reached the NCAA tournament in five of the last eight seasons. (Ames *Daily Tribune* photo)

Orr's competitive side often is unleashed at courtside through clashes with officials. ''I don't hate basketball officials,'' he says. ''It's a hard job. I'm not saying they should be perfect, but I sat back a long time and didn't say a word. In nine years I never got off the bench and never got technicals, but it made no difference. It seems to me that if you can intimidate them, you'd better do it. (Bobby) Knight seems to do a pretty good job, because everyone is scared to death of him.'' [*below*] Orr yells instructions to the team, 1991. (Ames *Daily Tribune* photo)

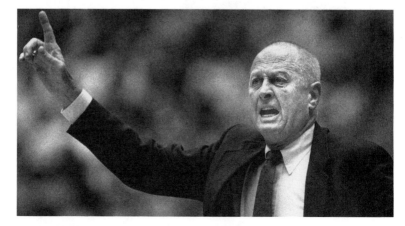

Celebration time at Hilton. Orr calls Iowa State basketball fans "phenomenal. I love them so much, when you don't win, it just kills you." Ticket sales went from less than 7,000 in the year before he arrived to sellout crowds over the last several seasons. (Ames *Daily Tribune* photo by Darrell Goemaat)

Orr discusses a call with an official. (Ames *Daily Tribune* photo) [*below*] Although Orr can get emotional on game night, assistant coach Ric Wesley said Johnny "doesn't like to get angry or frustrated with his players. He puts players at ease. Guys are always comfortable around him." (Ames *Daily Tribune* photo)

A long day at Lawrence, Kansas, 1989–90 season. (Ames *Daily Tribune* photo by Dennis Magee) [*right*] Johnny's playful side came through in Iowa State's successful "Cooler Coaches" promotion, when he joined football coach Jim Walden in a takeoff of the well-known Bartles & Jaymes advertisement. The campaign included posters, TV commercials and a music video. (Iowa State University photo)

Orr said he hopes to keep coaching as long as he's healthy
and it's still fun. Cyclone football coach Jim Walden is
worried that the new breed of coaches won't show the
sensitivity that Orr has in taking a chance on players with
borderline academic records. "That's what Johnny Orr is
all about—giving a chance," Walden said. "He believes we
have to quit shutting doors on people academically. When
did it get so bad that an opportunity to fail is worse than no
opportunity at all? I'm nervous about the Coach Orrs
getting out of this coaching business." (Ames *Daily Tribune*
photo by Darrell Goemaat)

Orr's positive relationship with the media has been a critical part of his success. "He's honest, and that's important," said Fort Dodge sportswriter Bob Brown. "He's accessible and returns phone calls. His rapport with the media, more than his so-so win-loss record, has been very important to his success at Iowa State." (Ames *Daily Tribune* photo by Dennis Magee)

Johnny recently coached the Big Eight all-star team on a summer trip to Spain. (Ames *Daily Tribune* photo by Dennis Magee) [*below*] Orr in Minneapolis, March 1992, where he was installed as president of the National Association of Basketball Coaches (NABC). NCAA executive director and former Iowa coach Dick Schultz (*left*) and Michigan State coach Jud Heathcote are longtime friends. (Photo by Gene McGivern)

The most surprising player of Johnny Orr's Iowa State era has been Jeff Hornacek (*14*). Barely recruited out of high school, Hornacek became an All–Big Eight guard under Orr and has blossomed in the National Basketball Association. (Ames *Daily Tribune* photo by Jim Percival)

Johnny Orr will have a hard time leaving his job so long as Fred Hoiberg is on campus. Hoiberg's all-around play in his freshman season helped the Cyclones reach the NCAA tournament in 1991–92. (Ames *Daily Tribune* photo by Mark Davitt)

KCCI-TV sports anchor Heidi Soliday interviews Orr live at his 1992 roast. (Photo by Gene McGivern) [*below*] Indiana coach Bob Knight was a hit as a guest roaster of Orr at the April 1992 banquet in Des Moines. Knight told the gathering of 250 that there's "nobody I've enjoyed more and nobody I've respected more" in college coaching than Orr. (Photo by Gene McGivern)

in 1975, Robin, Leslie and Becky paddled to a national championship in war canoe. Robin was the first female coxswain ever to win a championship in the sport at the Canadian nationals.

Romie said the coaching life has its ups and downs, but the family generally has enjoyed its experiences. They're quite proficient at performing the wave: they've waved goodbye while departing from St. Louis, Milton, Dubuque, Madison, Amherst, Champaign and Ann Arbor on the way to the current stop in Ames. As their Rolodex grows, Romie puts a positive spin on that affiliation with moving vans. She considers it a chance to live in eight great places, while never being pushed out the door.

"We've always been lucky: we never had to leave somewhere, and there's a difference between going and leaving," she said, referring to Johnny's proud coaching record of never having been fired. "We always figured if people were good friends they'll still be good friends. Moving gave the girls a tremendous perspective in friendships and relationships, that they may or may not last. We lived in Madison four years, and our oldest daughter (Jenny) just hated to leave. I remember we had been living in Amherst, Mass., only four months when she said, 'If Gail doesn't write me soon I'm going to quit missing her.' "

On the flip side, Romie noted that moving to new jobs always brought a new challenge. "The thing about moving is that no matter what you've done before and what you've accomplished, you still have to work just as hard to make your reputation as you did to establish it in the first place," she said. "John always has been able to do that."

The hardest times came during the early years at Michigan, when the criticism of Johnny's coaching took a nasty personal tone. A student, Jim Barahal, made "Dump Orr" his platform to get elected to student government in the fall of 1973. "We both worked hard in Ann Arbor," Romie said. "I tried to fill every niche, do everything necessary to sell our program. But it wasn't always easy. They had these 'Dump Orr' signs at games just like you see those 'John 3:16' signs. That was tough on Jenny and Robin."

The patience of Romie also was tested, and she says it was hard to forget the criticism even after Johnny silenced critics with a successful run at Michigan. "It doesn't matter how many letters of apology you get three years later; what kind of person would step on someone else to further their own goals?" she asks. "John accepted it at face value. John never carried a grudge, never had self-pity. He was always upbeat, always ready to be objective." Romie said Johnny's ability to ignore Barahal's attack is an example of why he's had a 50-year career as an athlete and coach: "What's always impressed me is how fair John is. Some people, I'm sorry, but I can't be nice to. Sometimes I hold a grudge. But John isn't that way. A lot of people don't know John Orr. They think he has some grand ego, which isn't the case."

Romie said basic character values have made Johnny a success as a coach. "Coaching is something he really enjoys," Romie said. "He develops a relationship with each of his players. It's very genuine. People respect him, and it isn't like he's tough to be around. He gets involved in their projects, like in fund raising. He enjoys going out and speaking to groups. He comes back pumped up to the sky. It's his good nature, love of people and love of his job."

With that formula, it's no surprise to Romie that Johnny has been a hit at Iowa State. "A lot of factors made (Iowa State and Johnny) a great relationship," she said. "Like anything, you forget about the bad moments. God, it's a good thing, because 1989 was tough. And our first year was tough." Coming to Ames has been as rewarding for Romie as it has for the coach. "Before Ames, I didn't have much time to be a friend. I was too busy being a wife, mom and teacher. In Ames, I finally had time to be a friend," she said.

As a testament to how fulfilling the Ames years have been, Romie recalled an anecdote regarding Magic Johnson, who came close to signing with Michigan before he opted to stay near his hometown of Lansing to attend Michigan State. Regarded among the greatest impact players in the history of the National Collegiate Athletic Association (NCAA) or the National Basketball Association (NBA), Magic led the Spartans to a national title and then carried the Los Angeles Lakers to five NBA championships throughout the 1980s before his abrupt retirement in 1991. "Seeing Magic Johnson and seeing what a tremendous individual he is, I said I couldn't believe how our life would have been different if he'd have come to Michigan," Romie said. "But John said, 'You can't even think of that. We'd have never left Michigan and never come to Ames. We've had too much fun at Iowa State.'"

Robin said her parents' move to Ames was risky but was too great an opportunity to pass up. "How many people at age 50 get a chance like this to find out if they really are that good?" she asked. "It took a tremendous amount of courage to make that big of a change."

• All Grown Up

The Orrs remain close, with three of the daughters living in central Iowa and a fourth living in the Chicago area. The daughters are carrying on the family legacy well, with education, coaching and parenting among their primary activities.

Jenny graduated from Michigan in physical education and special education, and received a master's degree in educational administration from Northern Illinois. She currently is director of student activities at Downers Grove (Illinois) South High and recently retired from coaching high school swimming after 16 years. Jenny married John Davis, who is the girls' varsity assistant basketball coach at Downers Grove South in addition to being assistant police chief at Downers Grove.

Leslie graduated from Iowa State and teaches middle school in the Saydel school district, north of Des Moines, at Woodside Middle School. She's married to Craig Boylan, sales representative at Benson Motors in Ames. Their son, John Henry, the first grandson for Johnny and Romie, was born in 1989.

Robin received her doctoral degree in marketing nutrition and gerontology at Iowa State and teaches at Des Moines Area Community College. She also has a background as a swimming coach and tutor, and has run Phil Hubbard's sports camps. She received a master's degree in nutrition at Iowa State and a bachelor's degree in zoology and chemistry at Michigan.

Becky was an English major at Michigan and lives and works in Ames with a career in marketing. She's engaged to John Montgomery and will be married in May 1993.

"You get any combination of us together and it's like the greatest party," Jenny said. "It's something you can bring a friend, a husband or another couple into and it's just as fun. It's not just basketball stuff, either. In fact, it's almost more fun when it's not a basketball event. I don't know anything more fun than just getting together with my family."

Robin said, "We're all eternal pranksters. We have competitions at birthdays to see who can make people laugh longest, or who can be the tackiest with cards."

Leslie added that the sisters have an unusually strong bond. "We're always very supportive of each other. That's not to say we don't have disagreements. If someone is dating someone I don't like, I'd tell them. And they always did the same for me when I was single. We're a pretty close family."

• Memories

The Orr sisters say they have both unique and universal memories of growing up. "We've had a great life," Robin said. "Swimming took us a lot of places, and Dad took us a lot of places. We had a very different experience than most of my friends." At the same time, Becky noted, the sisters wore hand-me-downs and sacrificed like all kids. They had the loyal, lovable family pets—Boston bulldogs named Buckets, Maggie and Jigs—that simultaneously were a joy and a pain. "They tore the house up sometimes. Whoo! Boy, that was an experience," Johnny said.

Celebrity

Being the oldest, Jenny has memories of the time before Johnny Orr became a recognized figure nationally. "It was no big deal," she said of her dad's profession. "It's just what he did. I remember being in college and being aware for the first time that his job was much more in the public eye. I remember the first time I ever went through a hard time with it was at Michigan, leaving a football game with thousands and thousands of people leaving the stadium and having this guy (Jim Barahal) standing on the roof of a house with a microphone yelling, 'Dump Orr!' " The Barahal incident was a reminder to the Orr girls that even the best situations have challenges. "We were always reminded that fame was fleeting," Robin said. "The things that matter in life have nothing to do with fame."

The pressure in Ann Arbor was particularly hard for Becky, the youngest. "When I was in junior high, it was hard to understand how those people could be so wrong," she said. "I knew my dad wasn't a bad guy." Robin, then a freshman at Michigan, recalls Barahal handing her a leaflet, not knowing she was the coach's daughter. "I just told him, 'Could you wait a few years? He's paying for my education.' "

Robin said the incident reinforced her belief that you have to learn to bite your lip and not respond to criticism. "Like our mother, we're all fiercely loyal," Robin said. "We're not allowed to speak out, because whatever we say will be attributed to (Johnny). It probably saved us a lot of grief. Except for a few select people, nobody hears my opinion. I remember the first day I was at Iowa State, I had a professor tell me, 'I think your father makes too much money.' I said, 'Go tell him that.' "

The celebrity parent creates some unexpected benefits, too. "I remember meeting Wilt Chamberlain in an airport," Robin said. "I walked up to him and came up to his knee. People said,

'Wow, you know Wilt Chamberlain?' I just thought he's just another basketball player. Just another nice guy. He's just a person. I was never in awe of athletes." Becky recalled how access to free tickets to Michigan's basketball games could boost your popularity in junior high. "The guys were bound to like you," she said. "I gave tickets to all my friends." In another case when having a famous father helped, Jenny chaperoned a group of seriously handicapped students from her school on a trip from Chicago to Los Angeles. When the group went to a Dodger-Cub game, Jenny asked her dad to send a note to Cub broadcaster Harry Caray, in hopes that Johnny's ties would be influential in getting Harry to mention their group over the air for the parents watching back home. Sure enough, Harry gave a special welcome "to Johnny Orr's daughter, Jenny Davis's class from Downers Grove South High School." Romie recalls, "That meant so much to those parents. That might be the only time in their parents' lives these kids were gone for 24 hours."

Leslie recalls having a particularly great senior year in high school. Being a member of the bicentennial graduating class of 1976, it was particularly exciting to get to travel to Philadelphia, the bicentennial city, to watch Michigan reach the national finals that spring. "I thought I was pretty cool as a senior," Leslie said. "Then when I went back to Ann Arbor for my 10-year high school reunion, we had just beaten Michigan in the NCAA tournament in 1986. Then for my 15-year reunion, guess what? We just beat Michigan again in 1991." Leslie's elementary school students are impressed that she's related to the Iowa State coach. "My students come up to me and say, 'Mrs. Boylan, my dad doesn't believe you're Johnny Orr's daughter.' They get a charge out of it. I tell them that the ones wearing the Iowa State colors get to line up first for recess. That always makes the Hawkeye fans mad."

Despite living in five different cities growing up, the sisters said moving always seemed to bring new opportunities and friendships. "I always was excited about moving," Leslie said. "Part of that was we were always moving up. I remember leaving Wisconsin, I was so excited. I looked out the window as we drove away, and saw Suzy, my best friend, crying. I thought, 'Why is she crying? We could write letters. That would be fun.' I can remember playing in the field house at Massachusetts and running all the way up to the rafters."

"I loved growing up," Robin said. "My mother is a Pollyanna. We never 'left' anywhere; we always moved to somewhere better. Mother never allowed us to look at the dark side of it. Everywhere we'd go was going to be better. We were never allowed to complain. We were happy. We always had tremendous opportunity to do things."

Leslie noted that even today Romie "always makes sure there's something to look forward to. She even does that with Grandma Robinson. She calls Grandma at 5 o'clock every single day so Grandma has that every day to look forward to. She's always instilling that in us. That's important, because when you get down, it's hard to get up. She's one of the most productive people I know. We never were allowed to sit in front of the TV on Saturday mornings. We'd always be up cleaning the house. She'd always say, 'We've got to get something done today.' She always has been a real go-getter."

Being the youngest allowed Becky to spend more time with her parents. "Mother and I are like best friends," Becky said. "My mom is dynamite. Incredible. She's like my oldest sister Jenny; they don't waste a minute of a day, don't waste a second of a minute. I could never keep up. She's very sincere and cares about everyone she knows. Mom and I spent a lot of time together. Dad was traveling a lot, and my sisters were gone. We went out to eat together a lot."

Being a wife, teacher and coach herself, Jenny has a special appreciation of how hard her parents have worked. "I have a tremendous respect for my dad, but I'm probably more sensitive to the commitment Mom made. She supported him and stuck with him." Leslie added, "Mother has maintained her personality throughout. If she didn't, she wouldn't have survived. It's tough because as a coach's wife you have to be a strong person yourself, but you have to be able to drop everything to fill a role. She's always prepared. You never know who Dad will bring home from the golf course. We always had to make sure the house was clean."

"A lot of relationships break up in that stress that comes with coaching," Jenny said. "The great thing about my parents is not only did their marriage survive, but it nurtured and grew in that situation." Robin added, "Sometimes you forget to give your parents credit. They've been extremely wise in things they've done. They did a super job of not screwing us up. Mother trained us to be independent and trusted us more than anyone."

Education

Education was another priority that Romie and Johnny stressed, and they've been generous in paying for college and postgraduate studies (although Johnny joked that he wouldn't pay for tuition to Michigan State, Indiana or Ohio State). "They taught us when we were very young that a woman with a college degree had the same earning potential as a man with a high school diploma," Becky said. "They taught us you have to look out for No. 1."

Leslie said her parents were especially patient with her decisions in college. She attended Eastern Michigan for 3½ years but decided she didn't want to graduate with a physical education major. She opted to take a break from school, moved to Colorado for a year and lived with a girlfriend, and eventually took a job making ice cream cones. She then moved to Arizona but couldn't find a job. Johnny and Romie later welcomed her back home without judgment. "They weren't happy about me quitting school, but they didn't stop me. They were really understanding," Leslie said. "I learned a lot, even though it was the hard way to learn it. But I'm glad I did it. A lot of my friends got their degree, got married and later found out they never did anything in their life." Leslie finished her degree at Iowa State.

Jenny said her parents preached a simple philosophy: " 'Do what you believe in; appreciate what you have; work hard for it; and do the best you can.' The versions of that come out very differently in what we've chosen to do, but we all understand that . . . The biggest thing my mother ever said was that it was important that we had our own identity, particularly as our dad's identity got stronger."

Athletic experiences

As it turned out, their own athletic experiences turned out to be a large part of the Orr sisters' identities. "My mother made a real effort to get us involved in different things in every town we lived in," Robin said. "In Massachusetts, she got us interested in dance. In Urbana (Illinois), we got into a high-powered gymnastics program. The other thing we always were encouraged to do was to play golf. We'd be at the golf course from 6 a.m. to noon. Mom popped for a hamburger at lunch, and we'd spend the afternoon at the pool. We started swimming (competitively) because that's where all our friends were at night . . . We were busy. We swam eight hours a day. We'd leave at 5 in the morning and get home at 10 at night."

The daughters say Johnny didn't follow the stereotypes and push his daughters to excel in sports. "Dad wasn't a typical sports dad," Jenny said. "He didn't expect you to be real competitive. He just wanted you to enjoy sports and have something to do. He loved for you to try different things. He values the chance to play golf with Mom, and he wanted us to have things to do with a husband or a friend. He got a motorcycle, but we were the ones who got to ride it. Two of my sisters have tried skydiving, and my husband and I learned sailing, and now we really like to golf together. He was proud of us, but the stories he would tell were not about winning some race. I remember one of my sisters slipped at the start of a swimming race and fell off the block. Instead of quitting, she still swam the race, and he always said how proud he was that she finished."

Robin added, "The only thing Dad ever said about sports was 'Don't quit before you're done with your commitment, and give 100 percent when you're there.' I remember coaching and having certain parents come up to you and say, 'What can I do to get my kid to swim faster?' Then I'd think, 'Have you considered suicide?' because they'd probably improve if they didn't feel so much pressure."

Becky said Johnny strives to let his family share in his success. "Once I was in high school I broke my back, and he dedicated a game to me," she said. "Another time I was sick in the hospital for the Kansas State game, and he came and apologized to me for getting kicked out of the game. I thought it was funny because he didn't have anything to apologize for. He's very loyal. He has a lot of integrity. He believes in following the rules. He would never go out of his way to hurt anyone. I only hope I'm as wise as my parents someday. Sometimes, I wish I could be more like them."

The daughters say that Johnny is measuring up well as a grandfather, too. "I enjoy my grandson, John Henry," Johnny said. "He wasn't even two years old and already he could hit a golf ball, and he knew how to shoot a basket. He recognizes all kinds of sports on TV. He wears me out in a hurry. He likes to go boating, but he doesn't like to go slow. He looks likes he's going to be a center on the football team. He's a chunky guy, but I was chunky, too, as a toddler."

• Retirement?

Leslie said it's hard to envision the thought of Johnny retiring from coaching. "I think he'll die doing it," she said. The Orr sisters speculate that Johnny will remain busy whenever he leaves basketball. "He gets a lot of joy from coaching," Becky said. "But when he retires, it will give him a chance to do the things he likes. Basketball season really stresses him out." Robin warned, "Dad better get a big-time hobby, or we'll have to shoot him. Whenever he's sick, and is around the house, he's as annoying as hell. He'll just do something else. He loves golf. If Iowa State is smart, they'll try to keep him to do fund raising."

Jenny said the best part is that whenever Johnny waves to the Hilton crowd for the final time, he can feel proud. "My dad's career is like a fairy tale come true," she explained. "When you can do what you want, work hard at something you believe in and it all works, it's like a fairy tale. He's a great person. He's very sincere, and he does things for the right reasons. It's great that other people recognize that. He has a tremendous ability to appreciate what he's got. He appreciates being alive today. He appreciates being recognized. He remembers who helped him get where he is, long after other people have forgotten. He's very good at giving other people credit. If you were shoveling snow with him, it would always be 'Look what *we* did, Jenny,' and that made you feel special."

"I always felt most fortunate to be in this family," Robin said. "There's a certain amount of luck involved in birth. Still to this day we have a lot of fun as a family. I know a lot of people and families where it's not like that. Sure, we had disagreements, but we always worked things out. Our parents leave us alone and allow us to live our own lives. If I had to pick what kind of family to be in, I would pick my own family. That's a real tribute, mostly to my mother. You can't pick your parents, but I've always said that if life is a crapshoot, I got a good set of dice."

Johnny said Romie and his daughters have been an inspiration to him. "My family is pretty close, particularly the girls and their mother," Johnny said. "We always have good picnics and parties. We have a great time when everyone gets together at the Lake Panorama home. We play golf, boat, swim. Everyone has their own bedroom out there—that's why we have so big a place. It's fun to have everyone close by. My daughters are all different. I like them all. They're all pretty good kids."

"My position in Iowa is unique. I can't exactly tell you why. I never have figured that out. Here in Iowa, you're much more in the public eye than in other jobs. Here, whoo, you can hardly eat or go anywhere without somebody wanting your autograph or wanting to talk to you. But I don't mind that. I've been in places where it has been the other way around, where they don't care at all. Coming out to Iowa State was like getting a fresh start. Everyone has been so nice to me. I've never known a coach who has been treated like I was by the fans. Here, you feel so badly for the fans when you lose. It wasn't always like that at Michigan."

• Testimonial

How is Johnny Orr regarded by his peers in coaching, his colleagues at Iowa State and the people who cover him in the media? Research compiled for this book suggests that Orr has scores of friends and admirers. The bad news for Johnny comes when you factor in the inverse rule of testimonials: The nicer folks are with their tributes in the book, the more aggressive they'll be at the microphone at the subject's retirement roast.

If that holds true, Johnny may have to call out extra security for his eventual goodbye party. Unless they implement a 45-second shot clock, Orr's retirement roast might run longer than an NBA season. All because this coach has worked for, worked with and worked above an array of interesting people and personalities. A tough crowd? Look for the head of Missouri's rowdy "Antlers" student group to offer the invocation. Bob Knight will claim that Woody Mayfield has been hired as on-site rules chief at the Panorama Golf Course . . . Bo Schembechler will reveal that Jim Barahal is running for Congress in Michigan and needs a platform . . . Max Urick will warn that the *Des Moines Register* has opened a news bureau in Panora to be staffed by investigative reporter Tom Witosky . . . Cyclone head football coach Jim Walden will announce Johnny's selection as grand marshal of the Veishea Parade—the Veishea Riot 5-Year Reunion Parade, that is, set for Welch Avenue in May 1993 . . . Bill Frieder will announce that he hired Joe Falls to write Johnny's eulogy for two reasons: (1) he's had Johnny dead and buried before, and (2) it'll give Orr incentive to stay alive that much longer.

A disclaimer is appropriate at the outset of this chapter. Dozens and dozens of people who know Orr well were interviewed for this book. The majority of these sources have a connection with the coach. Thus, seldom was heard a discouraging word. Many of their observations are printed here, not to elevate but to help define Johnny Orr. Why is he so well liked? What are his coaching philosophies? How does he relate to players? How does he deal with the media and the public? How is he regarded in the coaching profession? What has he meant to Iowa State?

The testimonials in this chapter come from four sources: (1) other coaches, both at Iowa State and other schools, (2) assistants, past and present, (3) players he's coached, and (4) media representatives.

• Other Coaches

Johnny's income, visibility, power and ego make him a prime target for jealousy or resentment among his colleagues on Iowa State's athletic department staff. While internal conflicts have popped up, colleagues say Orr's 12 years generally have been marked by harmony. Johnny had a fallout with football coach Jim Criner, which is no surprise given their drastically different personalities. In another rift, Orr's relationship with the Cyclone women's basketball coaches soured in 1991. Johnny was irked that after 10 seasons, the men's program was forced to share the prime practice time slot in Hilton Coliseum with the women's team. Johnny also resented the pressure from the women's staff to share an academic advisor assigned to men's basketball. That same year, Johnny said he was hurt when his boss, athletic director Max Urick, refused to support Orr's appeal of a one-game suspension assessed by the Big Eight Conference for criticism of officiating.

However, Iowa State athletic staffers interviewed say Orr has been a friend to the entire athletic department, and vice versa. Their appreciation of Johnny goes beyond the feeling, as one coach put it, of "If football and basketball don't win, we don't have a salary."

Iowa State colleague Ron McEachran, an assistant track and field coach, said Johnny's personality works because he's sincere. "He doesn't have to pay attention to an assistant track coach," McEachran said, "but he does. He isn't too big for others."

"With Johnny, what you see is what you get," said Iowa State assistant wrestling coach Les Anderson. "He's not a split personality, and he's not two-faced. People like him. He's honest. He doesn't mince words."

"I think hiring Johnny Orr was probably the greatest move Iowa State ever made," said Frank Randall, Iowa State head athletic trainer throughout the 1970s and 1980s. "Everything about him is very positive. He's a winner. He goes out of his way to meet people. He has a great personality. He puts everything into perspective. There was never any doubt he was going to be successful here. It was just a matter of fact: we're going to win, it's just a matter of time. What was good was the fact that he didn't get uptight about doing it overnight."

When Criner stormed into Ames, he talked boldly of taking a team to the Orange Bowl. Many people say that sent Criner off on the wrong foot in Cyclone Country. Instead of adopting an Orr-like approach of patience and pragmatism, Criner blitzed ahead with a win-immediately philosophy. Granted, Criner was unproven as a Division I-A head coach and didn't have the long-term job security that Johnny enjoyed, yet Criner's hard-charging style took its toll and contributed to the circumstances that prompted his dismissal. Criner had the greatest of intentions in bringing winning football to Iowa State, and worked as hard and as long as anyone could ask, but his rigid and authoritative approach made enemies. It's believed that some of those enemies contacted NCAA investigators or cooperated when contacted by the investigators. As a result, Iowa State found itself facing serious charges of rules violations involving Criner's football program. To show the NCAA it was serious about policing itself, the school fired Criner late in his fourth season of a five-year contract.

That firing, the NCAA investigation and subsequent probation and a steady decline in revenue from lost football ticket sales sent the morale of Iowa State coaches and fans plummeting during the 1986–87 school year. Colleagues said Johnny's value to Iowa State never was greater than in that critical time. "He kept us afloat during a rough time," explained Rod Wilson. "In terms of fund raising and fan interest, he rallied the troops and kept morale up. If Johnny wasn't here, we might be down to 12 sports right now from 21 because of money. And had we not hired Johnny Orr, we wouldn't have gotten (Cyclone football coach) Jim Walden."

"Johnny really became a great ambassador for the entire Iowa State athletic department and the entire university," Cyclone track coach Bill Bergan said. "In the coaching staffs previous to the Johnny Orr era, there wasn't really the cohesiveness and mutual respect among the total athletic program at Iowa State. Johnny emerged as a leader in our ranks."

"There probably isn't a coach in the nation with a little better than .500 record who has the type of support that Coach Orr does," said Ed Gagnier, the former Cyclone gymnastics coach and now Iowa State's director of athletic development. "His eagerness to help the football program has been important. Orr could do just about what he wants, and when he endorsed Jim Walden and publicly accepted him, that gave our fans a big boost. The relationship wasn't the same with basketball and football before Walden came here."

Walden added that he's puzzled how anyone couldn't enjoy Johnny. "If you know Johnny and don't like him, I think you've got a problem," he said. "You might not like him if you don't know him. But anyone that's ever played 18 holes of golf with him and or sat and had a beer with him will like him. He is an absolute delight to spend time with. I don't get to spend as much time with him as I'd like. There isn't a football coach in America who could possibly have more fun with the basketball coach as I do. And I love George Raveling and enjoyed our time together (on the coaching staff) at Washington State, but this is the best situation I can imagine. I guess it's because my sense of humor and John's are similar. I love to hear him tell his old coaching stories."

Walden said people are drawn to Johnny. "What sets Coach Orr apart is that he's totally himself," Walden said. "He likes himself and loves what he's doing, and it shows. People like being around him for that reason. He's one of those people you like to be liked by. People like Bobby Knight like to be liked by Johnny Orr."

Walden said he's still amazed at how many different people are friends with Johnny, from all over the country. "He knows everybody," Walden said. "Never in my life have I met someone like him. Everywhere I go, people come up to me and ask me to tell Johnny Orr hello. This guy can call Jack Nicklaus and Nicklaus knows him."

Walden said coaches not only appreciate Orr's personality, they like what he stands for. Walden said Johnny is admired for his decision to leave the prestige of Michigan to come to the less-visible Iowa State. "When he left Michigan for Iowa State, it tells you coaching is more than the position or the place and status. He is admired for that," Walden said. "He has done marvelous things with not always the best programs."

The support goes beyond lip service. Former *Des Moines Register* sportswriter Bob Dyer said that Johnny went out of his way to help former Drake coach Tom Abatemarco after Abatemarco's much-publicized firing following a Bulldog player revolt in 1990. "Johnny talked to some of the Drake players," Dyer said, "and they told him they weren't trying to ruin (Abatemarco's) career or get him fired, they just wanted some changes. But outside people stepped in and it got out of control. When John heard that, he went to bat for Tom. A lot of guys say they'll do it, but never follow through."

Abatemarco said his respect for Orr grew through the ordeal because Johnny wasn't obligated to help him. Johnny lobbied for Abatemarco at the National Association of Basketball Coaches (NABC) meeting when it wasn't necessarily the popular thing. Abatemarco's coaching future was hanging in the balance when Orr stepped forward, and Johnny's support was instrumental in Abatemarco's hiring as an assistant coach at Colorado.

"When I came to Drake, I really didn't know him and he didn't know me," Abatemarco said of Johnny. "When I went through the controversy at Drake, he was real kind to me. He stepped in and helped me get the Colorado job. He supported me at the NABC meeting. There was no reason for him to do that. We were not particularly close. I think Johnny Orr is one of the legends of the game. I think he's one of the top 10 coaches in the country. When you talk about the Bobby Knights, the Dean Smiths, you say Johnny Orr. His record shows it. We feel (his) is a model program for us to emulate at Colorado. He has a clean program, his kids do well in grades, he plays exciting basketball. I still get chills when they play 'Here's Johnny,' even coaching the other team."

Johnny went out of his way to embrace Jim Gibbons when the latter was an unproven 25-year-old hired as Iowa State's wrestling coach. "Johnny always identifies with younger coaches," Gibbons said. "He's willing to give advice and share the stories. He relates to what it's like to be a young coach. A couple of times when wrestling was struggling, he called me up and said, 'Gibby, I want you to keep your head up. We've got to stick together. Keep your spirits up.' When I first started, he put his arm around me in public and said, 'This is our guy.' He was probably at the peak of his popularity at the time, and the decision to hire me may have been controversial then because of my age. But Johnny basically put his arm around me and said, 'Cyclones, this is our guy—you're going to be all right.' He kept things real positive. That was a big thing for me. He made the transition easier for me with our alumni and friends of Iowa State. I'll definitely always look up to him and always consider him to be a great friend."

Here's a sampling of other opinions on Johnny, given by some big names in college basketball:

Arizona coach Lute Olson

"When I think of Johnny Orr, I think: (1) great guy, (2) tremendous sense of humor. The only time you'll ever see him in a bad mood is when he's lost a game. I enjoyed competing against him when he was at Michigan and at Iowa State. I think we always handled (the Iowa-Iowa State rivalry) in a competitive but friendly manner, and that's not always easy to do. We even made some appearances together to diffuse any of that rivalry. One thing about him: Don't ask him a question if you don't want to hear what's on his mind. Most people in the public eye are very selective with their words, and if there's a doubt, it's probably better not said. But that's just not the way Johnny is. That's probably the greatest compliment to him. Johnny is Johnny, take it or leave it, like him or don't like him. That's how he is."

Former Kansas coach Larry Brown

"Johnny's Iowa State teams didn't always have the great size, but he had some real athletes. I never won in Hilton Coliseum, but I always liked going there. The fans were great, and the atmosphere was special. I really liked his kids—Hornacek, Grayer and Thompkins were all good people. If you can accept losing, I don't mind losing to a guy like John. He runs a clean program. John always gives you credit after a game, he doesn't make excuses. He's very competitive, he wants to beat you, but he's fun to be around when it's all over."

Arizona State coach Bill Frieder

"I can't think of a better person for a guy to work for. My seven years I worked for him probably were my most enjoyable in basketball. Not only is he a good person, he was a good boss and a good friend. He gave you credit, he wasn't insecure, and he made people know that you contributed. That's probably why our families developed such good friendships.

"One time at Michigan, *Sports Illustrated* was in there for a story on our program and saw how involved I was with the team. Somehow it came out in the story that I was taking credit for the success of the team. I was so down in the dumps and really hurt after that story was printed because it gave the wrong impression. So at the end of the week, John sent me a check with a note that said: 'Bill, here's a $500 bonus. Thanks for helping so much in our program, especially helping me do my interviews for *Sports Illustrated*. I love you. John.' That's the kind of guy he is.

"He didn't want to hire me at first (in 1973) because he was afraid he might get fired and he was concerned about my well-being. He said, 'You've got tenure at your job.' But I wanted to come in the worst way, and he finally brought me in. I was really happy to be a part of the best seven years in Michigan basketball history. I always admired that he never took basketball out of the office with him. He could walk away from it, while it stays with me."

Michigan State coach Jud Heathcote

"The times I've been around John, I've always had a good time. He seems to radiate enthusiasm in everything he does. John is very highly respected by coaches around the country. They look upon him as sort of a coaches' coach. We coached against each other in a lot of games. I remember that overtime loss to Iowa State (in December of 1985) when (Jeff) Hornacek was a senior and (Scott) Skiles was a junior. That was a classic game. They beat us on a last-second shot. But the most competitive thing we were involved with was the recruitment of Earvin Johnson. That was my first year at Michigan State. I think Earvin's mind told him to go to Michigan, because Johnny had them established as a top program. But his heart was always at Michigan State, because that's where his home was, in Lansing. Eventually, he took a chance and came with us, and we convinced him that he could *be* the program.

"I think John never quite got the recognition in (Michigan) that he deserved. The Detroit papers are just brutal. Even with the great seasons Bo Schembechler had, if they'd lose a bowl game you'd think they lost all their games from the stories they wrote. Yet if you went around the country and asked people knowledgeable about basketball who the top 10 coaches are, Johnny Orr would be on most of those lists."

Heathcote again (at the Johnny Orr roast, April 1992)

"In all honesty, I don't know why I'm here. I never liked

Johnny Orr. When he was 5-years-old, he fell out of the ugly tree and hit every branch. When he was in fifth grade, he lost all communication skills—he broke the knuckle on his middle finger.

"I think so much of Johnny Orr that if I ever get diagnosed with having a terminal disease, I'd like to spend it with Johnny Orr, because ladies and gentlemen, I guarantee you, two weeks with Johnny would seem like a lifetime.

"When I think about Johnny Orr, I think that Johnny is the best friend a guy could ever have and the best guy a friend could ever have. He's a credit to our profession, to his family and to everyone he comes into contact with. I don't believe that you people, and maybe some of you do, know how lucky you are to have Johnny as your coach. He calls everybody 'Coach.' But I'm thrilled he calls me coach, and I'm also thrilled we both call each other friends."

Indiana University coach Bob Knight (at the Johnny Orr roast, April 1992)

Here's a telegram for you:

DEAR JOHN

IT'S ALWAYS BEEN A REAL PLEASURE TO PLAY AGAINST YOUR TEAMS. PLEASE THE NEXT TIME YOU COME DOWN TO PLAY, YOU COME AND LEAVE HALLIHAN AT HOME.

SINCERELY
BILLY TUBBS

University of Southern California and former University of Iowa coach George Raveling (at the Johnny Orr roast, April 1992)

"Johnny Orr has one of the most interesting shoe deals I've ever heard of. Reebok is paying Orr $50,000 a year to endorse Nike.

"I've known John Orr for many years, and I want to advise you this: If you need a friend (*pause*) get a dog.

"Here's a guy who could have been anything he wants, and why he chose himself I'll never know.

"In all seriousness, he's a friend, he's a coach, he's a man. He's a man for all seasons and all reasons. I feel sincerely that one of my pleasures in life was to get to know Coach Orr and rub shoulders with him. It's made me a better human being. Each one of you who follow Iowa State basketball is most fortunate to have John Orr as your basketball coach."

Broadcaster and ex-coach Dick Vitale

"John has a great sense of humor, and behind it all, he has a great knowledge of the game. He's a tremendously fierce competitor who hates to lose. He and I used to have some great battles when I was coaching at Detroit. I think we played a big role in Michigan not winning the national championship in 1977. They had to play us in the NCAA tournament, and it was an emotional game. I remember wearing a maize and blue outfit into the arena. He got mad at me for wearing the Michigan colors, but it was all part of the ploy. They were ranked No. 1 in the nation, and even though they beat us in a close game, it was so physically and emotionally draining they had nothing left when they came back to play North Carolina-Charlotte, and they got knocked off.

"I remember the time at Detroit when we got the chance to play Michigan in our arena, and we played one of the great games in Detroit history. We were so emotionally charged up because Michigan was like Goliath and it was a big game to my kids. Near the end of the game, I was sprinting all over the place and I left the court. I think John thought I was hot-dogging it, and I probably was. I am a hot dog, I guess that's part of my act. But it was done out of excitement, not disrespect. I have nothing but respect for Michigan.

"Johnny had a hell of a lot more success than me, and he coached a lot longer than I did, and I've always had a tremendous amount of respect for him. The Big Eight Conference has become absolutely dynamite. You could have a good team and still finish in the middle of the pack. I'd love one time to (broadcast) a game at Hilton Coliseum. I hear it's a real happening."

• Assistants

Another tribute to Orr is the number of coaches who worked for him and went on to become college head coaches. Jack Leaman (Massachusetts), Jim Dutcher (Minnesota), Bill Frieder (Michigan and Arizona State), Fred Snowden (Arizona), Jim Boyce (Eastern Michigan), Charlie Harrison (East Carolina) and

Steve Antrim (Wisconsin-Milwaukee) are past or current head coaches who previously worked for Johnny. Another colleague, Tom Nissalke, worked for Orr in the University of Wisconsin freshman program 30 years back and went on to coach the NBA's Cleveland Cavaliers. Orr also coached at Wisconsin with D. Wayne Lukas, who's regarded today as one of horse racing's leading trainers.

Johnny predicts that all of his current Cyclone assistant coaches—Jim Hallihan, Ric Wesley and Steve Krafcisin—will make outstanding head coaches. Yet all three, and others on his previous staffs, say that working as an assistant under Johnny is more attractive than a lot of smaller head-coaching jobs. Orr gives his assistants responsibility and is a fair boss, they say, and his connections can be valuable to a coach seeking a job in the future. Harrison, hired in 1980 as Orr's first assistant coach at Iowa State, once said, "When Johnny Orr asks you to be his assistant, anybody in his right mind would be a fool to turn down a chance to work with him."

The flip side of retaining bright assistant coaches and giving them authority is that it can trigger criticism of the head coach's ability. America wants its presidents, news anchors and head coaches to be strong. While Johnny's personality and recruiting ability are roundly praised, some question whether Orr measures up as a game strategist. The old *Sports Illustrated* rap that Johnny "can't lead his team out of the locker room" was hard for Orr to live down at Michigan, even with his subsequent national success. One theory is that Johnny is where he is today primarily because he's had the Dutchers, the Frieders and the Hallihans as his brain trusts. Such criticism might surface because the Johnny on display at courtside is more of an analyzer than an aerobics instructor. Sure, there's an occasional wing-tip stomp under his seat, plus the customary face-to-face encounters with the refs, but Johnny's not big on waving, pointing and calling out formations. He never subscribed to the coaching club that loosens the tie, throws off the jacket and jumps around the coaching box like a rock singer in concert. Once the ball goes up, he thinks the word "coach" is more of a noun than a verb, unlike some of the telegenic coaches of the 1990s. Yet colleagues say the Orr mind is always working.

"He doesn't overcoach," said Wesley, who calls his boss "O" and has been with Johnny since his arrival in Ames in 1980. "O doesn't let his ego get in the way of coaching. He puts less stock in how much a coach can control the outcome. During the game, he's such a good listener, he takes in suggestions, absorbs them and makes up his mind. He's secure in himself. He's not afraid to take input from coaches or players. He has a sharp mind. You'll say 'Man, that guy is hot.' And he'll say, 'I'll say he's hot. He's hit 7 of 9.' "

Perhaps the bigger question is this: even if Orr's assistant coaches are extremely visible and pivotal to his success, is that a negative, or actually a strength? Many times in coaching, the verb *delegate* has the same connotation as *Watergate*. Johnny's assistants say he's confident enough in himself and his abilities to hire good people and let them do their jobs. A spot on Orr's staff isn't like the token vice-presidential nominee on the presidential ticket.

"He's always been a guy who surrounded himself with guys who complement him," Hallihan said. "At Michigan or at Iowa State, the time demands away from the court with the press, (booster) club, and outside appearances make it necessary to give your staff responsibility. I think it's the sign of an excellent leader to hire people and allow them to do their jobs. Some coaches have to make every decision, and not only do you kill yourself trying to do that, it's not as good when you don't get more people's input. On the bench, he listens to the things I have to say, but he's still the one who makes the decisions."

Hallihan said Johnny's experience as an assistant coach makes him sensitive to the needs of his own assistants. "When he hired me, he was looking for a guy who possibly had been a head coach, someone who was a family-type guy and a floor coach," Hallihan said. "He doesn't have time to look at hours and hours of film himself so he wanted someone to help plan the practices and make suggestions. On most staffs, the older assistant is in charge of recruiting and is on the road most of the time. I have a family now, so I'm not a guy who wants to be gone. I've only missed one game and one practice in eight years, and I'm very grateful for that."

Wesley said a key to Orr's success is that assistants and players feel comfortable around him. "My first reaction as a kid growing up in Michigan was that he was a different type of coach. He's refreshing," Wesley said. "He has that easy-going manner about him. He doesn't have that military approach. At Michigan, he was more in the background and he let his players take the forefront. When I came here to work as a graduate assistant, the first thing that hit you was how down to earth he was. I appreciate that he never puts on that air of superiority. He puts people at ease, like you've known him all your life. He's easy to talk to, and easy to be around. Everyone feels like they know him. Everyone feels like O is their buddy."

Hallihan noted, "Everyone likes Johnny Orr. Most coaches you'll get a lot of different opinions on. He's a fierce competitor, but people say he's a great guy. He never talks about people, he's always supportive of other coaches. He's always available to go somewhere and make an appearance."

Hallihan said Orr thrives on being able to help people, whether at marquee golf tournaments or simply through personal calls and appearances. "Johnny's the guy that makes all those events go," Hallihan said. "He doesn't have to do any of that—he could tell them he's too busy. He goes over to Boone to the YMCA camp every summer for a camp they have for kids with cancer. It's always the week of his birthday, and they have a big birthday cake for him. He has a very caring heart, particularly for kids. He adds something, he adds a happiness to these things. I remember a guy got hit by a car while riding on his buggy and was in critical condition in the hospital. He said he wanted to see Johnny Orr, so Johnny went over and visited the guy."

Steve Krafcisin has been associated with several prominent coaches—he played collegiately and reached the Final Four under famous coaches Dean Smith (at North Carolina) and Lute Olson (at Iowa); he played for ex-Marquette coach Al McGuire on an international team; and came to work on Orr's staff in 1987. Krafcisin offers this perspective of his first five years working for Orr: "When I first came here, I really was surprised at how well Coach Orr is liked. What's the mystique? Now I know why. My first day I came here when I got the job as his part-time coach, I came from Dubuque with one of my roommates. Coach Orr drove us around for like three hours looking at apartments. He treated my roommate, Scott, like he was Quinn Buckner, or even one of his own kids.

"I knew there was something special. His charisma and his love for people really stand out. He's not worried about the fishbowl. I've never been with him in a restaurant when he says, 'Let's get out of here.' He likes that interaction with people. When you look at Coach Orr, you see a guy who enjoys life, not a guy obsessed with winning. If there are some people, say Iowa Hawk fans, that don't like him, it's because they don't understand him. If they met him, they'd change their mind."

Wesley said Johnny's background as a standout player has helped him relate to his own standout players. "He wasn't just a good athlete, he was a great athlete in high school. Now he always has that ability to get along with his best player. He knows what they're going through. He puts players at ease. Guys are always comfortable. They're always allowed to keep their egos intact. He's not big on always showing them 'I'm the boss.' Guys can start out shooting 0-for-5 and still come back and have a good game. He lets their personalities really emerge."

Orr's assistants say Johnny is careful in how he vents his competitive energy. "For the most part, he doesn't like to get angry or frustrated with his players," Wesley said. "Some guys yell at their players, and some guys yell at their assistants. I think that's why sometimes he gets on the officials. I think the good officials know that, and they don't take it personally."

Colleagues say Johnny puts more stock in hard work than in great credentials, whether he's evaluating recruits or assistant coaches. That comes through in several decisions he's made, including a bold one to elevate the 25-year-old Wesley from part-time to full-time coach in 1983. "I really appreciate the fact that O was not afraid to give me the opportunity when he hired me as a full-time assistant," Wesley said. "He had a lot of guys who certainly were as qualified or more qualified. I'm not a guy that was a great player, but I had been loyal to him, and I think I did a good job. I don't think a lot of coaches would have done that. But he thinks a guy deserves a chance, whether it's a Jeff Hornacek, Marc Urquhart, or Ric Wesley."

Wesley said Johnny's experience and instincts come through in his recruiting philosophy. He said Orr looks for hard workers and isn't obsessed with blue-chip lists and labels, as his unusual success with walk-ons attests. "It's hard for a lot of coaches to start a guy who wasn't a recruited guy," Wesley said. "Sometimes it's like a self-fulfilling prophecy. You recruit a guy and you're convinced you've got to play him to justify that. O sees it for what it is, and it doesn't bother him to start a walk-on kid. He figures that if you deserve it, he'll give you a chance. I think he's really fair. I remember the first game Dick Breitbach ever started for us was in the first round of the (1988) NCAA tournament against Georgia Tech. Here's a kid who played three years at (NCAA Division III school) Loras and came here and walked on. He just kept working hard and improving, and when it looked like he could help, Coach had no hesitation to put him in. He had a great game, too."

Wesley added, "In recruiting, Johnny's a team guy. He's not a second-guesser. We talk it over, go from there, and don't look back. He always believes the guys you have on the team are more important than guys we're trying to get. He likes little guys. Big guys drive him crazy if they can't run and press. He likes to be a smaller team because it makes you work harder than other guys. It's easier to motivate them if they know they don't have the size."

Alluding to his love for hard workers, Orr often has said he didn't have the desire to coach in the NBA. "I couldn't coach guys who made more money than me," Johnny said. Yet Krafcisin said Orr is the kind of guy pro players would appreciate. "He's not a rah-rah guy, not always saying let's do it for the team," Krafcisin said. "He says we're here to play basketball, just go out and put the ball in the basket. Here's your opportunity. I can't help but think Coach Orr would have been a great pro coach. He was a player himself. He looks at an individual and knows what he can and can't do. He won't overcoach them. He's more of an orchestrater than coach. He likes simple plays and likes guys to use their bodies and their talent. The pro game is like his style. One of his strengths is his ability to keep guys at ease. His system isn't written in stone. He's not as much of a guy who says, 'OK, let's have a four-hour practice today.' In the pro game, running is their forte, and in the last three or four years when we've run, we've won. He doesn't want to get bogged down in a half-court game. He likes to put pressure on their defense instead of (allowing) the defense to put the pressure on you."

Milwaukee-Wisconsin coach and former Orr assistant Steve Antrim

"Probably the biggest impact he had on me was that he really made the game fun for the players, with the pressing and running style. Before I worked for him, I was a little more disciplined, both in on-court style and how I acted around my players. But I looked at him, and as big as he is in the business, if he was that loose, I certainly could be, too. I really needed that because I was so tight in games, I was tied in knots. His big thing is to have guys be so relaxed, and to play really hard.

"We do a lot of things (at Wisconsin-Milwaukee) that I took from him. Now, we have a team meal before the game like he always does. That was something he was big on, and it helped lighten the load on road trips. The players always were comfortable around him. When he comes in the room they don't get quiet. The same banter goes on.

"I had way too big of an ego when I came to work for him. For a guy who is as big as he is, he had very little ego. He thinks the players win and lose the games, and they do. A lot of coaches try to make everyone think that the coach controls the games, and they try to let everyone know it by standing up and yelling instructions every 10 seconds. But John lets the flow go to the players.

"On a bad game, we'd go into the locker room at halftime, and all the coaches would gather, and instead of getting on them, he'd say to us, 'Tell me about something we're doing well.' He liked to keep it positive. In practice, if a drill is going well, he runs it until they drop. If the drill is going bad, he stops it. He sets it up so you can't have a bad practice. I think his basic philosophy is that you don't have to teach them about the game as much as you just let them play. With John, everything doesn't have such a consequence. Before I came to work for him, when I'd go to put a player in, I'd think and analyze it so much. I think what the guy can't do, but his outlook is 'Let's give him a try.' The year before I came to Iowa State, that's what happened with (Jeff) Hornacek and how he got his chance.

"John isn't patient enough for the half-court game. John likes to pretend he doesn't coach at all, but he loves to coach the fast break. His big thing is that you can't get on them about making mistakes. When you make the long pass, you're going to chuck it into the stands sometimes. But he says you can't get upset; you just go ahead and throw it. It's the same with the press. You can't run the press if you're afraid to give up a layup or two."

• Players

Several former players who were asked about Orr said he was fun to play for and easy to be around. Two players from Orr's first Cyclone team, Mal Warrick and Jon Ness, said the coach's personable style made the transition from previous coach Lynn Nance to Orr an easy one. "Coach Orr has the ability to motivate and manage in an unorthodox manner," Warrick said. "I had the unique experience of playing for five different coaching staffs (including interim coaches at Purdue and Iowa State), and Orr's style was much less rigid and less militaristic than the others, yet more effective, in my opinion. This led to players being more responsible for their performances and work habits in practice, which rolled over into game performances."

Ness said Johnny is an interesting blend of fun and competitiveness. "He's one of the most witty, fun-loving, funny individuals I've ever known," said Ness. "Beneath the humor is a man who hates to achieve anything less than his team is capable of achieving. He has the natural ability to encourage his players and instill a desire to work harder. It's very difficult not to like Coach Orr, even if you're an Iowa Hawkeye fan."

Ness said Orr is best known for his humor, but behind the joking is a sensitive guy. "The lasting impression I gained from my experience with Coach Orr is the close rapport he developed with his players. He relocated the coaches' locker room to put it next to the players, enabling him to joke around with the players before and after practices, shower together, and reinforce that basketball issues stay on the court. He always made time if a player wanted to discuss issues. He ran the program in a manner that would enable his players to enjoy their college experiences and look forward to competing. He treated the seniors fairly, even though it would have been easy to overlook us and begin to build the program with new players."

Ron Harris and Mike Born both said Orr's positive outlook sticks in their memory. "When I first came here, we weren't always winning, and we didn't draw that many fans, but Coach Orr always has been so positive," Harris said. "He always told us to hang in there, and pretty soon we'd pack Hilton. My last year (1983–84) we got to the National Invitation Tournament (NIT) and the following year they catapulted into the NCAA tournament. Coach Orr put Iowa State on the map. Before that, I'd go back home to Chicago and people didn't know Iowa State—they thought I meant Idaho State."

Harris has worked for several years in a management job in Marshalltown, Iowa, but he said he almost wasted his chance that Iowa State offered. "I left Ames after my fourth year because I had a chance to try out for the Continental Basketball Association (CBA) team in Fort Wayne, Indiana," Harris said. "I made it to the last cut, but I was an in-between player—not big enough to play forward and not enough of a shooter to play guard. When I signed a contract to try out, I lost my chance to receive my scholarship, and I didn't finish my degree. I was married at the time, and I went back to Chicago and hung out. I wasn't going anywhere, though, and Coach Orr eventually brought me back. (Iowa State athletic director) Max Urick and Coach helped me get back my scholarship aid to finish up. He told me that I was his first player and it wouldn't look good if I didn't finish up and graduate, so I eventually finished up. Of the first recruiting class he brought in, I think we all graduated."

Born recalls that during his junior year (1987–88), Iowa State jumped to a 16-2 start and was ranked in the top 10 and top 20 nationally. "Then we hit a seven-game losing streak," Born said. "The thing I remember most is that all through that losing streak, Coach Orr was so positive every practice. It was almost unreal."

Walk-ons like Born, Breitbach and Scott Howard said Orr treated them on an equal plane with scholarship players. "I owe a lot to Coach Orr," Born said. "He gave me a shot. He told me he couldn't promise anything, but he gave me the opportunity. Then it was all on my shoulders."

Breitbach said, "There aren't too many coaches that would let a player come from a Division III school and walk on like he did with me. He has an open mind, and he gave me a fair shot. I think it worked out for both of us. He's a very fair guy."

Howard said, "I wasn't a starting player, yet he has always treated me well since my year with him. The thing that impressed me about Coach Orr was that he has never forgotten who he was. Through all of his success, he has remained humble, funny and caring. I've also been impressed by his ability to step back from the game during the off season."

Ex–Iowa State player Tom Peterson

"Johnny often came across like a dad. The way I looked at it, he didn't have any sons, so we were like his sons. He was hard on us at times, but he's a nice man and very caring. There were a lot of funny things, too. I remember how he always stomped his foot, wearing those big wing tips, when he got mad during games. I thought he was going to break his foot."

Milwaukee Bucks guard and former Iowa State All-American Jeff Grayer

"I made the statement when I was at Iowa State that Coach Orr is not only a coach, but he's a good friend. I still look at him that way, as a guy I'll always look up to. Not only could you talk with him about things concerning basketball, but private things, too. At times, he really got you loose and you'd really laugh at him. He's a funny man, but at the same time when it comes down to business, he's a serious guy. He's a fair man, and all anyone wants is equal treatment. You might be a superstar, but everyone was treated equally. If I skipped class, I ran drills like everyone else. I never had any regrets about going to Iowa State. The people there were lovely, warm, everything Coach Orr said they would be. As far as basketball, it spoke for itself. Johnny Orr prepared me well for pro basketball. He made me into an all-around player."

Philadelphia 76er and former Cyclone Jeff Hornacek

"Right off the bat I could tell he was a player's coach. I think he cracked a joke the first time I saw him, and that's the type of coach you like to play for. I felt more comfortable as the years went on. As a player, if you saw something on the court, you could go right to him and talk about it and most of the time he'd let you use it. He's open to that type of thing. One thing I learned from Coach Orr is to let guys have a free reign on the court. Especially now in the NBA, guys seem to play a little better when they aren't roped down and don't have to go to this spot or that spot."

Former Michigan All-American Rickey Green

"Johnny Orr is very outgoing. He kept you pretty loose. With a lot of coaches, you get bored with basketball, but he made it fun. He knows talent and lets guys go out and utilize it."

Former Cyclone Gary Thompkins

"It was a great four years here. I still remember being in seventh grade at the University of Michigan basketball camp and Johnny Orr told me he was going to recruit me to Michigan. Even now, Coach Orr still helped get back into school and get me to finish up my degree. I was out for a few years, but he told me if I graduated, he'd help me get a job in coaching, but first I have to get my degree, and I'm getting close."

• Media Representatives

Of course, the previous testimonials could apply to virtually any prominent college coach. But Orr's presence and popularity transcends the basketball court. His ability to relate so well—not only to the public and to his colleagues in the Iowa State athletic department, but also to the media—has enhanced his other accomplishments.

"I think we'd all take an Orr whenever we could," said former Ames *Daily Tribune* sportswriter John Akers, now a sportswriter for the *San Jose Mercury News*. "He's candid. He lets you know what's going on beneath an exterior that's apparent to everyone. And he's entertaining. That's a rare combination. He returns my phone calls, too, even though they're long distance."

Orr generally is sincere enough—and wise enough—to treat reporters fairly and help them do their jobs. Johnny is regarded to be easily accessible and a good interview in one-on-one situations. Reporters note that while Orr sometimes is a "quote machine," he occasionally displays an abrasive side during postgame press conferences, especially after games with more at stake. One media criticism of Johnny is that he's too defensive at these times. For example, after an emotional two-point loss to favored Oklahoma during the 1989 Big Eight tournament, he was asked if his 17-11 Cyclones deserved an NCAA tournament bid. "I don't think there should be any question," an irate Orr retorted. "I don't understand you people."

Here's what some Iowa sportswriters have to say about Orr:

Jeff Burkhead, former Ames *Daily Tribune* staffer

"One of the more significant incidents I recall involving Orr and the media occurred at his Michigan homecoming (in Ann Arbor) during the 1989–90 season. Even though the then-defending national champion Wolverines spoiled Orr's first trip back to Crisler Arena since he left Ann Arbor in 1980, after the game at the end of the press conference, the reporters (most of them from Michigan) gave Orr a hand. It's the only postgame press conference I've attended where the media applauded a coach. Michigan hasn't forgotten Johnny Orr."

Former *Des Moines Register* sportswriter Bob Dyer

"John's like Dick Vitale. Vitale still remembers when he was a high school coach in Jersey making $13,000 a year. John has made himself a comfortable living—I wouldn't call him wealthy—but that's never changed him. He still has a lot of high school coach in him. I've never felt he feels he's more important than anyone else."

Fort Dodge *Messenger* sportswriter Bob Brown

"He sticks up for his team, even if they stunk up the place. He does *a la* Bob Knight embarrass reporters, mainly TV reporters, who in a press conference ask dumb questions. But his relationship with the media is excellent. He's honest, and that's important. He's accessible and returns phone calls. His rapport with the media, more than his so-so win-loss record overall at ISU, has been very important in his success at Iowa State."

Former Iowa sportswriter Mark Neuzil

"Iowa Hawkeyes football coach Hayden Fry lives several miles outside of Iowa City on a large acreage surrounded by fences. During the height of his popularity, in the mid-1980s, the name on his mailbox read 'Smith.' Orr, on the other hand, has a house just as lavish, but it's within the city limits. Every writer who has ever done an Orr profile of any consequence has been invited to his home, along with a photographer. Many have been overnight guests. Fry would sooner have Bo Schembechler, Don James and Tom Osborne as houseguests than a journalist."

Ames writer Dan Davenport

Davenport, who has covered Johnny's teams since 1983, said he thinks Orr said and did the right things when he came to Iowa State. "The guy talks on the people's level so much," Davenport said. "He made them laugh, win or lose. Once he started winning, his popularity snowballed."

Davenport penned an eight-page story on Johnny in 1989 for the Iowa State University Alumni Association magazine, *Visions,* and said the project ranks among his favorites. "It's fun to do a story like that when you know a person, but then you find out a lot of things you didn't know about him," Davenport said. "When you go places with him, ride in a car or hear him speak, you get another perspective on him. Wherever there's people, he really lights up."

Here's an excerpt from Davenport's story, regarding Johnny's rapport with Iowans:

> Orr says he's visited more towns and more people than anybody else in the state, politicians included. While he's a bit of a braggadocio, he says this matter-of-factly . . . Though he scoots into most Iowa homes via TV, it's through public appearances that he's developed his constituency . . . Orr headlines more than 100 annual meetings, banquets and golf outings each year. If you're an Iowa business or charity and you want an event to be a success, put Orr's droopy, bloodhound mug on it. The Iowa Department of Economic Development did. So did charitable organizations like Variety Club and the Muscular Dystrophy Association . . . Earle Bruce, Hayden Fry, Maury John, Lute Olson and Tom Davis all have won more often, yet none developed a following that so cleanly

slices through every imaginable demographic sect . . . Maybe
Iowans fell for Johnny Orr because, like a soft, old sponge, he
soaked in their affection, and, with just a squeeze of
appreciation, gave it right back.

Sports broadcaster Pete Taylor

Taylor, who has broadcast Iowa State sports for more than 20
years and joined the Iowa State's athletic department in 1990 as
a fund raiser, said Orr is among the most recognized people in
Iowa. "I would say he's at least in the top four in the state of
Iowa as far as recognition, with (Governor Terry) Branstad, (Iowa
coaches) Hayden Fry and Tom Davis," Taylor said. "Everything
about Johnny Orr is recognizable—you don't forget him." Taylor
went on to say that Orr's visibility has greatly enhanced the university's image. "I don't think you could place a dollar amount
on John's value to Iowa State," Taylor added. "It would be astro-
nomical. I know from my career being in the media that the cost
of advertising and public relations would add up in the millions
of dollars."

Both as a broadcaster and a fund raiser, Taylor said the presence of Orr and football coach Jim Walden was a big lure to join
Iowa State full-time. "I can't imagine having a better situation
any place anywhere in the country," Taylor said. "I can't say
enough about those guys. Even though Hawkeye fans may have
had some better teams than Iowa State, I think they're a little bit
jealous of Iowa State people when they see that association between the fans and Orr, and between the fans and Walden."

Taylor sees a paradox in Johnny's personality. "I think he's a
Jimmy Stewart–type guy," Taylor said. "He's homespun, gener-
ally appears to be a nice guy. He plays the role of a super nice guy.
But don't kid yourself: he is a smart man. I don't know what his
IQ is, but he's very intelligent."

Taylor likens Johnny's bond with his players to that of a father. "I remember coming back from Indiana (in December of
1989) after Iowa State was drilled by 30 points. All the way
home, Johnny was feeling badly about that game. He was mad at
some of his players, but we got (home) to that airport, and it was
20 below zero out and the wind was blowing, yet he wouldn't
leave that parking lot until all the guys got their cars started and
had driven away. It was kind of like your dad—he's mad at you,
but still looks out for you."

Former Ames broadcaster Mark Mathew said you can tell a
lot about a coach by the way his players regard him. "The funny

thing, after all these years, I've never heard a former player have a bad thing to say about him," Mathew said.

The appreciation of Johnny isn't limited to the Iowa media. When writer John Feinstein wrote *A Season Inside,* a collection of first-hand observations of college basketball teams and games in the 1987–88 season, one of his many stops was Ames and Hilton Coliseum. Feinstein, who was following the Kansas Jay-hawks to profile Coach Larry Brown, recalled, "It has been exactly seven years since Johnny Orr shocked the college basketball world by leaving Michigan to come out here to Iowa State. Orr had one of the top programs in the country at Michigan, but big money and long-term security lured him away. He has built a solid program at Iowa State and become a local folk hero."

". . . he's a friend, he's a coach, he's a man. He's a man for all seasons and all reasons. I feel sincerely that one of my pleasures in life was to get to know Coach Orr."

—GEORGE RAVELING

"I think this is a good thing. I hope you make sure this roast is public so those professors understand what I'm doing here. Maybe they can help us out a little bit and return the favor."

—JOHNNY ORR

"I don't think there are any more loyal fans than those here at Iowa State. I can't imagine if Nebraska went 5-6 in football how their fans would react. The fans here are phenomenal—just loyal, supportive people. I love them so much, when you don't win it just kills you. It eats at you because the fans are so involved. That's part of why I take so many speaking dates. I know those Cyclones are going to come out if I'm going to be there."

"I love the people, the fans, the games, the practices, the players. I'm going to retire here and stay here because I love Iowa. But I don't feel as comfortable in my job as I did before. That's not going to affect how hard I work, but I just don't feel as relaxed about my job."

"If I was going to start out in coaching today, the way it is now, I don't think I'd go into it. There's no question it's not as much fun. It's too much of a business. As long as I was healthy, I would have wanted to coach until I was 70, no question. But now I don't know what will happen."

• Johnny Speaks Out

The 1940s were the years Johnny Orr made his identity as a great athlete. The 1950s brought his transition to his career as a successful high school teacher and coach. The 1960s were years of risk taking, with four job changes between 1959 and 1968 and a leap from high school to college coaching. The 1970s at Michigan produced soul searching followed by triumph, with national exposure for Orr and his program. The 1980s marked his career pinnacle with his bold move to Ames and the revival of the stagnant Iowa State program.

With the 1990s here, the question is: What's in store for Johnny Orr?

Along with many positives, there have been some trying times in Johnny's quest for fulfillment and satisfaction. On one hand, Orr says he's a lucky man: he points to good times at home with his wife and family; loyal colleagues at work; players who keep him feeling young and productive; many Cyclone fans and friends who genuinely touch his heart; memories you can't put a price tag on. The coach is elated with his 1991 recruiting class and their immediate impact in 1991–92, and he's confident his Cyclone teams will be even better in 1992–93 and beyond. Certainly, Orr wants to leave coaching on a winning note. He'd like nothing more than to guide an Iowa State team on a Big Eight Championship run and return to the NCAA tournament—not because his clock is winding down, but because he always coaches to win.

But more than that, Johnny is searching for some inner peace, enough to let him walk away with a smile after four decades in coaching. Some days, the joy is missing. The disillusionment appears when Johnny considers that the game he's played, coached and forged a strong bond with is changing. The rules, the academic expectations, the recruiting, the pressure, even the personalities continue to evolve in a direction that bothers the 65-year-old coach. Johnny admits that retirement from coaching—a prospect he said he hoped would wait until age 70—looks more attractive every year, primarily because of this changed environment. "My job certainly has changed," Orr says. "I've always been treated well, but the philosophy is different. I'm looking at various options now that I never did the last couple of years."

Johnny said his frustration has nothing to do with his salary. It has nothing to do with two Cyclone losing seasons to start the decade. It's not about winning and losing at all, he says, except he feels what's being lost is common sense and fairness by the decision makers in college sports. A lot of things, Johnny says, just drive him nutty. This time, he's not smiling.

Here's Johnny, speaking to these subjects and many others.

• Climate for Reform in College Athletics

"I don't think things are much worse today in college sports than they were 10 years ago or 20 years ago. Part of it is that newspapers and TV today publicize these events more often and more widely. If a guy gets arrested at Purdue—boom!—it's on CNN that night.

"I think we have to be careful with this reform movement. Now Congress is talking about getting into it. Holy cow, that would be a mess. The university presidents are getting into it. A lot of people jumping in with ideas don't know a damn thing about it. I think the university presidents should be informed, but they hired athletic directors and they hired coaches, and they should let them do their jobs. The presidents have a lot of other important things to do without getting into something they don't have the expertise in.

"It used to be that the athletic directors had the power in college athletics. Now the faculty representatives who represent the presidents have all the power. It's like with this Athletic Council at Iowa State. Why should an English professor make decisions about basketball? I wouldn't think of going into his department and telling him what classes to teach or who to hire. He knows nothing about my job.

"If you cut basketball scholarships from 15 to 13 as the NCAA proposed, that's not a big deal with me, because it's hard to keep guys happy if you can't play them. But to cut the number of assistant coaches—that makes no sense. This is supposed to be about helping the student-athlete. Now you have the people who can help the players, and now you're going to cut them out.

"It just seems like everything today is going against coaches. Sure, the public image of college athletics is more negative today, and we've had a lot of problems. So now it's time to jump on us. I don't like that they're taking the free enterprise out of coaching. They want to take away all the camps and shoe contracts. It's like they want the coaching jobs to go back to the way it used to be when nobody could make any money.

"You watch, if this keeps up, the coaches will go into collective bargaining. They'll get united and say you're not going to take away our scholarships, our assistant coaches, our TV shows or shoe contracts. If they can get the players together with them, they'll go into the Final Four weekend and the night before the first game they'll say, 'Sorry, there's no game.' Then you're going to see some fast action. They're not going to lose that $2 billion in TV money. Hopefully that will never happen, but if they push some of these things, the coaches are going to draw the line. I've been on the National Association of Basketball Coaches (NABC) board of directors for six years now. I think they should let the coaches set the rules and hand out the punishments."

• Cheating

"What is cheating? I think it's when you induce someone illegally to come to your school, or if you get someone a car or pay them so much money. I've never bought a player. But what happens when it comes wintertime and you have a guy who doesn't have a winter coat? And I've had kids like that. To me, if you don't help them, there's something wrong. I don't know of a coach in America who wouldn't help someone in a case like that.

"As far as the cheating that goes on, if you know someone is doing it, you just don't schedule games against them. The only ones you have to play are the ones in your conference, so if I have proof someone in my league is cheating—proof and not just hearsay—I'll turn them in.

"You hear a lot today about recruits getting $500 to visit a school. Those coaches at those inner city high schools will tell you that. You say to them, 'Will you come to my conference commissioner and tell him what you just told me?' Then they say, 'No, I can't do that.' They're afraid it will hurt their kid, their school or themselves. So how are you going to catch anybody if the star witnesses won't talk?

"Here's another thing: It used be that the guys who were cheating were guys who were about to lose their job. They'd go into the final year of their contract knowing they had to win, so they'd do anything to save their job. Now you see honest guys like (ex-Dayton coach) Don Donoher get fired, with time left on his contract, because he didn't win enough. What does that tell guys who don't break the rules?

"There are too many rules. Some are impractical, some are bent because of a fear that others are bending rules, and coaches are afraid to lose their advantage. There are some minor rules that schools bend. Like you're not supposed to call a recruit more than once a week. Now if three or four schools are working hard, and you know the other schools are calling him twice, are you going to just call him once? Does the kid know if you call him once it's because that's a rule, or does he think you don't want him as badly? Then there's a rule about only one coach being away from campus at one time. Like (Duke coach) Mike Krzyzewski says, 'If we have our recruiting trips planned, and there's some bad weather, I'm not going to break my back to fly home in bad weather two hours sooner.'

"A freshman ineligibility rule would help some of these problems if you gave them four years to play, but they only want to give them three years. I bet the percentage of graduates would triple. Now, they've lost their incentive to stay in school if they're done playing in four years."

• Coaches' Shoe Contracts

"I think people have a misunderstanding about these shoe contracts. There are 300 Division I head coaches, and maybe 800 head coaches when you count Divisions I, II and III. Out of the 800, you're talking about maybe 50 guys who have nice shoe contracts. We didn't just show up and have it handed to us. We're the guys that worked for $3,000 a year, and taught five classes and coached all sports. We worked on one-month contracts. We earned this over a period of time.

"I started out with Pro-Keds for $1,000 a year, two pair of shoes for all my players and $2,000 sponsorship fee for my basketball clinic. I signed a three-year deal. I thought that was fantastic. Later, I got a five-year deal with Pony, and then a four-year deal with Reebok. Those were more lucrative. They have to select you because they like you and you can represent them.

"And there's another thing: we're so worried about money, I get $10,000 worth of shoes and equipment donated to Iowa State every year because of this shoe contract. You multiply that over the years I've been here, and that's a nice chunk of money. But nobody at Iowa State has ever come up and thanked me for those shoes and that revenue. And as far as our basketball camps, that's not just something handed to us. We pay $2,100 to rent Hilton Coliseum for a week, and now we have to pay $3 per person in camp to the university. We never had to do that before."

• Iowa State University Administration

"First, I think of Dr. (W. Robert) Parks, the former university president. I had a close relationship with him. He used to come to practices some, and sometimes he'd come into the locker room. He was like your buddy.

"I'll always appreciate Lou McCullough, the athletic director who brought me here. Because of Lou, there's no doubt in my mind that my first five years here, this was the best college basketball job in the country. Lou McCullough made that possible for me. He let me spend carte blanche, although I never took advantage of it and overspent.

"But a lot of that has changed now. McCullough left Iowa State in a very controversial thing (he resigned suddenly in 1982, effective at the end of the school year). I tried to find out what happened and I called Dr. Parks, and he said there's nothing I could do—Lou was leaving, and that's the way it's going to be. There was talk about a sexual harassment complaint. If there was anything to it, I'm sure it wasn't anything Lou did as much as some things he might have said. He joked about things in the office and some of those things were misunderstood. Times have changed and people are more sensitive today to things that are said.

"I like Max Urick and Dave Cox, and I'll always appreciate their work in getting me here. One of the hard things for me, though, was having Lou as my boss and then having a change. Lou was so much like (Michigan athletic director) Don Canham with his philosophy. Canham put football and basketball up front, and everything else depended on them. If we had a bunch of coaches at a Michigan booster gathering, and a tennis coach would speak longer than one minute, Canham would say, 'Cut him off.'

"It's the same thing when they change presidents at the university. I had the great relationship with Dr. Parks, and he left. Then came President (Gordon) Eaton. I was just starting to get to know Eaton and Charlie McCandless (the vice president overseeing athletics) real well. I think they were starting to understand us and our problems, when Eaton left for another job. Things were going fine, they gave us support. (Football coach) Jim Walden and I sat down with Dr. Eaton and had a real good meeting, then four days later, boom!—he's leaving.

"Our athletic department under Max Urick has a different type of leadership entirely. Like I said, I like Max, but he has a different style than I was used to with Canham and McCullough. And now the way things are, they don't let the athletic directors do their job. They have vice presidents overseeing athletics. It's gotten so bad that I know an athletic director from another school who was at the NCAA meetings ready to vote, and his university president took the paddle right out of his hand and voted the opposite way.

"It used to be that you have to get football and basketball going, because they are the revenue-producing sports and the visible sports. Then if you have money for everything else, great. Now everything is treated equal, no matter what. When I first came here, we never had to share Hilton Coliseum for practices with women's basketball. I never minded if they practiced when we were done. But we wanted to practice early for our players' benefit and so we could have time if we went out and recruited at high school games in the evening. It's

not a men's vs. women's thing—it's a revenue sport vs.
nonrevenue. A lot of schools in the country don't even let the
women's teams play *games* in the arena, let alone share
practice times. This Title IX (federally mandated equality) rule
is interpreted at different schools in different ways. I don't
agree with some of the things they push on you. I'm for
women's athletics 100 percent—if you have the money, great,
spend it. But if you don't have the money, what are you going
to do? I'd hate to see us drop any sports, but I don't know how
we can continue to fund them unless we can find some other
way to finance it. We're one of only two schools in the Big Eight
(along with Nebraska) that have all (21) sports.

"The problems I have are all minor things. Iowa State has
been good to me, but on the other hand I took over a program
that was losing $500,000 a year and now we have a $1 million
annual profit. We're to the point where we can't make much
more in basketball—you can only raise ticket prices so much.
If we continue to lose money as an athletic department,
sometime, someone is going to have to make some cuts. That's
going to be a bad situation.

"I don't need more money, I want to make that clear. I've
got a good retirement, I own a home, I own cars. But it's
frustrating sometimes. We run our program with a $1 million
surplus. I do what I have to do to fill the arena. But we get
nothing back for that. My assistant coaches can't get a raise
with all the state cutbacks. How do you justify that? (In 1991)
we had the ninth-best recruiting class in the country (according
to magazine rankings)—Jim Hallihan, Ric Wesley and Steve
Krafcisin did a great job making that happen. But there's no
raise, no bonus. What incentive do they have to do that again?
Our pride is not going to let us do less than our best, but
there's a principle here. When you take the incentive out, it
takes a lot out of it."

• Iowa State Coaching Colleagues

"Jim Hallihan is a very good coach. His idea is that the
team is more like a family. He gets a lot closer to players, for
instance, than I probably do. He has done a great job for me.
Ric Wesley has a very hard job to get a kid to come here, since
he recruits in the middle of Big Ten territory. Ric found Victor
Alexander. He spots those kids in camps. He's getting us some
great players. He got us Julius Michalik in 1991, and UCLA,

Kentucky and a lot of schools wanted Juli. The most important thing is that my coaches have been so loyal.

"I've worked with three different football coaches at Iowa State. I really liked Donnie Duncan (the Cyclone coach from 1979 to 1982, now the University of Oklahoma athletic director). He's one of the few athletic directors in the Big Eight with any guts. There are a lot of spineless guys in there now.

"Jim Criner (the Iowa State football coach from 1983 to 1986) was a different experience entirely, different than anywhere I'd ever been. I think he's a very knowledgeable football guy, but he basically tried to do everything himself. Boy, he had a lot of changes in (assistant) coaches, about 20 or so, and something had to be wrong. I think it was like something you'd see in the movies where he thought, 'You have to win or you'll be fired.' One time I tried to explain that to him, but I don't think he believed me. That was a difficult period there.

"Jim Walden (Cyclone football coach since 1987) is a terrific guy. When they hired him, I think he was the best guy at the time that Iowa State could have hired. His personality is tremendous, and he's optimistic. He has a great coaching staff. They're terrific teachers, they've been with him for years, so you know he's a solid guy. Having Jim Walden here has been a bright spot for me. He's fun to go to the outings with. I don't think Iowa State could have a better guy as its football coach.

"I've enjoyed all the coaches here at Iowa State. One disappointment I had was losing Gerry Gurney as academic advisor a few years back. We've had some good people helping us in that academic counselor role, people who the players really like. Even now, we have somebody really good who wants to work solely with men's basketball and she has plenty of work. But other coaches want her to work with their athletes, so we're having a big fight over that."

• Basketball Officials

"I don't hate basketball officials. When I was in the Big Ten, Bob Knight and I did more than anyone to help officials get more money. It's a hard job—a very hard job. I think we should pay them more. I would do anything I could to make it better for them. But when I go to the rules meetings, then I see the things they don't call, I get mad. Like the rule about staying in the coaching box that caused the problem when we played Kentucky in the 1992 NCAA tournament.

"I'm not right all the time. I'm not saying they should be perfect, but I sat back a long time and didn't say a word. In nine years I never got off the bench and never got technicals, but it made no difference. It seems now that if you can intimidate them, you better do it. Knight seems to do a pretty good job, because everyone is scared to death of him.

"I think officials should be like the coaches and players— they should be jacked up for those games. Sometimes coaches and players have bad games, sometimes officials have bad games. I do think that officials should be held accountable for anything controversial, particularly something that happens at the end of the game. I was absolutely sick when that (official) threw Dean Smith out of the (1991 NCAA semifinal) game. You have to use some common sense. If I were the commissioner of officials, that official would have been tossed out of working college basketball games.

"I don't like to protect officials. They should be held accountable. They should have to march up to that press conference and explain what they called and why. There are a lot of times I don't want to go up there to those press conferences, or let guys in my locker room, but I do it. The same rules should apply to them. We treat them like they're sacred. I'm not talking about every game, I'm talking about controversial games. They say there's no way in the world the officials would go for that. I say, yeah, the gutless guys wouldn't, but the guys who have been working a long time would.

"In most instances my disagreements with officials are not a personal thing. There are some guys I don't ever want to work my games, though. I can't forgive the guys who never admit they're wrong. I made Woody Mayfield famous with all the problems we've had. I got him (hired into) the NBA—they wouldn't have known who he was otherwise. A lot of officials are good friends of mine. When we went on the Big Eight all-star trip to Japan, we traveled with the officials and had dinner and drinks with them and had a hell of a time. In the past, you'd see some officials out and you buy them a round of drinks, and they'd buy you a round, and that never affected anything. But now it's like a new breed. They won't say anything to you. They won't explain any calls. It's almost like they're against you instead of being neutral. Like the one who said to me early in the game, 'They told me about you.' What an attitude to have. You used to ask a guy what he called and he'd explain it and often he was right and you'd understand. Or you'd call them or write a letter after the game and they'd give you an explanation, and often you'd say, 'Well, I hadn't thought of that.' Now you can't call them or write to them or say anything about them. I think we need more communication, not less.

"I got suspended (for the first game of 1991–92) for saying some things (at the 1991 Big Eight tournament postgame press conference) that were completely misunderstood. I complimented Missouri on winning, and I never had any excuses for losing. I never said anything about the game officials. But now that Victor Alexander had played his last game, I wanted to get something off my chest. Because he was a big guy and he didn't fall down and doesn't say anything, he never got any foul calls even though people hammered him all four years. That's all I said was they didn't treat him fairly, and it frustrated me. I had received a reprimand before for talking about officiating, so they take this comment as a criticism of officiating, and I get a one-game suspension.

"Now you take that (1990) Missouri-Colorado football game with the fifth down mistakenly allowed. Do you realize the ramifications of that mistake? Colorado might not have been in the Orange Bowl, let alone be national champions, and Missouri might have gone on and won a couple more games. Somebody should be held accountable for that. Did they fire those guys? No, they got a one-game suspension. That's the same thing I got, and you tell me what's worse."

• Iowa State–Iowa Athletic Rivalry

"I have great respect for the University of Iowa athletic program. They're just like we are with the problems of location, and being in the Big Ten is even more difficult. The other Big Ten schools you play and recruit against have so much more talent so close to their school. I think the situation for me was helped with Bump Elliott being there as athletic director (until 1991), and our friendship going so far back to Michigan.

"I always respected (former Iowa basketball coach) Lute Olson. I think he's a great coach. He's doing a hell of job at Arizona. I think he's a happy guy down there and he loves it. I think his personality has changed some and he's more loose. I think that was a good move for Arizona and a good move for Lute. Our relationship was never bad, but we weren't close friends. I think our relationship got a little better when I came to Iowa State because he always beat us then. I think we had won 12 of the 14 games against Lute's Iowa teams when I was at Michigan.

"George Raveling (Olson's successor) is on the National Association of Basketball Coaches board of directors with me. He's a heck of a guy and a very good friend. He's getting that program turned around at Southern Cal. He wasn't as happy in Iowa City's environment, where people seem to know where you are all the time. He's more at home in the Los Angeles metro environment. When George came to Iowa, there was so much pressure on him to beat Iowa State. That was a killer for him when we beat them three times in a row. He said he'd rather be dead than lose to Iowa State. We joke about that a lot.

"I've known (current Iowa basketball coach) Tom Davis a long time, too. I saw him play in college. I helped him get his first job in high school coaching. I've followed him during his career, and he's been very successful everywhere he's been, except for some years at Stanford. He's done a good job at Iowa, and I have a good relationship with him. I have a good relationship with his assistant coach Bruce Pearl, too. I've made jokes about the Hawks, but I've never said anything bad about Tom Davis. I hope the Hawks have great success every time they play except when they're playing us.

"Hayden Fry, I consider him a friend. I think he's a heck of a football coach. We used to be with the same shoe company, and we went on a trip together with the company once. Now we get asked to do a lot of promotions for things that have to do with the state of Iowa—we just filmed a commercial for the Iowa National Guard. He's done great things with that program. I remember what those Iowa teams were like when I was at Michigan. Michigan just drilled the Hawks. Even in basketball, my biggest thing was to get my players to take the Hawks seriously.

"Before Jim Walden came, I know all the football coaches at Iowa State put a lot of stock in beating the Hawkeyes. That rivalry was big at first. I do think if you're the Iowa State football coach, before you're totally accepted by the fans, you have to beat the Hawks.

"I always enjoyed going over and playing in the Amana golf tournament. I went over (in 1991) to the Hogan Hawkeye Tournament and played with Tom Davis and (Northern Iowa basketball coach) Eldon Miller, and Hayden Fry followed us around for eight or nine holes. There were more people

watching us than were watching the pros. I even got some
criticism at this end from people who say, 'You shouldn't go
over and help the Hawks raise money.' Well, they're going to
raise money whether I come there or not. I think it works out
well because I get a lot of exposure for Iowa State, too."

• Relations with Bob Knight and Other College Coaches

"I met some great coaches in the Big Ten. My best friend
probably was Bob Knight. Knight gave me one of the most
bitter defeats I ever had. No, it wasn't in the national finals. It
was that overtime (Michigan) loss in Bloomington that let
Indiana stay undefeated and win the Big Ten championship (in
1976). We came back and won the Big Ten the next year. Once
the games were over, we've been able to be pretty good friends.
One of the difficult things for me was when Bill Frieder and
Knight had that falling out recently, because they're both good
friends of mine. It's funny because Frieder threw a surprise
50th birthday party for me, and Knight came in and stayed at
Frieder's house. But now they aren't speaking, and that's
tough. I don't agree with everything Knight has done and all of
his philosophies, but of all the coaches in the country, he's
probably my favorite.

"There are some coaches I don't get along with, but I
respect them all. Some I respect more than others. Overall I
think I have good relations with other coaches. It's just like
anything else, you disagree some of the time but you get along
most of the time. I do think that some guys who people think
are great coaches are overblown. It's the situation that makes
them a great coach.

"Lou Carnesecca is a guy I really like. Jud Heathcote and
Eldon Miller are guys I like a lot. I respect Jerry Tarkanian
(former University of Nevada-Las Vegas basketball coach
who had an ongoing feud with the NCAA over alleged rules
violations in his UNLV program). I think to be critical of Tark is
unfair. Most people in that same situation would do the same
things he's done. UNLV is just a different place. If I was there,
I'd probably have done some of the same things. I hate that he
has to quit because of some personal vendetta.

"We had the best basketball coaches in America in the Big
Eight at one time. I still think it's one of the better conferences.
Basketball is now as well thought of as football in the Big

Eight. I think my favorite guy in the Big Eight was Larry Brown. I enjoyed playing him, and I like everything about him as a coach. He's a hell of a coach and a hell of a person. I remember a guy that was always tough to beat was Moe Iba. When you played Nebraska, if you weren't ready to play, you were going to get your butt kicked. It was never over until the final whistle blew. I respect Billy Tubbs. I admire the way he gets guys to play for him, although I don't agree with some of his decisions."

• Rapport with African-American Athletes

"Race has never been a big deal with me. I'm going to be perceptive and fair and be honest with people. All I look at with any athlete is, 'Can this guy play? And if he's a good kid, can we get him in school?' I will say this: I certainly don't think that blacks have the same opportunities as whites as far as education goes in some high schools.

"We've come a long way with the whole race issue. When I hired Fred Snowden (at Michigan), he was the first or one of the first black assistant coaches in the Big Ten. In the early 1970s, there was a lot of tension over race. Michigan State had a big player boycott, and I was the first guy in the country to have five blacks starting for him. That was a bad deal for me to face. The whites were mad because we had so many blacks, and the blacks were mad I was a white guy coaching instead of a black with so many black players. I ended up the loser in the deal. Once a parent of a recruit told me, 'You have 10 blacks and two whites.' Never until that moment did I think of that. So I told him, 'If that bothers your kid, this is not the place to go.'

"I had three different black assistants during the 12 years at Michigan. I asked my players at Iowa State if it made any difference if we had a black coach, and I've never had a player tell me it makes a difference."

• Recruiting

"One of the reasons I've been around so long is that I think I'm a pretty good judge of talent. It doesn't take a genius to see that the great players are prospects. The hard part is judging the other guys who aren't as developed yet. Is he going to just be another player, or can he be great? My teams that have had success, like at Michigan in 1976, were ones where I had two great players and three guys who played great because they were playing with great ones. Not that I've made all correct picks. I've missed on a lot, too.

Recruiting is out of control, there's no question about that. Now we build them up too much. They have those all-star games, and kids feel like they have to get to those summer basketball camps to get a scholarship. Recruiting also has changed in that there's more focus on certain skills. It used to be simple—if we liked him, we tried to get him. Now in the last five years, recruiting has changed so you try to replace a guy with a guy with specific skills.

"We came so close on some guys—particularly Clark Kellogg (from Cleveland, who went to Ohio State), Magic Johnson (from Lansing, Mich., went to Michigan State) and Glen Rice (from Flint, Mich., went to Michigan).

"I had Magic Johnson in my summer basketball camps. You knew from the beginning he was going to be great. Yet it's funny how after high school, people didn't know him yet. I begged them to take him on the national all-star game—now it's the McDonald's All-Star game. Some guy dropped out, so they took him, and he was the best guy there. They took him to some games in Europe, and he was great. We tried to get him to sign, but as soon as he got back from Europe, there were 5,000 people waiting in the airport at Lansing to meet him. If we would have had him at Michigan, we would have won the national championship. He still is Magic. I love him still.

"That was close with Rice, whoo. He just didn't sign early like he wanted to because of his coach. I remember going to see him (as Iowa State coach) with (assistant coaches) Ric (Wesley) and Jim (Hallihan). It was a Saturday night, and Mrs. Rice was going to church. Hallihan said he thought (Michigan coach Bill) Frieder had been there to the church, so we decided we'd better go. The assistant pastor was very influential with Mrs. Rice—he was helping the family make its decision. They invited me to speak to the congregation, so I took them up on it. I got up to the pulpit and told them I had a lot of black kids on my teams. I told them that I coached Wayman Britt and Barry Stevens from Flint, and I told them we wanted the Lord to send us Glen Rice. I really got into it—I was fired up.

"When we hung that phone up with Glen Rice (after he chose Michigan), we were depressed, man. If we'd have had him with Jeff Grayer and Jeff Hornacek, who knows? But it goes to show if you're close on those caliber of guys, you're on the right track. And you have to savor the guys you do sign, like Phil Hubbard, Rickey Green, Mike McGee. And some of my favorite players were the overachievers, like Wayman Britt, Steve Grote, Ron Virgil and Jeff Hornacek.''

• Relations with the Media

"I've always gotten along with the Iowa writers and media. Pete Taylor, Eric Heft and Mark Mathew have been terrific on my radio and TV shows. I've worked with a lot of good writers at the *Des Moines Register* and around the state. The only hard thing has been all the turnover of sportswriters in town here at the Ames *Daily Tribune*. I think we've had some outstanding young writers, and it's disappointing to see them leave because they can't make a living. You just get to know them and they get to know you, and boom!—they're gone. We've probably had 10 different sports guys at the *Tribune* since I came to Iowa State.

"I always got along with the press at Michigan except for one guy—(*Detroit News* columnist) Joe Falls. I had just won the Big Ten championship and Rickey Green was named to the All-American team. But Joe Falls said if I didn't win the NCAA tournament, I was a complete failure. He and I never got along after that. He made me so mad I threw him out of my office, but I never should have done that. One time he wrote a big piece saying I should be fired. (Michigan athletic director Don) Canham read it and wrote me a letter and said, 'As long as I'm here, you'll be my basketball coach.' Looking back, I don't hold anything against Joe Falls. Some of the things he wrote were great. But he was the kind of guy who wasn't going to let it end, and I wasn't either, and that was a mistake. My backers really hated him. But it's just his nature. Man, he gets on those Tigers.

"I don't think at Michigan the press ever will say the basketball coach is a great coach. Dave Strack won three Big Ten championships and went to the NCAA tournament, and did phenomenal things, yet no one thinks he was a great coach. It's like with Bill Frieder and now Steve Fisher. They say they're good recruiters, but they can't coach. That's not how *I* feel, but that's just the way it goes. And with football, you're either a great coach, or you'll be out of there in a hurry.''

• Michigan Colleagues

"I don't understand the people who say Frieder can't coach. I saw him take two Flint (Northern High School) teams in high school to state championships. After he won the first time, they graduated 11 of the 12 players (all except Wayman Britt), and he came back and won the state championship again. Winning a state title is hard to do in Michigan, especially with a whole new team. I really wanted to hire him at Michigan, but I was worried whether we could pay him enough to make it worth his time. Canham didn't pay the head coaches much, and it was even worse for the assistants. Bill said he'd come for nothing—I think we were able to come up with about $8,000—and he never griped about his pay. Bill did a great job working for me. I think the way his Michigan career ended (with his move to Arizona State on the eve of the 1989 NCAA tournament) changed Bill and made him a little bitter. He called me at 3 o'clock in the morning and said he was leaving to take the job at Arizona State, and I said, 'Have you told Bo Schembechler (his athletic director)?' He said he tried to reach him but hadn't yet. I think he should have talked to him before he decided he was going. I don't think Bill thought Bo would take the team away from him. I think he thought he'd get to coach them in the NCAA tournament. Bo's fair, but he's a big Michigan guy.

"I remember when Bo Schembechler came to Michigan, I thought he was one of the meanest guys I'd ever met in my life. As I got to know him, I gained a great respect for him. I found him to be a soft guy, very fair, very organized. His first heart attack completely changed his personality. I think he was a more feeling, fun person, and he was even a greater coach. I think he's one of the greatest coaches of all time.

"Working for Don Canham was so great. He was a genius the way he sold and marketed our sports programs. He was one of the smartest guys I ever worked for. He was the boss, no question about that. There was never any animosity when I left Michigan. He just said he knew I'd do well. All he ever said about Iowa State was make sure that whatever they promise, get it in writing.

"The only conflict I ever had with Don Canham was he refused to pay me more. He did that with everybody, with Bo, too. I'd go in there and talk my ass off, and it would be no different. I saw how much the other guys were making in the conference. I helped Jim Dutcher get the coaching job at

Minnesota and he got $10,000 more than I did already. It was more of a pride thing. Big Ten coaches would get together and say, 'Hey, Orr, I see you got another $500 raise. What's the matter with that guy (athletic director) of yours?' (Bob) Knight always pressed that. His assistants would tell my assistants what they made, and we weren't paying anything.

"But as far as our operating budget, there was nothing Michigan wouldn't do. Canham revolutionized college sports. He was so far ahead of other schools in the promotions, it was unbelievable. When he started we were getting about 80,000 at football games, and he really marketed that and got it to 103,000. He understood that the players would only be there for two to three years at a time, so he really pumped the coaches, Bo and me. With Don Canham, you knew who the boss was. If he called a meeting, no one was absent—even the janitor would show up. I think he was the most powerful man in the state of Michigan.

"Before Canham there was Fritz Crisler. He was something. I remember one time in my first season, as an assistant coach, I went to Fritz and asked him if I could get some expense money to attend a basketball clinic. Fritz looked at me and said, 'John, you're a Michigan coach. You don't go to clinics. You *are* the clinic. People pay to listen to *you*.' So I didn't get to go to that clinic, man. Fritz was tight with the money like Canham, only he didn't invest the money like Canham did.

"I played golf with a lot of the big guys at General Motors, Chrysler and Ford. I played golf with Gerald Ford when he was the President of the United States. Ford helped me get Mike McGee to sign with Michigan. Mike was from Omaha, and President Ford was born there. Mike and his mother were there to visit the campus the same time President Ford was there. Bo Schembechler and I were with Ford, and I asked him if he'd talk to this young man and his mother. He said, 'Sure.' He went over and said, 'Mike, it's nice to know you. I'm from Omaha, too.' After that, Mike's mother Mae wanted him to come to Michigan.

"I also was a partner in an Ann Arbor restaurant—Thano's Co. Some friends invited me to be a limited partner, in part to help secure a liquor license. Because of the restaurant, I went back and forth to Michigan quite often the first year I was in Ames. It was a good restaurant, but the overhead costs were killing us, so we ended up closing."

• Michigan Teams

"We had a little team (in 1976–77), but we outrebounded almost all of our opponents. Man, they could jump. We were ranked No. 1, but we were upset in the NCAA tournament by North Carolina-Charlotte, led by Cedric Maxwell. Cedric really hurt us. We played them in Lexington, but first we had to play Detroit. Because they were our rival, our guys were a little too keyed. We beat them, but then we had a letdown in that next tournament game and got beat by Charlotte. Nothing against Charlotte, but Rickey Green was injured, and even though he played, he wasn't sharp.

"I thought we had two teams at Michigan with the chance to go to the national finals. On the first one (in 1974–75), Campy goes pro on me. The second time in 1977–78 Phil Hubbard hurts his knee at the World University Games and has to lay out that year. Dick Vitale was the coach for the Pistons and they drafted him after his junior (fourth) year in 1979, but they shouldn't have done that, because he was not ready to play. Had he come back to Michigan another year, he would have gone higher in the draft, and we could have had a great team, because by then we had Mike McGee coming in. But Phil got it in his mind he might get injured again and he'd never play pro ball, so he signed a pro contract. He did play a lot of years in the pros and was a good NBA player, but he wasn't what he could have been if he hadn't hurt that knee.

"Phil was the perfect kind of athlete. He was excited for his teammates, and their success didn't bother him one bit. He made the U.S. Olympic team as a freshman. He played hard all the time and you never had to give him a pep talk. Had he not gotten injured, he would have been the all-time greatest player in Michigan history, and one of the greatest in college basketball history. But I remember that big knee brace—he just couldn't do the same things after he had to put that on."

• Leaving Michigan for Iowa State

"I had a great time at Michigan. People say football overshadowed us, but our teams were good there most of the time. We had plenty of success. The main reason I left was I didn't have a long-term contract, and I couldn't make any more money. I was making $15,500 as head coach when I started there in 1969, and when I left after my last year (1979–80), I was making $33,000—I think I was ninth highest paid among the coaches in the Big Ten. It wasn't that Iowa State paid me so much, it was the fact they gave the opportunity to make money with a TV show, a radio show and a camp. It was up to me to do it. At Michigan, I didn't have a TV show or a radio show.

"Looking back, there are two things I wish I would have asked for in my Iowa State contract—an attendance clause, and an NCAA bonus. But I had no idea we'd ever get to the NCAAs, that was the furthest thing from my mind. And I didn't expect us to get a sellout. I was hoping we'd get up to 8,000-9,000 people.

"Coming out to Iowa State was like getting a fresh start. Everyone has been so nice to me. I've never known a coach who's been treated like I was by the fans. Here, you feel so badly for the fans when you lose. It wasn't like that at Michigan."

• Job Opportunities

"I went after more than a hundred different jobs early in my career. I applied for jobs at Iowa and Iowa State back when I was at Dubuque. The Iowa job opened up again (in 1964) when I was at Massachusetts, and my name was mentioned. I was interested, but I didn't apply for that, and I never even got an interview. Forest Evashevski was athletic director at the time, and he had his mind made up that he wanted to hire Ralph Miller.

"Because he was a good friend, I think Bump Elliott would have liked to hire me at Iowa after Lute (Olson) left, but I was at Iowa State, and he couldn't do it, and I couldn't do it, either.

"Since I went to Michigan, I haven't actively tried to get any jobs, although I've been called about some. I was interested when the athletic director job at Illinois was open in 1976. I had a lot of friends at Illinois from growing up there. They wanted to hire me as basketball coach once, but the athletic director wouldn't hire me. So when the athletic director job opened and I got an interview, I talked to Canham about it. He told me not to go down there 'like a pansy' but to be direct and spell out everything I wanted. So I told them I wanted to do all the hiring, and I wanted complete control for five years, and then if they didn't like what I was doing, they could get rid of me then. Well, they said they weren't sure they could promise that. That probably was not the way you should act when you're trying to get a job, but I wasn't ready to quit coaching yet, anyway, and I figured I had a job, and if I can't get the job on my terms, I didn't want it. It came down to me and (Neale Stoner), and they offered it to the other guy."

• Charity Work

"I enjoy doing it. It makes you feel good. I'm actively involved with four golf tournaments: Variety Club of Iowa, Muscular Dystrophy Association, American Diabetes Association (sponsored by the Ames and Ankeny Kiwanis clubs), and the MS (multiple sclerosis) tournaments. The Variety Club of Iowa has the biggest golf tournament in Iowa— we had 366 golfers in one day (in 1990). When it first started, we made like $1,000. (In 1990) we raised almost $50,000 in one day. We've had people like Jud Heathcote, Larry Brown, Bob Knight, Abe Lemons, Sonny Smith, Tommy Heinsohn, Jerry Tarkanian, Barry Switzer, Earle Bruce and Jack Pardee make appearances to speak.

"At one time or another, we try to help practically every charity in Iowa that comes along. We participate in a lot of auctions and benefits. And autographs—I don't know how many basketballs we autograph a year, but it's a lot of them. One guy made a particular impact. This Iowa State basketball fan, Bob Ash, came into my office and asked me to sign a basketball. The poor guy had ALS (amyotrophic lateral sclerosis, Lou Gehrig's) disease, and a few months later he died from it. We did a public-service spot taped here at Hilton and sat in Bob's seats. You remember those things."

Heard at Johnny's Roast

"When I think about Johnny Orr, I think that Johnny is the best friend a guy could ever have and the best guy a friend could ever have."

—JUD HEATHCOTE

"It was nice of all of you to come here but I'll tell you one thing, I have to be honest with you: If I would have had to pay $200, I'd have never paid it. I'm glad you did, but I can't believe I gave this damn money away."

—JOHNNY ORR

"I've never thought about what people will say when I'm gone. I hope people say I rejuvenated the basketball program. I think we've done a good job. But I don't worry about people's reaction too much. I think we have fans that will come out and support you, no matter who coaches here next. I think if a guy comes in here and tries to hold the basketball, there certainly will be griping."

"I'm not sure when I'll retire. As I've always said, the biggest factor is my health. The decision doesn't have anything to do with what players I have coming back. I'll leave when I'm ready to get out."

• Thanks for the Memories

How will Johnny Orr be remembered when he leaves the coaching box later this decade? When the coach makes his final stroll from the dressing room to courtside, and the Iowa State pep band strikes up "Here's Johnny," what will stick in people's minds?

He'll be remembered as a paradox: the intense competitor during the season who's a cutup at the summer golf outings.

People in Michigan will remember his great games against Bob Knight and the Hoosiers, some exciting runs in the NCAA tournament, and Orr players like Campy Russell, Mike McGee, Phil Hubbard and Rickey Green.

Colleagues around the country will remember his courage in leaving a national power to start fresh at Iowa State.

In Ames, they'll remember his humor at Tuesday Cyclone Club luncheons and the life he breathed into Hilton Coliseum. They will recall the intensity of those nose-to-nose encounters with officials and remember the flu-stricken Orr collecting enough energy for a smile after Iowa State's stirring 1986 NCAA tournament victory over Michigan in the Metrodome.

At home, Johnny's loyal family will recall his rapport with his players and with people. "My dad is the fairest man I know," Robin Orr said. "He has an incredible ability to cut through a lot of crap and get to the point. He has a tremendous acceptance of all people. He has a way of making people feel welcome in that dumb, country-boy style. People don't know how sensitive he is, how warm and caring. A betting man never would have believed he'd ever make it out of Taylorville, if you'd known the way he grew up. I think that's made him more effective when he goes into the inner city and recruits players. He sees potential in people. He thinks opportunity makes a big difference in people's lives. I went to that Reggie McKenzie dinner (in 1991, when Johnny received a humanitarian award), and I'd never been to a more moving banquet in my life. It's nice to be proud of someone you're related to. He truly adores his players, and he's very loyal to them."

People who have endured the previously mediocre history of Iowa State basketball say it will be difficult to replace Orr. "He's made this a terrific job in college athletics," said Iowa State sports broadcaster Pete Taylor. "It'll be impossible to replace him. But there will be a lot of people interested. Who wouldn't want to come to sellouts every year? You don't have to have Orr's personality, but you have to have *a* personality."

Here's this author's theory: the best tributes to Johnny Orr won't surface for another five, perhaps even 10 years. Someday, though, people will notice the void. History will stamp him as a classic. Not always right, not always a winner, but always genuine. If the money, greed and reformers haven't ruined college sports by early next century, the new breed of robot coaches will do the next worst thing: they'll put us to sleep. Orr's candor and his style will be missed in tomorrow's politically correct atmosphere, where coaches speak carefully and nobody rocks the boat, even when the boat could use a decent shaking. The underdogs will lose an ally when Johnny leaves.

"The attitude has changed in college athletics over the last 13 years," Johnny said. "In my first five years here, not one person asked me how many of our kids graduate. Now, that's on everyone's mind. What people don't see is that I've had high school coaches beg me and parents beg me. They say, 'Take our kid for one year—even if he fails, it's better than him not getting a chance at all.' But now if you take them, they have to graduate. Hopefully, they're all going to make it, but if they don't, you can't say they're not better off for having their chance. There's something to look forward to when an opportunity is there."

Orr said dozens of his current and former players have blossomed because they were given an opportunity some want to deny. "Phil Hubbard was not a good student at Michigan, because he was going to be a pro player," Johnny recalls. "And he was a pro, but when he hurt his knee and there was some doubt whether he could keep playing, he looked at it differently. He eventually graduated from Michigan with almost a B average. With the right chance and the right motivation, people can accomplish anything."

Yet judging by the reform climate that's sweeping Iowa State and the NCAA, such success stories seem less likely to occur. "The school's approach to admitting inner-city kids has changed," Orr said. "They're raising all the standards. The attitude toward junior-college players is a lot different than when I came here, too. If the inner-city kid had the same chance as the kid at Ames High or (West Des Moines) Dowling, they'd have qualified. I think we should do everything to help them.

"I think if a person has ability, whether it's in athletics or whatever it's in, and they have a desire to go to college, we should admit them, and give them a chance, and help them when they get here. Don't just shut them off because they can't get a certain test score or a certain grade point (average)."

"I understand John," Cyclone football coach Jim Walden said. "We're both rebels against the new elitism. We came from somewhat poverty, but we didn't even know we were in poverty. But we're both survivors, because we had some concerned coach, or a beautiful history teacher, who believed in us. We're both products of having a chance in the system. I think we're both afraid of where we'd be if we didn't have those people providing that chance for us. But the modern philosophy is 'To hell with them.'

"We're losing our sense of sensitivity. I'm sensitive, and I think Johnny Orr even is beyond my sensitivity. He'll bring in the stray cats and stray dogs. That's what he's all about—giving people a chance. He figures they're better off here playing basketball with him for a couple of years than the alternative. He believes people need a chance, and he believes we have to quit shutting doors on people academically. When did it get so bad that an opportunity to fail became worse than no opportunity at all? As parents, we don't accept that, we don't tell our kids not to try. But we're letting schools do it to our athletes. I'm nervous about the Coach Orrs getting out of this business. I'm nervous about the modern-day coaches who say, 'If they don't do a 3.0 (grade-point average), I won't recruit them.' It's the Carneseccas, the Ray Meyers, the Orrs who are a dying breed."

Walden said he's concerned with today's "hot shot" coaches who'll lead the profession in future years. He wonders whether they'll carry on Johnny Orr's sensitivity. "The older guys coached for the fun of it," Walden explained. "They parked cars and coached tennis in high school, and lined the fields and drove the bus and made nothing (financially) doing it. That's Johnny. He represents a throwback. Everyone over age 50 still in coaching is in the end of that breed. We're the old dinosaurs. We know about a budget: trying to have the kids get one more day out of their shoes. It doesn't bother us if we don't have gold-colored doorknobs.

"We have too many young (coaches) today going from college to college to college as graduate assistants. They don't really know what coaching is all about. It's a little like the son starting at the corporate level of his dad's business instead of down in the warehouse."

Cyclone assistant coach Steve Krafcisin said working with Orr has given him a different outlook on coaching. "There are probably coaches I could have learned more Xs and Os from, but I've learned so much here about people and how to handle people," Krafcisin said. "If you ever get down on a player, and everyone does sometime, Johnny gets it back into perspective. One of his favorite sayings is, 'Remember, without these guys, we wouldn't have jobs.' He says giving up on kids is the wrong thing to do. The kid suffers in the end."

Des Moines Register sports columnist Marc Hansen said Orr will be remembered in two contexts. From a numbers aspect, Orr will be heralded for his breakthrough Cyclone teams of 1984 through 1988, and his impact on Iowa State basketball's surge in attendance. From a human interest standpoint, Hansen sees a cover boy, not for *GQ* magazine, but for the *Saturday Evening Post.*

"He's one of the old-school coaches," Hansen said. "He's done everything. He coached in high school. He coached football in high school, too. How many guys reach the national finals who used to coach high school football? He's a character. He's not a blow-dry image. When you get right down to it, he's just a guy with a whistle.

"When people look back at Johnny's era at Iowa State, they'll talk about when Orr had it going. I think people will look back at 1984 through 1988 as the golden era. It will be a part of Iowa State's lore. There was a time when Johnny Orr had the best program in the state. The amazing thing is he comes here and wins over Cyclone fans, and packs the place, and 10 years later his winning percentage is at .500. That must say something about his charisma. For that, I give the guy even more credit.

"The celebrity college coach is here to stay. Orr's not a CEO type, like basketball coaches and football coaches are starting to become. He's not one of these guys with the big entourage and a big brigade of assistants. He answers his own phone. With Orr, it's kind of like a mom-and-pop operation, and he's like Pop."

Longtime Orr observers think a permanent tribute to Johnny is appropriate. Former Ames *Tribune* sportswriter John Akers, who covered Iowa State basketball during Johnny's run to respectability, said, "I hope after he retires, someone thinks enough of him to erect a statue—hand clenched in victory, smiling, a wrung-out towel over his shoulder—just outside Hilton Coliseum." Krafcisin said, "Johnny's done so much for Iowa State, sometimes I think he's underappreciated by the university. When he goes, they're going to have to name a building after him. He truly loves Iowa State and the Ames community. The fact that he's going to retire here in Iowa at Lake Panorama is great."

What will Cyclone basketball life after Johnny bring? "Like anything else, and Johnny will be the first to tell you, things move on," Walden said. "He won't just disappear. He'll be very visible in the community and in the state. It's much different when a coach leaves and takes a job in another state than when you retire. People know it's over, and they accept it. I'm sure people will be saddened, but they'll be proud he ended his career here just like he said he would.

"But I'm dreading it. I'm sure I'll like whoever comes in next, but there's no way it's going to be like the way it was with John," Walden laments. "I love the assistant coaches over there now. For me it will be hard. I'm selfish. I'm not going to like life after him as much. I'll tell you, whoever comes in can have a lot of 20-win seasons, but he better have a sense of humor. The lock-jawed young bucks who come in here might win 20 games, but they'll be out of here. After (the Iowa State 1990–91 team) started with a 1-8 record, you could have taken the top 100 young coaches in the country and I don't think any could have won 10 games (Iowa State closed 12-19). The coaching job John and his guys did was amazing."

Cyclone assistant coach Jim Hallihan said one of Orr's greatest gifts to Iowa State has been his cultivating an atmosphere that will make his successor's job easier. "It will be tough for anybody to follow him, but there is great support at Iowa State, and that makes a big difference," Hallihan said. "At Iowa State, a bad crowd at a Cyclone Club outing is 150 people. At East Tennessee State (where Hallihan formerly coached), a great crowd was 50 people. Iowa State is still a first-class school, with a first-class program, in a first-class league."

Yet Hallihan, like all Johnny Orr fans, doesn't look forward to the day the music dies for this colorful coach.

"The most difficult thing will be the day we don't hear 'Here's Johnny,'" Hallihan said. "That'll be like not having 'The Star-Spangled Banner.'"